The Cham

1995

FOOTBALL & HURLING

Dedicated to Trish, John Brian and Sarah Marie

By the same author
Football Captains 1940 - 1993
Wolfhound Press, 1993

The Championship
1995
FOOTBALL & HURLING
The Complete Record

BRIAN CARTHY

Wolfhound Press

First published 1995 by
WOLFHOUND PRESS
68 Mountjoy Square, Dublin 1

British Library Cataloguing in Publication Data
A catalogue record for this book is avaliable from the British Library.

ISBN 0-86327-516-8

Cover design: Joe Gervin
Cover and colour photographs: Inpho, Dublin
Book design and layout: Wolfhound Press
Typesetting: Wolfhound Press
Colour film: Typeform Ltd, Dublin
Printed in Ireland by Colour Books, Dublin.

Contents

Left: Anthony Daly, captain of the victorious Clare Hurling team, with the Liam McCarthy Cup.

Below: John O'Leary, captain of the winning Dublin Football team with the Sam Maguire Cup.

Introduction

S alute the hurling men of Clare and the football men of Dublin. Champions of Ireland 1995! Congratulations!

Never-say-die Clare conquered Everest after a gap of eighty-one years in one of the most momentous All-Ireland Hurling Finals in the annals of the great game. An equally determined Dublin team defeated Tyrone by just a point to claim the Sam Maguire Cup some twelve years after Tommy Drumm's team of twelve beat fourteen-man Galway in the 1983 Final. John O'Leary played a key role in the 1983 victory, but he went one better in '95, becoming the first goalkeeper since Billy Morgan in 1973 to captain an All-Ireland winning team.

Clare hurlers first senior success on All-Ireland Final day since 1914 sparked off tumultuous celebrations right around the Banner county. Substitute Eamonn Taaffe sent them on their merry way with a priceless goal near the end and then a point each from mighty captain Anthony Daly and Jamesie O'Connor ensured that Croke Park was turned into a sea of saffron and blue. Anthony Daly's speech equalled his masterpiece on Munster Final day and by the time he had finished tears were falling like raindrops! To crown a wonderful day, selector Tony Considine took the microphone for a rendition of the Banner anthem, 'My Lovely Rose of Clare'.

The following Monday night tens of thousands converged on the centre of Ennis to welcome home the victorious team with the 'missing person', the Liam McCarthy Cup. Earlier Anthony Daly and his team were given a heroes welcome on arrival at Shannon Airport before they began their very emotional trip to Ennis. It is a week-end that will be talked about as long as fires remain burning in the county of Clare! There was magic in the air and a extra spring in the step of Clare people everywhere! Offaly captain Johnny Pilkington and his team accepted defeat graciously. Never easy. Only one team can ultimately win the biggest prize in hurling and in 1995 that team was Clare.

What of Dublin's victory two weeks later? It was a long time coming and the Dubs deserved their moment in the sun! It promised to be one of the most intriguing finals in recent times, but sadly it never lived up to expectations. Both sides produced just a sprinkling of top class football in the opening half, but what followed after the break was poor in the extreme. Charlie Redmond gave the Dubs supporters plenty to cheer about after 26 minutes when he scored the only goal of the game. Dublin led at half-time by, 1-8 to 0-6, but they suffered a big set-back fourteen minutes into the second half when Redmond was sent off by referee Paddy Russell. The drama was only beginning! It was all very confusing. The referee called Charlie aside a second time and the brilliant Dublin forward eventually made the lonely walk to the line.

There was further controversy at the very end when Tyrone had what appeared a perfectly legitimate equalising point by Sean McLoughlin disallowed by the referee who adjudged that Peter Canavan handled the ball on the ground while passing to his colleague.

The final whistle sounded very soon afterwards and Dublin were crowned All-Ireland champions for the twenty-second time!

Tyrone County Board intimated afterwards that they were considering appealing the result because Charlie Redmond stayed on the field for a few minutes after being sent off. Later in the week the Ulster champions decided against appealing. Peter Canavan scored 11 points for Tyrone to underline once again why he is widely acclaimed the best forward in Gaelic football. The Games Administration Committee later handed Charlie a three months suspension and cautioned him about his much publicised criticism of referee Paddy Russell.

There were many highpoints in the 1995 GAA calendar of events but one player more than any other grabbed the bulk of the headlines. In the space of a few short months, Jason Sherlock has become the most talked about and the most sought-after sportsman on these islands. He is in direct competition with international pop stars like Boyzone in the popularity stakes. Jasonmania is certainly sweeping the country. Jason was given an incredible reception when he made his senior championship debut as a substitute against Louth at Navan on June 18. He was in the starting fifteen thereafter and underlined his poaching skills with a goal against both Laois and Cork.

Laois beat Carlow by one point in the Leinster quarter final? Or did they? Coming up to full time Laois substitute Mick Turley struck a speculative shot which appeared to have gone wide but referee Noel Cooney allowed the 'winning' point after consultation with the umpires. Television pictures later revealed that Turley's finish was wide of the posts. Laois sportingly agreed to a re-fixture and the men from the O'Moore county emerged victorious by 3 points in one of the most exciting games of the entire championship. Laois County Board was presented with a special 'Fair Play' award before the game by Bank of Ireland to mark the county's sportsmanship in offering the re-fixture.

Colin Kelly turned in a match-winning performance for Louth as they dumped favourites Kildare out of the championship in the first round in the Lilywhites home patch in Newbridge; Meath had impressive early round wins in Leinster but were no match for a rampant Dubs in the provincial decider and eventually lost by 10 points.

There were shocks galore in Ulster. What's new? Donegal put their League Final defeat by Derry quickly out of their minds and turned in a fine display to beat the All-Ireland champions Down by 6 points in the preliminary round. The 1992 All-Ireland champions were then trounced by rank outsiders Monaghan in the quarter final at Ballybofey. There were more shocks to follow! Thirteen-man Tyrone defeated hot favourites Derry, and Cavan got the better of Monaghan to set up the first provincial decider between the counties since 1956. Tyrone were deserving winners of the Anglo Celt Cup but as Cavan manager, Martin McHugh said afterwards: "Remember, we were only three points behind with seven minutes left in the game."

The old order was restored in Munster! Cork and Kerry met in the provincial decider at Fitzgerald Stadium in Killarney. Kerry were unable to capitalise on a dream start which saw Eamon Breen score a goal after just two minutes and the once mighty Kingdom lost again. Cork have now won seven of the last nine Munster titles on offer1 One crumb of consolation for the Kingdom supporters: Kerry's total of 7-12 against Tipperary in the Munster semi-final was the highest recorded in the entire 1995 football championship!

Leitrim's first defence of a Connacht title since 1928 ended in disappointment as Galway corner forward Niall Finnegan kicked over the winning point for the Tribesmen in injury-time in the provincial semi-final. Galway emerged as the real surprise packets of the championship. Bosco McDermott's men defeated a fast-improving Sligo team after a replay; then accounted for Leitrim by a point in the next round and easily defeated Mayo in the final to emerge Kingpins of Connacht for the first time since 1987.

Galway's superb performance against Tyrone in the All-Ireland semi-final went a long way towards restoring pride in Connacht football. Tyrone full forward Peter Canavan was the match-winner on the day with a personal tally of 1-7.

In the other semi-final, Jason Sherlock's first half goal breathed life into a struggling Dublin team and completely altered the course of the game. Cork never fully recovered from that set-back, yet still lost by only 3 points. Interestingly, Cork failed to score a goal in the entire championship campaign. As already documented the Dubs delivered Sam to the capital city for the first time in twelve years with a none too convincing win over Tyrone in a controversial game.

Sunday June 4 was the day the journey began in earnest for the hurling men of Clare. It very nearly turned sour for Anthony Daly's team in the Munster semi-final when Kevin Murray struck the ball to the net to edge Cork 2 points in front with one minute left to play. Substitute Ollie baker guaranteed himself a special niche in Clare folklore when he rescued the Banner county's championship with a priceless goal.

Gary Kirby scored 12 points as Limerick defeated Tipperary in a thrilling Munster semi-final by a solitary point. Tipp had to line out without suspended pair Paul Delaney and Michael Ryan, but manager Fr Tom Fogarty made no excuse afterwards and conceded the Shannonsiders' deserved win.

Clare ended the sixty-three Munster famine with a 9 point win over Limerick in the final. All past failures were forgotten! Captain Anthony Daly's speech summed it up succinctly: "It's been sixty-three years of the long road back from Thurles and Limerick, but this baby's coming home tonight."

Laois hurlers were extremely unlucky to lose to overwhelming favourites Kilkenny in their first round championship game at Dr Cullen Park. The League champions were holding on to a narrow 2 point lead when a Fint Lalor goal-bound shot was brilliantly saved by substitute goalkeeper Joe Dermody.

Offaly survived a spirited second half rally from Wexford but still won comfortably by 7 points to set up a Leinster Final meeting with Kilkenny.

No team would have lived with the All-Ireland champions on that wet July Sunday in Croke Park. It must surely rate as the best team performance of the year. Offaly were magnificent on the day and ruthlessly brushed aside the Kilkenny challenge.

As expected, Galway beat a brave Roscommon side in the first Connacht Senior Hurling Championship Final for seventy-two years and Down defeated Antrim after a replay in Ulster. In the All-Ireland quarter final at Ruislip, Down, without ever reproducing the form shown in the Ulster Final replay, still has 7 points to spare over London.

Offaly proved much too good for Down, and Clare had 5 points to spare over Galway in the All-Ireland semi-finals.

The meeting of Offaly and Clare in the Final generated huge interest right around the country and abroad. Would Clare bridge an eighty-one year gap, or would Offaly become the first team from the county to win back-to-back All-Ireland crowns? It appeared the Leinster champions would claim the Liam McCarthy Cup when Johnny Pilkington first-timed a ground shot to the net in the second half, but substitute Eamonn Taffe saved the day with a Clare goal. Soon it was over and, against all the odds, Clare were the 1995 All-Ireland Hurling Champions!

What about the minnows in 1995? The Westmeath/Carlow preliminary round was one of only 2 games in which 9 goals were scored: the final score, Westmeath 6-6 Carlow 3-14, also represented the third highest aggregate score in the '95 Hurling Championship. The highest aggregate score of the championship was recorded at Dr Cullen Park in Carlow on Sunday June 4 when Wexford annihilated Westmeath by 6-23 to 1-7.

Sport has been a part of my own life since I was a child growing up in the townland of Ballymore near Strokestown in County Roscommon. Back then summer holidays were spent around the foothills of Sliabh Ban with family and friends playing football and hurling, making the hay and saving the turf. Household names like Mick O'Connell, Eddie Keher, Jimmy Doyle, Tony Doran, Enda Colleran, Joe Lennon, Dermot Earley, Gerry O'Malley, Jimmy Murray and dozens more helped create my own dream. The legendary Michael O'Hehir was then the voice of sport, and those vibrant living commentaries combined with the games I watched and the talk I heard inspired my childhood ambitions. Soon I was out in the fields near home kicking a football or wielding a caman doing imaginary commentaries on imaginary games. The years have rolled on and the dream of a young boy has finally come true. It is a wonderful privilege to be now commentating on Gaelic games for RTE Radio Sport. There are so many to whom I owe a great debt of gratitude. My heartfelt thanks to you all. This year I have travelled thousands of miles doing interviews with inter-county hurlers and footballers and then each Sunday commentating on the big championship games. It has been the best sporting year of my life and I look forward to many more great days and great years covering Gaelic games. Here's to 1996!

Brian Carthy
October 1995

THE ALL-IRELAND FOOTBALL FINAL
1995
Dublin & Tyrone
CROKE PARK
REFEREE:PADDY RUSSELL TIPPERARY
RESULT:DUBLIN 1-10 TYRONE 0-12

There are two images of All-Ireland Football Final Day 1995 that will linger in my mind long after the all too-few positive aspects of the game itself have become a distant memory. I will never forget the concentration on Peter Canavan's face as he wrestled with the ball in the dying moments of the game after losing his footing. Everything that could go wrong, went wrong. Yet the brilliant full forward was somehow able to turn around what appeared to be a hopeless situation and, against all odds, deliver what looked a perfectly legitimate pass to Sean McLoughlin. The Tyrone half back sent the ball over the bar to level the game. But referee Paddy Russell disallowed the score because, as he viewed it, Canavan handled the ball on the ground.

During the few seconds the ball was in the air, I saw a footballing genius in action as he considered his options. Canavan was one of the real heroes of All-Ireland '95. The Errigal Ciarain man registered 11 scores for Tyrone in the final, the same as the entire Dublin team, and yet he ended up on the losing side! The reason Tyrone lost this game is simple. Apart from Peter Canavan, the only other player to score was Jody Gormley. No one man can win an All-Ireland on his own. Not even one so great as Canavan!

The second image of All-Ireland Final day '95 is the smile on the face of Dublin manager, Dr. Pat O'Neill. Here is a man who has gone through the wringer with Dublin teams of recent years, but the smile on his face after the game was finally over revealed everything. More than anything else, Dr. Pat was a relieved man; relieved that Dublin had at last won an All-Ireland title after a twelve year drought! The following Monday night, I watched him again as he stood on top of the open decked bus bringing the victorious Dubs through the streets of Dublin, and he looked like a man without a care in the world.

He was devastated after last year's All-Ireland Final loss at the hands of Down. Now the Dubs had finally delivered. It mattered little to the manager that it was an uninspiring game and that Dublin only scored 2 points in the second half; what mattered to everyone involved with the team was that the Dubs won! The manner of victory was irrelevant. Dublin have played some vintage football in recent years and yet failed to win the ultimate prize, so the old adage that 'it's better to win a bad game, than to lose a good one' seemed to apply in this case.

Dublin won this game through hard work and sheer determination. Conditions at

Croke Park were perfect for one of the most eagerly awaited finals of recent years. Outsiders Tyrone, endeavouring to make it five-in-a-row for the province of Ulster, started in blistering fashion. Peter Canavan kicked over 2 frees inside four minutes and the All-Star set up Jody Gormley for Tyrone's third point. The Dublin defence appeared a little uncertain early on but Paul Curran and Keith Barr responded to the Tyrone challenge with vigour. Very soon it was Tyrone who found themselves under pressure: Dessie Farrell and Jason Sherlock began finding gaps in the Tyrone defence and Paul Bealin assumed responsibility for Dublin in the midfield sector.

Keith Barr opened the scoring for Dublin with a long-range free and further points from Charlie Redmond and Paul Clarke levelled the game after ten minutes play. Dessie Farrell was now coming into his own and he kicked 3 valuable points before Sherlock's hard work paid off when he laid on the pass for Charlie Redmond's goal twenty-six minutes into the game. Dublin had moved 5 points clear, 1-8 to 0-6 at half-time. The supporters on the Hill were in full voice! Tyrone had failed to deliver on their early promise and Canavan, with 5 points, was their only forward to make a significant impact .

The same player was quickly to the fore after the break! He kicked 2 points from frees and one from play and suddenly there were just 2 points separating the sides. Farrell calmed Dublin's nerves with a point on 44 minutes, but incredibly nearly twenty-three minutes elapsed before another score was registered.

If the scores were in short supply in the second half, there was more than a fair share of controversy. Charlie Redmond, injured in the week leading up to the game, received his marching orders after 14 minutes of the second half for retaliation. Over two minutes later, Charlie was still playing to his heart's content. The referee approached him again and ordered him off. It was a bizarre episode. Paul Clarke assumed the role of free-taker, but he was off target on a number of occasions. Dublin failed to put away their chances and Tyrone weathered the storm. Canavan narrowed the gap to just 2 points with the game's first score for nearly twenty-three minutes, but Clarke made amends for earlier misses with a good point from play.

The Dubs defence was now under intense scrutiny; Canavan pointed 2 frees to reduce the deficit to the minimum and when Sean McLoughlin sent the ball over the bar in injury time, everyone was certain there was going to be replay for the first time since 1988! Paddy Russell deemed otherwise and adjudged Canavan handled the ball on the ground. He awarded a free out to Dublin, much to the annoyance of Tyrone supporters.

The sound of the final whistle soon after was sweet music to the ears of the Dublin players and their long-suffering supporters. The 12 year wait was over and Dublin were crowned champions for the twenty-second time! Some of the Tyrone players were certain that the game had ended in a draw, unaware that McLoughlin's point had been disallowed. Tyrone full back Chris Lawn told me later that he only realised Dublin had won when he saw their supporters streaming on to the field at the end. He was devastated when the scoreboard revealed his worst fears. Dublin had beaten Tyrone by a single point, 1-10 to 0-12.

Action of the All-Ireland Final – Stephen Lawn, Tyrone, and Dessie Farrell, Dublin. See Colour section for Dublin team.

Tyrone County Board intimated afterwards that they were considering appealing the result because Charlie Redmond stayed on the field for a few minutes after being sent off. But later in the week the Ulster champions decided against that course of action.

Captain Ciaran Corr expressed the view that the Tyrone players were not interested in winning an All-Ireland medal in the boardroom. He felt Tyrone never played to their full potential and ultimately paid the price. "When you're beaten, you're beaten. The County Board may be thinking of an appeal, but as far the players are concerned, Dublin are the All-Ireland Champions." Tyrone players were devastated after the game but the plain and simple truth is that too many of their players, try as they did, failed to deliver the 'big performance' required of them to win on All-Ireland Final day. Peter Canavan produced another superb display and kicked 11 points, but he was the only Tyrone forward to score. But this is a very young Tyrone side, and with Art McRory and Eugene McKenna re-appointed as joint team managers, a bright future beckons."

Celebrations began in earnest as thousands of deliriously happy navy and blue clad supporters raced on to the pitch to acclaim their heroes. Immediately after the game, I interviewed Charlie Redmond for RTE Radio Sport as he made his way up the steps of the Hogan Stand. He was disappointed at having been sent off but expressed himself 'delighted' that the Dubs had finally delivered on their promise. I also spoke with birthday boy, Ciaran Walsh; injured player, gentleman Jack Sheedy, who was trembling with emotion, and I even got a word with the Chairman of the County Board, John Bailey. All sang the one tune. 'there's nothing in the world to compare with winning an All-Ireland'.

John O'Leary and the team attended a civic reception in the Bank of Ireland centre in College Green on the following Monday evening. Afterwards the players

Tyrone Back row 1 to r: Paul Devlin, Jody Gormley, Seamus McCallan, Sean McLaughlin, Finbarr McConnell, Ciaran McBride. **Front row 1 to r:** Pascal Canavan, Ronan McGarrity, Chris Lawn, Stephen Lawn, Ciaran Corr, Fay Devlin, Fergal Logan, Ciaran Loughran, Peter Canavan

and substitutes were given a heroes welcome when introduced to the huge crowd by popular RTE presenter, Des Cahill. The players and mentors then boarded an open-top bus for an emotional journey through the city centre where many thousands more loyal Dublin supporters crammed the streets. It was a joyous occasion for everyone concerned. Thousands of Tyrone supporters also turned out to welcome home the losing finalists and to thank them for their wonderful effort during the year.

And so the Sam Maguire Cup came back to the capital city for first time in 12 years, but for a courageous Ciaran Corr and his Tyrone team it was a case of what might have been. But, remember, there's always next year!

Scorers Dublin: Dessie Farrall 0-4; Charlie Redmond 1-1; Paul Clarke 0-2; Jim Gavin 0-1; Keith Barr 0-1; Paul Curran 0-1. **Scorers Tyrone:** Peter Canavan 0-11; Jody Gormley 0-1.

D U B L I N

	JOHN O'LEARY	
CIARAN WALSH	PADDY MORAN	KEITH GALVIN
PAUL CURRAN	KEITH BARR	MICK DEEGAN
PAUL BELIN	BRIAN STYNES	
JIM GAVIN	PAUL CLARKE	DESSIE FARRELL
CHARLIE REDMOND	JASON SHERLOCK	MICK GALVIN

Substitutes: Pat Gilroy for Keith Galvin; Robbie Boyle for Mick Galvin; Vinny Murphy for Dessie Farrell

T Y R O N E

	FINBAR MC CONNELL	
PAUL DEVLIN	CHRIS LAWN	FAY DEVLIN
RONAN MC GARRITY	SEAMUS MC CALLAN	SEAN MCLOUGHLIN
FERGAL LOGAN	JODY GORMLEY	
CIARAN CORR	PASCAL CANAVAN	CIARAN LOUGHRAN
CIARAN MC BRIDE	PETER CANAVAN	STEPHEN LAWN

Substitutes: Mattie Mc Gleenan for Ciaran Loughran; Brian Gormley for Stephen Lawn; Paul Donnelly for Seamus Mc Callan

LEINSTER SENIOR FOOTBALL
CHAMPIONSHIP FIRST ROUND
WESTMEATH & WEXFORD
WEXFORD PARK
REFEREE: TOMMY HOWARD KILDARE
RESULT: WESTMEATH 0-13 WEXFORD 1-3

When the two sides met in the O'Byrne Cup Final in March, the game finished level, but Westmeath refused to play the allotted extra time. The Leinster Council later decided to award the Cup to Wexford.

There was never any danger of this championship meeting ending in a draw as a disappointing Wexford team could only register a single point in the entire second half. That paltry return summed up what was a frustrating afternoon for the home county against a Westmeath side that produced a second half performance of real quality.

Wexford manager Liam Fardy made it clear in the week leading up to the game that it was going to be an extremely difficult assignment, particulary with a number of his key players out through injury. Fardy had to plan without captain, Ger Halligan, Michael Kavanagh and long-serving midfielder Louis Rafter. Rafter made an appearance in the second half while Barry Kirwan played despite going down with pneumonia a week before the game.

Westmeath had to line out without star midfielder Noel Lynch who was forced to quit the game after suffering a serious eye injury while playing hurling in London.

Westmeath's first half display gave little indication of what was to unfold after

Westmeath Back row l to r: John Murray, Ollie Keating, David Mitchell, Ciaran Ryan, Martin Flanagan, Michael Fagan, Aidan Collins, John O'Brien. **Front row l to r:** Ger Heavin, John Fleming, Michael Broder, Rory O'Connell, Dermot Brady, Larry Giles, John Cooney.

the break. Wexford right half forward, Scott Doran, from a penalty, scored the only goal of the game after 34 minutes which meant that his team, despite playing against the breeze, was on level terms at half-time. There was a much improved performance from the Midlanders after the restart. Midfielders, John Cooney and Rory O'Connell, exterted their influence, and a point apiece from Rory O'Connell and John Fleming, and 3 from frees by top scorer, Ger Heavin, put the game out of Wexford's reach fifteen minutes before the end, by which stage Westmeath led by 0-10 to 1-2.

Wexford's only score of the second half came after 56 minutes from substitute, Jason Lawlor, although Scott Doran was deprived a goal when David Mitchell brought off a superb save. The Westmeath goalkeeper also denied Billy Dodd a goal in the opening half with another first class save.

Westmeath's win was marred by the injury to half forward, John Murray, who was stretchered off in the second with a suspected cruciate ligament injury.

The game marked Michael 'Spike' Fagan's thirteenth championship campaign in the maroon and white of Westmeath.

Scorers Westmeath: Ger Heavin 0-5; Larry Giles 0-3; John Fleming 0-2; Aidan Collins 0-1; Rory O'Connell 0-1; John Healy 0-1. **Scorers Wexford:** Scott Doran 1-1; John Hegarty 0-1; Jason Lawlor 0-1.

WESTMEATH

	DAVID MITCHELL	
MICHAEL BRODER	JOHN O'BRIEN	DERMOT BRADY
OLIVER KEATING	AIDAN COLLINS	MICHAEL 'SPIKE' FAGAN
	JOHN COONEY	RORY O'CONNELL
MARTIN FLANAGAN	CIARAN RYAN	JOHN MURRAY
JOHN FLEMING	LARRY GILES	GER HEAVIN

Substitutes: John Healy for John Murray; Paul Aherne for Martin Flanagan; Anthony Coyne for Ciaran Ryan

WEXFORD

	JOHN COOPER	
CIARAN ROCHE	JOHN O'GORMAN	RICHIE PURCELL
SEAMUS KAVANAGH	JOHN DUNNE	PADRAIG O'GORMAN
	JOHN HARRINGTON	IAN WICKHAM
SCOTT DORAN	GREG WATERS	BARRY KIRWAN
JOHN HEGARTY	JIM BYRNE	BILLY DODD

Substitutes:Darragh Ryan for Jim Byrne; Louis Rafter for Greg Waters; Jason Lawlor for John Hegarty

Wexford Back row l to r: John O'Gorman, Greg Waters, Ian Wickham, John Harrington, John Dunne, Richie Purcell, Jim Byrne, Barry Kirwan. **Front row l to r:** Seamus Kavanagh, Padraig O'Gorman, Ciaran Roche, John Cooper, Billy Dodd, John Hegarty, Scott Doran.

SUNDAY MAY 28
LEINSTER SENIOR FOOTBALL
CHAMPIONSHIP FIRST ROUND

LOUTH & KILDARE

ST. CONLETH'S PARK, NEWBRIDGE
REFEREE: PAT CASSERLY WESTMEATH
RESULT: LOUTH 0-13 KILDARE 0-11

Colin Kelly emerged as the scoring hero as Louth withstood a late Kildare challenge to pull off a shock victory in this late evening game televised live by RTE. Man of the match, Kelly, from the Newtown Blues club, scored 7 points as a determined Louth team showed tremendous composure at crucial stages of the game to send the much fancied Lilywhites tumbling out of the championship. Kildare created numerous scoring opportunities but the old malaise was very much in evidence throughout the seventy minutes and they paid a heavy price for their inability to pick off scores.

Traditionally, Louth are a hardy championship team and their deserved two point win set them up for a second round meeting with Dublin. It also made up for their disappointment of failing to gain promotion to Division One earlier in the year after losing in a play-off to Tyrone.

It was always felt that Louth had the players to exploit any weaknesses in the Kildare set-up and the return to the fold of brothers, Seamus and Cathal O'Hanlon was a huge boost to the Wee County's prospects. Louth defeated Kildare in the '91 Championship during Mick O'Dwyer's first year in the managerial hot seat, and Dermot Earley was anxious not to suffer the same fate in his inaugural year in charge of the Lilywhites.

Kildare's cause suffered a setback midweek when Johnny McDonald was handed a one-month suspension by the County Board after being sent off in a club game. The ban precluded the Naas club man from taking part.

Louth left a vacancy in the left corner forward position and that was filled by Ollie McDonnell after he successfully came through a late fitness test.

The teams were level on four occasions during the opening half, by the end of which Kildare, with the breeze at their backs, led by 0-8 to 0-5. Dennis O'Connell, with a point from play, increased Kildare's lead shortly after the restart, but Louth fought back tenaciously and Stefan White reduced the deficit with a good point. Kildare were struggling at this juncture and Louth hammered home their advantage. Colin Kelly kicked two points and Ollie McDonnell levelled the game after 46 minutes with a point from play. It was the moment of truth for Kildare. Almost immediately, Denis O'Connell edged Kildare in front with a point and the Clane man scored his third of the second half one minute later to increase the Lilywhites lead.

Colin Kelly kicked a point for Louth after 48 minutes and Brendan Kearns levelled the game for the sixth time with his first point of the afternoon. Ollie McDonnell and Kelly again registered the last 2 scores of the game to fashion a great victory for Louth. Kildare supporters found it difficult to comprehend how their team, despite an abundance of possession, failed to get the vital scores near the end. Incredibly, Kildare failed to raise a flag in the final twenty-three minutes due to a combination of wayward shooting by their forwards and some heroic work by the Louth defence. Kildare scored just 3 points in the second half, all from Dennis

Louth Back row l to r: Brendan Kearns, Gerry Curran, Davy Mc Donnell, Gareth O'Neill, Niall O'Donnell, Stephen Melia, Seamus O'Hanlon, Ken Reilly. **Front row l to r:** Colin Kelly, Stefan White, David Reilly, Ollie Mc Donnell, Cathal O'Hanlon, Peter Fitzpatrick, Alan Doherty.

Kildare Back row l to r: Jarlath Gilroy, Peter Mc Connon, Packie Cahill, Brian Fahy, David Fennin, Christy Byrne, Sean Mc Govern, Dennis O Connell, Tom Brennam, Anthony Rainbow, Graham Dunne, Davy Dalton, Denis McCormack, Martin Lynch, Enda Murphy. **Front row l to r:** Glen Ryan, John Whelan, Noel Donlon, Paul Mc Cormack, Niall Buckley, Ken Doyle, Declan Kerrigan, Sos Dowling, Seamus Byrne.

O'Connell. That bare statistic sums up what was a bitterly disappointing afternoon for a team that has promised much but delivered little in recent years.

Scorers Louth: Colin Kelly 0-7; Alan Doherty 0-2; Ollie McDonnell 0-2; Brendan Kearns 0-1; Stefan White 0-1. **Scorers Kildare:** Niall Buckley 0-4; Dennis O'Connell 0-3; Seamus Dowling 0-1; Sean McGovern 0-1; Declan Kerrigan 0-1; Paul McCormack 0-1.

L O U T H

	NIALL O'DONNELL	
PETER FITZPATRICK	GARETH O'NEILL	KEN REILLY
DAVY MCDONNELL	STEPHEN MELIA	GERRY CURRAN
DAVID REILLY		SEAMUS O'HANLON
CATHAL O'HANLON	COLIN KELLY	ALAN DOHERTY
BRENDAN KEARNS	STEFAN WHITE	OLLIE MCDONNELL

Substitutes: Pat Butterly for Alan Doherty; David Staunton for David Reill

K I L D A R E

	CHRISTY BYRNE	
BRIAN FAHY	DAVY DALTON	SEAMUS DOWLING
KEN DOYLE	GLEN RYAN	ANTHONY RAINBOW
SEAN MCGOVERN		JOHN WHELAN
DECLAN KERRIGAN	DENNIS O'CONNELL	NOEL DONLON
PAUL MCCORMACK	MARTIN LYNCH	NIALL BUCKLEY

Substitutes: Graham Dunne for Paul McCormack

SUNDAY MAY 28
LEINSTER SENIOR FOOTBALL
CHAMPIONSHIP FIRST ROUND

MEATH & OFFALY

PAIRC TAILTEANN, NAVAN
REFEREE: PAT O'TOOLE LONGFORD
RESULT: MEATH 1-15 OFFALY 1-5

This was a real Jekyll and Hyde performance by Meath. Sean Boylan's men were outplayed for long periods of the opening half, but were totally dominant after the break as the Offaly challenge collapsed in dramatic fashion. Remarkably, favourites Meath failed to score until the twenty-fifth minute of the first half, by which stage Offaly had registered 1-4, much to the amazement of the home supporters.

A vicious downpour of sleet and rain and the loss early on of Graham Geraghty with a facial injury appeared to knock Meath off their stride. Offaly, with wind advantage, played some inspired football in the first half and got their just reward when Mick Casey took advantage of a mistake in the Meath defence to score the opening goal of the game. But Meath profited from the switch of Cormac Murphy to centre half back to keep tabs on Ronan Mooney. It was a shrewd move by Sean Boylan. Murphy stabilised the defence and Brendan Reilly was much more comfortable thereafter at wing back. He scored 2 points and made a valuable contribution.

Tommy Dowd opened Meath's account after twenty-five minutes; Brendan Reilly

Meath Back row l to r: Graham Geraghty, John McDermott, Conor Martin, Cormac Murphy, Martin O'Connell, Brian Stafford, Jimmy McGuinness, Brendan Reilly. **Front row l to r:** P.J. Gillic, Oliver Murphy, Evan Kelly, Robbie O'Malley, Trevor Giles, Tommy Dowd, Enda McManus

Offaly Back row l to r: Ken Kelleghan, Vinny Claffey, John Ryan, Ken Furlong, Sean Grennan, David Coffey, Ronan Mooney. **Front row l to r:** Tom Coffey, David Foley, Alan Kelleghan, Peter Brady, Finbar Cullen, Brendan Flynn, Michael Casey, Pat Daly.

added another soon after and then 2 points from newcomer Evan Kelly closed the gap to just 4 points at the interval, Offaly 1-5 Meath 0-4.

Meath played some exhibition football in the second half and Offaly were totally outclassed. The Midlanders were so out of sorts after the break that they were unable to register a single score. Extraordinary, by any standards! Colm O'Rourke, dropped from the Meath starting line-up for the very first time in his career, made a significant contribution when introduced early in the second half. O'Rourke, who made his championship debut in 1976, scored 1-2 and his mere presence seemed to cause consternation among the Offaly back line. Meath scored 1-11 in the second half and in the process played some outstanding football. It was Meath's first competitive game since March and despite the slow start, Sean Boylan had to be reasonably satisfied with his team's performance.

Scorers Meath: Evan Kelly 0-5; Colm O'Rourke 1-2; Tommy Dowd 0-3; Brendan Reilly 0-2; P.J. Gillic 0-1; Trevor Giles 0-1; Brian Stafford 0-1. **Scorers Offaly:** Pat Daly 0-4; Mick Casey 1-0; Ronan Mooney 0-1.

MEATH

	CONOR MARTIN	
ROBBIE O'MALLEY	MARTIN O'CONNELL	ENDA MCMANUS
GRAHAM GERAGHTY	BRENDAN REILLY	CORMAC MURPHY
P.J. GILLIC		JOHN MCDERMOTT
JIMMY MCGUINNESS	TREVOR GILES	EVAN KELLY
TOMMY DOWD	BRIAN STAFFORD	OLLIE MURPHY

Substitutes: Tom Hanley for Graham Geraghty; Jody Devine for Jimmy McGuinness; Colm O'Rourke for Ollie Murphy

OFFALY

	KEN FURLONG	
TOM COFFEY	KEN KELLEGHAN	DAVID FOLEY
ALAN KELLEGHAN	SEAN GRENNAN	FINBAR CULLEN
DAVID COFFEY		JOHN RYAN
BRENDAN FLYNN	RONAN MOONEY	VINCENT CLAFFEY
PETER BRADY	MICK CASEY	PAT DALY

Substitutes: John Kenny for Vincent Claffey; James Grennan for David Coffey; Mel Keenaghan for Brendan Flynn

SUNDAY JUNE 11

LEINSTER SENIOR FOOTBALL
CHAMPIONSHIP QUARTER FINAL

MEATH & LONGFORD

PEARSE PARK, LONGFORD
REFEREE: MICK CURLEY GALWAY
RESULT: MEATH 4-15 LONGFORD 0-10

The gulf between Division One and Division Four was clearly in evidence as Meath brushed aside the Longford challenge with considerable ease. When the teams last met in the championship in June 1990 at Pairc Tailteann in Navan, Meath emerged winners by 12 points; on this occasion their margin of victory was seventeen points. The final scoreline does scant justice to a courageous Longford side who only trailed by 4 points twelve minutes into the second half. But then Meath's superior strength and team-work came to the fore and the Longford effort crumbled.

Colm O'Rourke was recalled to the team after his surprise omission from the starting fifteen against Offaly. The Longford team was badly weakened by injuries. Or perhaps more to the point, an injury crisis! Among the players unable to take part were Niall Caslin, Liam Belton, Raymond Kenny, Kieran Kenny and Ciaran Fox. Furthermore, preparations for the championship suffered a demoralising setback when manager, Tom O'Donoghue, resigned after a number of players failed to turn up for a challenge game.

Although there was never the slightest danger of a shock result, Meath's long-serving manager, Sean Boylan and his selectors, All-Ireland winning captains, Mick Lyons and Joe Cassells could hardly have been overly enamoured with their team's slow progress in the first half with a near monopoly of possession.

Despite playing against a stiff breeze, Meath led at half-time by 1-5 to 0-5, with the goal coming from corner forward, Colm Rourke. Michael O'Brien from the Civil Service Club in Dublin was Longford's most industrious forward and he scored 4 points in the first half to keep his team in touch.

It was only a matter of time until Meath took complete control, and 2 goals in quick succession from Evan Kelly paved the way for a landslide victory. Ten players scored

Meath Back row l to r: Graham Geraghty, Colm O'Rourke, John McDermott, Evan Kelly, Cormac Murphy, Martin O'Connell, Brian Stafford, Brendan Reilly. **Front row l to r:** P.J. Gillic, Jody Devine, Robbie O'Malley, Conor Martin, Tommy Dowd, Trevor Giles, Enda McManus.

Longford Back row l to r: Frank McNamee, Michael O'Brien, Padraic Farrell, Paul McCormack, John James Reilly, Brian Greene, Jimmy Tully, Eddie Farrell. **Front row l to r:** Colin Hannify, Gerry Lynn, Dessie Barry, Joe O'Donnell, Seamus Killian, Cathal Lee, Seamus Gallagher.

for Meath while just three players found the target for Longford. Meath outscored Longford by 3-10 to 0-5 points in the second half to comfortably secure a semi-final meeting with Wicklow.

Still, the midlanders had something to cheer about near the end when midfielder, John James Reilly from the Rathcline club, closed the scoring with 2 points. But by then, Meath had their job done, and Colm O'Rourke had showered and was on his way to Carrick-On-Shannon to work for RTE Television on the live televised Connacht Championship game between Leitrim and Galway. A footballer's life is not an easy one!

Scorers Meath: Brian Stafford 1-3; Evan Kelly 2-0; Colm O'Rourke 1-2; Tommy Dowd 0-3; Jody Devine 0-2; Graham Geraghty 0-1; Brendan Reilly 0-1; PJ Gillic 0-1; Trevor Giles 0-1; Ollie Murphy 0-1. **Scorers Longford:** Michael O'Brien 0-5; John James Reilly 0-3; Dessie Barry 0-2.

M E A T H

	CONOR MARTIN	
BOB O'MALLEY	MARTIN O'CONNELL	ENDA MCMANUS
GRAHAM GERAGHTY	CORMAC MURPHY	BRENDAN REILLY
PJ GILLIC		JOHN MCDERMOTT
JODY DEVINE	TREVOR GILES	EVAN KELLY
COLM O'ROURKE	BRIAN STAFFORD	TOMMY DOWD

Substitutes: Jimmy McGuinness for Evan Kelly; Ollie Murphy for Colm O'Rourke; Colm Coyle for Brendan Reilly

L O N G F O R D

	BRIAN GREENE	
PAUL MCCORMACK	CATHAL LEE	PADRAIC FARRELL
COLIN HANNIFY	FRANK MCNAMEE	SEAMUS KILLIAN
JOHN JAMES REILLY		EDDIE FARRELL
JIMMY TULLY	JOE O'DONNELL	SEAMUS GALLAGHER
DESSIE BARRY	GERRY LYNN	MICHAEL O'BRIEN

Substitutes: Richie Culhane for Joe O'Donnell; Niall Caslin for Eddie Farrell; Paul Victory for Seamus Gallagher

SUNDAY JUNE 11

LEINSTER SENIOR FOOTBALL CHAMPIONSHIP QUARTER FINAL

WICKLOW & WESTMEATH

PAIRC CHIARAIN, ATHLONE

REFEREE: PAT MCENEANEY MONAGHAN

RESULT: WICKLOW 0-9 WESTMEATH 0-3

The meeting of the only two Leinster teams never to win a senior football provincial title generated a great deal of interest beforehand. But the game never lived up to expectations and a good number of the home supporters had left the ground long before referee Pat McEnaney blew the full time whistle. Westmeath's seven point victory over Wexford in the first round had instilled confidence in the side and hopes were high right around the county. It was felt that the team had the talent and commitment to make an impact in the championship. Not good enough to win outright, but certainly good enough to ruffle a few feathers along the way!

In the end, it was Wicklow who proved too strong for a strangely subdued Westmeath side in a drab game before a crowd of over 6,000. Wicklow are always formidable opponents in the championship and manager, Dave Foran, the former Dublin star, admitted afterwards he was well satisfied with his team's performance.

Westmeath forwards never really functioned on the day and their miserable tally of three points underlined the dearth of talent in the scoring department. The withdrawal through injury of half forward John Murray was a setback Westmeath could have done without.

Much was expected of Mattie Kerrigan's team, but they missed far too many opportunities and none of their forwards scored from play. In fact, apart from 2 frees from Ger Heavin, the only other Westmeath man on the scoresheet was wing back Michael 'Spike' Fagan after 29 minutes of the first half.

Three points from top scorer, Conan Daye, and 2 points from former All-Star Kevin O'Brien, left Wicklow in front 0-5 to 0-2 at half-time. Fergus Daly continued his dominance at midfield in the second half while Westmeath had little good fortune in front of goal. Corner back Michael Broder was unlucky not to score a goal for Westmeath after 42 minutes when his fisted effort came off the crossbar and the rebound was cleared. The Wicklow defence, marshalled by brothers Hugh and Billy Kenny, held firm at all times. Conan Daye scored 3 points for Wicklow in the second half while their other point came from substitute, Joe Clancy.

Wicklow were also guilty of missing scorable opportunities and a more accomplished team would have made them pay dearly for their tally of 16 wides.

Scorers Wicklow: Conan Daye 0-6; Kevin O'Brien 0-2; Joe Clancy 0-1. **Scorers Westmeath:** Ger Heavin 0-2; Michael Fagan 0-1.

Wicklow Back row l to r: Ronan Coffey, Billy Kenny, Raymond Danne, Darren Coffey, Tommy Murphy, Pat O'Byrne, Fergus Daly, David Whelan. **Front row l to r:** Kevin O'Brien Mick Murtagh, Brendan Brady, Damien McMahon, Hugh Kenny, Conan Daye, Paul Allen.

W I C K L O W

TOMMY MURPHY

PAUL ALLEN	HUGH KENNY	BILLY KENNY
DAMIEN MCMAHON	MICK MURTAGH	BRENDAN BRADY

FERGUS DALY   DARREN COFFEY

DAVID WHELAN	PAT O'BYRNE	RONAN COFFEY
CONAN DAYE	RAYMOND DANNE	KEVIN O'BRIEN

Substitutes: Joe Clancy for David Whelan; Darren Behan for Ronan Coffey

W E S T M E A T H

DAVID MITCHELL

MICHAEL BRODER	JOHN O'BRIEN	DERMOT BRADY
OLIVER KEATING	AIDAN COLLINS	MICHAEL FAGAN

JOHN COONEY   RORY O'CONNELL

MARTIN FLANAGAN	CIARAN RYAN	PAUL AHEARNE
JOHN FLEMING	LARRY GILES	GER HEAVIN

Substitutes: Alan McDonnell for Paul Ahearne; Anthony Coyne for Oliver Keating; John Healy for Ciaran Ryan

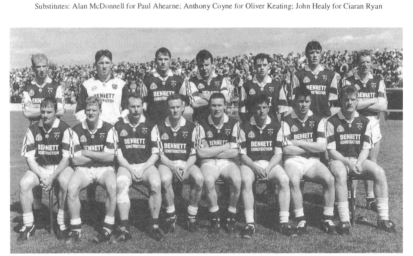

Westmeath Back row l to r: Ollie Keating, David Mitchell, Martin Flanagan, Aidan Collins, Ciaran Ryan, Rory O'Connell, John O'Brien. **Front row l to r:** Ger Heavin, John Fleming, Michael Fagan, Dermot Brady, Michael Broder, Larry Giles, Paul Ahearne, John Cooney.

Dublin Back row l to r: Dermot Deasy, Paul Bealin, John O'Leary, Sean Cahill, Brian Stynes, Paddy Moran, Mick Galvin, Keith Barr. **Front row l to r:** Paul Clarke, Dessie Farrell, Paul Curran, Mick Deegan, Vinny Murphy, Keith Galvin, Charlie Redmond.

SUNDAY JUNE 18
LEINSTER SENIOR FOOTBALL
CHAMPIONSHIP QUARTER FINAL

DUBLIN & LOUTH

PAIRC TAILTEANN, NAVAN
REFEREE: BRIAN WHITE WEXFORD
RESULT: DUBLIN 0-19 LOUTH 2-5

This game between old rivals Dublin and Louth will be remembered above all else for the incredible reception accorded championship debutant Jason Sherlock when he replaced an out-of-sorts Sean Cahill in the first half.

Nineteen-year-old Sherlock is an immense talent at both soccer and Gaelic football. He told me immediately afterwards that the highpoint of the game for him was Charlie Redmond asking him to take a close-in free. He was reluctant to take it but Charlie insisted and the Finglas youngster was relieved to see the ball float over the bar.

Twenty-year-old Keith Galvin was the only championship newcomer in the starting fifteen and the St. Sylvesters' clubman impressed sufficiently to suggest a bright future in the navy and blue jersey. Dublin were forced to line out without the injured Jack Sheedy and Ciaran Walsh but Louth faced a midfield crisis when David Reilly was ruled out through injury. It was a huge blow to the Wee County.

Man of the match, Charlie Redmond, kicked 9 points for Dublin, as Louth struggled to keep in touch for long periods of the game. Earlier in the afternoon, I had interviewed Charlie for RTE Radio Sport at his home just as he was about to sit down to watch the Rugby World Cup semi-final between New Zealand and England. He must have picked up some tips from the All-Black's powerhouse, Jonah Lomu, because for a man who always admits a dislike for first round championship games, 'Champagne Charlie' was in sparkling form. When Jason Sherlock was taken down in the small rectangle shortly after making his entry, everyone wondered would Charlie take the penalty. He had told me shortly after the All-Ireland that he would never again take a penalty and re-iterated the same view in our chat that very afternoon. He was as good as his word. Paul Clarke struck the ball well but Niall O'Donnell, the Louth goalkeeper, brought off an excellent save. I was doing commentary for RTE Radio on the game and said at the time: 'the saga of missed penalties for Dublin goes on and on and on'. Cathal O'Hanlon's goal late in the first half gave Louth a lifeline but they still trailed by 0-11 to 1-2 at half-time.

With the breeze behind them in the second half, Louth came out breathing fire and scored 1-2 without reply in the first eleven minutes. The goal from full forward Stefan White sent the Louth supporters wild with excitement. Inexplicably the Louth challenge crumbled soon after, as Dublin registered 8 points to Louth's tally of two in the closing twenty minutes.

Newcomer Keith Galvin rounded off a good day's work for himself and the Dubs with the final point of the game. A job well done. Next stop for the Dubs a semi-final meeting with Laois!

Scorers Dublin: Charlie Redmond 0-9; Paul Clarke 0-2; Mick Galvin 0-2; Dessie Farrell 0-2; Brian Stynes 0-1; Vinny Murphy 0-1; Jason Sherlock 0-1; Keith Galvin 0-1. **Scorers Louth:** Stefan White 1-1; Colin Kelly 0-4; Cathal O'Hanlon 1-0.

DUBLIN

JOHN O'LEARY

KEITH GALVIN	DERMOT DEASY	PADDY MORAN
PAUL CURRAN	KEITH BARR	MICK DEEGAN
	PAUL BEALIN	BRIAN STYNES
SEAN CAHILL	VINNY MURPHY	PAUL CLARKE
CHARLIE REDMOND	MICK GALVIN	DESSIE FARRELL

Substitutes: Jason Sherlock for Sean Cahill; Jim Gavin for Vinny Murphy; Enda Sheehy for Charlie Redmond

LOUTH

NIALL O'DONNELL

PETER FITZPATRICK	GARETH O'NEILL	BARRY O'CONNOR
DAVY MCDONNELL	STEPHEN MELIA	GERRY CURRAN
	SEAMUS O'HANLON	KEN REILLY
CATHAL O'HANLON	COLIN KELLY	ALAN DOHERTY
BRENDAN KEARNS	STEFAN WHITE	OLLIE MCDONNELL

Substitutes: Pat Butterly for Brendan Kearns; Alan Rooney for Ollie McDonnell; Kevin O'Hanlon for Cathal O'Hanlon

Louth Back row l to r: Brendan Kearns, Gareth O'Neill, Stephen Melia, Davy Mc Donnell, Barry O'Connor, Niall O'Donnell, Seamus O'Hanlon, Gerry Curran, Ken Reilly. **Front row l to r:** Colin Kelly, Alan Doherty, Ollie Mc Donnell, Cathal O'Hanlon, Peter Fitzpatrick, Stefan White.

SUNDAY JUNE 18
LEINSTER SENIOR FOOTBALL
CHAMPIONSHIP QUARTER FINAL

LAOIS & CARLOW

O'MOORE PARK, PORTLAOISE
REFEREE: NOEL COONEY OFFALY
RESULT: LAOIS 2-11 CARLOW 1-13

What appeared at first glance to be just another run of the mill championship game turned into one of the most exciting and certainly the most controversial of the entire series. A typical David and Goliath clash: Carlow, the no-hopers, against odds-on favourites, Laois, a side which appeared to have far too many aces up their sleeves to be unduly bothered by their neighbouring rivals.

Laois had an impressive League run which saw them top Division One before losing to Donegal in the semi-final, while Carlow had failed to gain promotion from Division Four. Interestingly, former Laois minor and under-21 player, Alan Bowe made his senior championship debut in the Carlow colours at right corner forward, one of eleven Eire Og players on the team. Laois announced their team on the Wednesday night preceding the game and left a vacancy at right corner forward to allow Tom Bowe sufficient time to recover from injury. The Stradbally clubman failed to satisfy Colm Browne and his selectors as to the state of his fitness and senior championship debutant Mark O'Brien took his place. Influential Laois forward, Hugh Emerson was not in the starting fifteen because of a long-term thumb injury sustained at work. Manager Colm Browne decided to push Emerson into action at half-time after it became abundantly clear in the opening 35 minutes that Carlow meant serious business. Both sides played some splendid football throughout but Laois relied far too heavily on their very skilful full forward, Damien Delaney, who scored 2-5 of his side's total. The teams were level at half-time and Laois with the breeze were expected to take control in the second half.

Instead, it was Carlow who grabbed the initiative with a goal from Anthony Keating. Garvan Ware and Sean Kavanagh continued to dominate the midfield exchanges as Carlow refused to bend the knee. But eight minutes from time, Delaney converted a Laois penalty from the rebound to level the scores. The drama was only beginning. Coming up to full-time, Laois substitute Mick Turley struck a speculative shot which practically everyone in O'Moore Park felt had gone wide but referee Noel Cooney allowed the winning point after consultation with the umpires. Carlow also felt aggrieved with the decision of the referee not to allow a close-in free to be re-taken. Substitute James Reid kicked the ball wide but insisted he never heard the whistle and the Carlow players wanted the free to be re-taken. Those controversial decisions clouded what otherwise was an outstanding game. Television pictures later revealed that Michael Turley's finish had gone wide. Carlow mentors and supporters were furious and their County Board lodged a request to the Leinster Council to

Leo Turley of Laois and Joe Murphy of Carlow.

Laois Back row l to r: Tony Dunne, Martin Dempsey, Adrian Phelan, P.J. Dempsey, Tom Conroy, Emmet Burke, Aidan Lacey, Leo Turley. **Front row l to r.** Damien Delaney, Michael Lawlor, Tony Maher, Denis Lalor, George Doyle, Eamonn Delaney, Mark O'Brien.

consider a replay. The Laois County Board sportingly agreed to a re-fixture and delegates attending an emergency meeting of the Leinster Council voted unanimously to accept the offer from Laois after first adopting referee Noel Cooney's match report. It was the first time video evidence was used to determine a score and ultimately decide the outcome of a senior championship game. A dangerous precedent? Not at all. Justice was done and common sense prevailed.

Scorers Laois: Damien Delaney 2-5; Mark O'Brien 0-2; Leo Turley 0-2; Tony Maher 0-1; Michael Turley 0-1. **Scorers Carlow:** Anthony Kearing 1-2; Johnny Nevin 0-3; Noel Doyle 0-2; Sean Kavanagh 0-2; Joe Hayden 0-2; Garvan Ware 0-1; Willie Quinlan 0-1.

L A O I S

	EMMET BURKE	
AIDAN PHELAN	MARTIN DEMPSEY	TOM CONROY
EAMON DELANEY	DENIS LALOR	AIDAN LACEY
TONY MAHER		GEORGE DOYLE
TONY DUNNE	PJ DEMPSEY	MICHAEL LAWLOR
MARK O'BRIEN	DAMIEN DELANEY	LEO TURLEY

Substitutes: Hugh Emerson for PJ Dempsey; Tommy Smith for Aidan Lacey; Michael Turley for Tony Dunne

C A R L O W

	JOHN KEARNS	
JOE MURPHY	JOHN WYNNE	JIMMY DOOLEY
WILLIE QUINLAN	HUGH BRENNAN	BRENDAN HAYDEN
SEAN KAVANAGH		GARVAN WARE
NOEL DOYLE	JOHNNY NEVIN	ANTHONY KEATING
ALAN BOWE	COLM HAYDEN	JOE HAYDEN

Substitutes: Jody Morrissey for Colm Hayden; James Reid for Anthony Keating

Carlow Back row l to r: Garvan Ware, Noel Doyle, Sean Kavanagh, John Kearns, John Wynne, Alan Bowe, Colm Hayden, Joe Hayden. **Front row l to r:** Anthony Keating, Joe Murphy, Willie Quinlan, Hugh Brennan, Brendan Hayden, Johnny Nevin, Jimmy Dooley.

SUNDAY JUNE 25
LEINSTER SENIOR CHAMPIONSHIP
QUARTER FINAL RE-FIXTURE

LAOIS & CARLOW

O'MOORE PARK, PORTLAOISE
REFEREE: PAT O'TOOLE LONGFORD
RESULT: LAOIS 1-16 CARLOW 0-16

B illed as the 'Battle Of The Barrow Part Two', it certainly lived up to expectations. Rarely had a game so gripped the imagination of the sporting public and all because of the controversy surrounding the first meeting. The Leinster Council voted unanimously to accept a very sporting gesture from Laois to allow the re-fixture after television pictures showed that Michael Turley's 'winning point' for Laois in the first game was wide of the posts. I must admit that I have rarely encountered such a happy atmosphere among supporters before any game. It was exceptional even by Gaelic games standards. In keeping with the mood, the Laois County Board was presented with a special 'Fair Play' award before the game by Bank Of Ireland to mark 'the county's outstanding sportsmanship in offering the re-fixture'. It was that kind of day!

One had to feel sorry for the previous Sunday's referee Noel Cooney who was unable to take charge of the re-fixture. He broke his wrist in a fall after colliding with a player while refereeing an Offaly senior championship game on the Friday night. It was cruel luck on the genial Offaly man. He himself realised the ball was wide only after he had watched the television pictures with his family on Monday night. He was unable to tell from his position on the field but his umpires were adamant the

Laois Back row l to r: David Sweeney, George Doyle, Adrian Phelan, Hugh Emerson, Emmet Burke, Tom Conroy, Tony Maher, Leo Turley. **Front row l to r.** Damien Delaney, Denis Lalor, Michael Lawlor, Martin Dempsey, Mark O'Brien, Eamonn Delaney, Tom Bowe.

Carlow **Back row l to r:** Garvan Ware, Jody Morrissey, Noel Doyle, John Kearns, Sean Kavanagh, John Wynne, Jimmy Dooley, Joe Hayden. **Front row l to r:** Johnny Nevin, Alan Bowe, Willie Quinlan, Hugh Brennan, Brendan Hayden, Joe Murphy, Anthony Keating.

ball had gone over the bar. Pat O'Toole from Longford was an excellent replacement in what was a riveting quarter final.

It was a glorious day, as boiling hot as any of the sun spots. The game represented all that the GAA strives for - pride, passion, skill, commitment, and the 12,000 or more sun-burnt supporters lapped it up. Laois left out defender, Aidan Lacy and forwards, Tony Dunne and PJ Dempsey from the first game with Tom Bowe, David Sweeney and Hugh Emerson taking their places. Jody Morrissey, grandson of the 'Boy Wonder', Tommy Murphy, replaced Colm Hayden in the Carlow team.

The general consensus before the re-fixture was that Laois had underestimated the Carlow challenge first time round and that the mistake would not be repeated. But Carlow manager and former Laois player, Bobby Millar, expressed the view that his players were eminently capable of rising to such heights again. He was proved right. Former Laois underage star, Alan Bowe, was listed to play at right corner forward for Carlow but spent the afternoon in a roving defensive role, with Laois full back Martin 'Miley' Dempsey in hot pursuit. It worked to perfection the first day, but the impact was less significant second time round. Carlow, favoured by the breeze, shaded the first half and Laois were a trifle lucky to be level at half-time. The hero of the opening thirty-five minutes was Laois goalkeeper, Emmet Burke, who pulled off three magnificent saves. Laois full forward, Damien Delaney, scorer of 6 points in the first half, had to retire injured at half-time and he was replaced by super-sub Michael Turley. Carlow surged 5 points clear eleven minutes into the second half as the Laois defence struggled to cope. It was then we saw the real character of Colm Browne's side and Michael Lawlor turned the game around with a well-taken goal. Lawlor was the Laois hero in the second half accounting for 1-5, underlining his class from both frees and play. Laois finished the stronger with 4 unanswered points to clinch a semi-final meeting with Dublin. It was as open and honest a game of football as one could wish to see with the expected tensions the championship inevitably brings. The perfect advertisement for Gaelic football.

Scorers Laois: Michael Lawlor 1-5; Damien Delaney 0-6; George Doyle 0-2; Leo Turley 0-1; Tom Bowe 0-1; Derek O'Connell 0-1. **Scorers Carlow:** Anthony Keating 0-6; Joe Hayden 0-3; Johnny Nevin 0-2; Garvan Ware 0-1; Noel Doyle 0-1; Sean Kavanagh 0-1; Jody Morrissey 0-1; Colm Hayden 0-1.

L A O I S

	EMMET BURKE	
ADRIAN PHELAN	MARTIN DEMPSEY	TOM CONROY
EAMON DELANEY	DENIS LALOR	GEORGE DOYLE
TONY MAHER		DAVID SWEENEY
TOM BOWE	HUGH EMERSON	MICHAEL LAWLOR
MARK O'BRIEN	DAMIEN DELANEY	LEO TURLEY

Substitutes: Derek O'Connell for Mark O'Brien; Michael Turley for Damien Delaney; Tommy Smith for Eamon Delaney

C A R L O W

	JOHN KEARNS	
JOE MURPHY	JOHN WYNNE	JIMMY DOOLEY
WILLIE QUINLAN	HUGH BRENNAN	BRENDAN HAYDEN
SEAN KAVANAGH		GARVAN WARE
NOEL DOYLE	JOHNNY NEVIN	JODY MORRISSEY
ALAN BOWE	JOE HAYDEN	ANTHONY KEATING

Substitutes: John Owens for Jody Morrissey; Alan Callinan for Joe Murphy

SUNDAY JULY 2
LEINSTER SENIOR FOOTBALL
CHAMPIONSHIP SEMI-FINAL
MEATH & WICKLOW
O'MOORE PARK, PORTLAOISE
REFEREE: TOMMY HOWARD KILDARE
RESULT: MEATH 3-14 WICKLOW 0-9

The vast difference between Division One and Division Four was once again underlined emphatically at O'Moore Park as Meath cantered into the Leinster Final. This semi-final meeting was effectively over almost as soon as it began. Meath had allowed both Offaly and Longford to grab the initiative early on in previous rounds but there was never any danger of repeating the mistake against rank outsiders Wicklow. Brian Stafford opened the scoring after one minute with a point from play; then All-Star Tommy Dowd crashed the ball to the net and Stafford followed with a goal after a mistake by Wicklow goalkeeper, Tommy Murphy. This left Meath in front 2-1 to no score with the game barely four minutes old. Disaster for the Garden County!

Indeed, by the time Wicklow registered their first score, a point from a free by Conan Daye after sixteen minutes, Meath had tacked on 4 more points from Jody Devine and Evan Kelly, and 2 from a rejuvenated Stafford. That early blitz rocked Wicklow as Meath sent out a stern warning to counties with ambitions of winning

Meath Back row l to r: Colm O'Rourke, John McDermott, Colm Coyle, Cormac Murphy, Martin O'Connell, Brian Stafford, Brendan Reilly. **Front row l to r:** P.J. Gillic, Jody Devine, Evan Kelly, Conor Martin, Tommy Dowd, Trevor Giles, Enda McManus, Robbie O'Malley.

the Sam Maguire Cup. Vintage Meath played some outstanding football in the first half and led Wicklow a merry dance; Sean Boylan's men were faster to the ball and so much more capable of picking off scores. Wicklow struggled in far too many areas and never looked capable of breaching a rock solid Meath defence.

The Meath full forward line of Colm O'Rourke, Brian Stafford and Tommy Dowd tormented the Wicklow back line and when O'Rourke, a man who played his first senior championship game back in 1976, scored Meath's third goal ten minutes into the second half, it was simply a matter of playing out time.

In fairness to the Wicklow players, they battled on against overwhelming odds

Wicklow Back row l to r: Billy Kenny, Paul Kenny, Raymond Danne, Fergus Daly, Tommy Murphy, Pat O'Byrne, Darren Coffey, Terry Allen. **Front row l to r:** Kevin Ó'Brien, Paul Allen, Brendan Brady, Hugh Kenny, Damien McMahon, Mick Murtagh, Conan Daye

but were always chasing the game after conceding those 2 early goals. Wicklow had their moments, particularly corner forward Conan Daye, who scored 6 points and was denied a goal by the crossbar in the second half and then soon after had a powerful shot brilliantly saved by a very alert Meath goalkeeper, Conor Martin. To compound Wicklow's misfortune, substitute David Whelan, who replaced Pat O'Byrne late in the game, was sent off after just three minutes on the field. Meath were forced to line out without wing back Graham Geraghty, but the experienced Colm Coyle turned in a tour-de-force performance. Geraghty was dismissed in a club game two weeks previously and received a one-month ban but Brendan Reilly, sent off in the same game, was handed a two-week ban, which allowed him to take his place at left half back against Wicklow.

Scorers Meath: Brian Stafford 1-5; Tommy Dowd 1-3; Colm O'Rourke 1-2; Evan Kelly 0-2; Jody Devine 0-1; Trevor Giles 0-1. **Scorers Wicklow:** Conan Daye 0-6; Paul Allen 0-1; Mick Murtagh 0-1; Kevin O'Brien 0-1.

M E A T H

		CONOR MARTIN		
ROBBIE O'MALLEY		MARTIN O'CONNELL		ENDA MCMANUS
COLM COYLE		CORMAC MURPHY		BRENDAN REILLY
	PJ GILLIC		JOHN MCDERMOTT	
JODY DEVINE		TREVOR GILES		EVAN KELLY
COLM O'ROURKE		BRIAN STAFFORD		TOMMY DOWD

Substitutes: Jimmy McGuinness for Jody Devine; David Beggy for Evan Kelly; Tom Hanley for Brendan Reilly

W I C K L O W

		TOMMY MURPHY		
DAMIEN MCMAHON		HUGH KENNY		BILLY KENNY
PAUL ALLEN		MICK MURTAGH		BRENDAN BRADY
	FERGUS DALY		DARREN COFFEY	
PAUL KENNY		PAT O'BYRNE		TERRY ALLEN
CONAN DAYE		RAYMOND DANNE		KEVIN O'BRIEN

Substitutes: Ronan Coffey for Paul Kenny; David Whelan for Pat O'Byrne; Mick Fitzpatrick for Terry Allen

Dublin Back row l to r: Paul Clarke, Mick Galvin, Paul Bealin, Sean Cahill, Brian Stynes, Paddy Moran, Keith Barr. **Front row l to r:** Paul Curran, John O'Leary, Jason Sherlock, Keith Galvin, Dessie Farrell, Mick Deegan, Ciaran Walsh, Charlie Redmond.

SUNDAY JULY 9
LEINSTER SENIOR FOOTBALL CHAMPIONSHIP SEMI-FINAL
DUBLIN & LAOIS
PAIRC TAILTEANN, NAVAN
REFEREE: BRIAN WHITE WEXFORD
RESULT: DUBLIN 1-13 LAOIS 0-9

The game marked the first full championship outing of Jason Sherlock and he made it one to remember with a second half goal that effectively ended the game as a contest and sent Dublin into the Leinster Final for the fourth consecutive year. As he proved against Louth when he came on as a substitute and forced a penalty, Sherlock once again underlined just how valuable he is to Dublin as a goal poacher supreme. He gave the Dubs an extra dimension and was very unlucky in the first half when his vicious shot hit the post and then later in the second half he set up a goal chance for Vinny Murphy with a touch of magic. The 'Travelling Hill' roared their approval on a day when Laois missed far too many scoring opportunities and failed to do themselves justice.

It could all have been so different had Damien Delaney scored in the opening minute when his shot whistled by John O'Leary's right hand post. A let-off for the Dublin defence who looked vulnerable in those early minutes.

Ciaran Walsh was a late replacement for injured full back, Dermot Deasy, but Keith Barr passed a late fitness test and took his place at centre half back. Laois forwards dominated the early exchanges and Damien Delaney made amends for his earlier miss by kicking 2 points. The full forward scored 3 points for Laois in the

Laois Back row l to r: David Sweeney, Adrian Phelan, Emmet Burke, Tom Conroy, Tony Maher, George Doyle, Leo Turley. **Front row l to r.** Damien Delaney, Denis Lalor, Tom Bowe, Martin Dempsey, Michael Lawlor, Hugh Emerson, Noel Roe, Eamonn Delaney.

opening half and Michael Lawlor registered the other 2 as the sides ended level, 0-5 apiece at half-time. Charlie Redmond's free taking was again of the highest standard and he struck over 4 points while Paul Clarke was the only other Dublin player to get his name on the scoresheet in the first half. Laois, favoured by the breeze, kicked 7 wides to Dublin's one in the opening half and they were to rue those missed chances.

Dublin left half forward, Paul Clarke, set the trend for the second half with 2 excellent points from play and those were followed by points from Dessie Farrell and Charlie Redmond to leave Dublin 0-9 to 0-5, ahead just five minutes after the restart. Against the odds, Laois battled back tenaciously with 3 points from Damien Delaney to one from Charlie Redmond, but 'The Dubs' had a ace up their sleeve in the shape of Jason Sherlock. Despite losing his boot, he scored a splendid goal thirteen minutes from time to seal this tie for the champions, who added 3 further points from Mick Deegan, substitute Vinny Murphy and Charlie Redmond. The Erin's Isle dangerman again emerged top scorer for the Dubs with 7 points to add to the 9 he scored against Louth. It was a tough, uncompromising game brightened by some patches of excellent football from both sides; Denis Lalor, Michael Lawlor and Damien Delaney were always a threat, but too many Laois players had off days and wasted much too much possession.

This was a pleasing performance from a Dublin point of view: there were times when the Dubs looked like champions in waiting; their defence was solid except for a brief period at the start and Keith Galvin once again emerged as a real find; the midfield pairing of Brian Stynes and Paul Bealin were always industrious, if not exactly dominant, and if the reshuffled forward line once again relied a little too much on the free taking of Charlie Redmond, there was enough to suggest they would be a handful for any opposition. Dessie Farrell had an outstanding second half; Paul Clarke once again proved his importance to this Dublin team while Jason Sherlock was the jewel in the crown. His goal poaching skills are second to none. Dublin have strength in depth and will be further boosted by the return of the injured pair, Jack Sheedy and Dermot Deasy, for the provincial decider against Meath.

Scorers Dublin: Charlie Redmond 0-7; Paul Clarke 0-3; Jason Sherlock 1-0; Dessie Farrell 0-1; Mick Deegan 0-1; Vinny Murphy 0-1. **Scorers Laois:** Damien Delaney 0-6; Michael Lawlor 0-3.

DUBLIN

JOHN O'LEARY

KEITH GALVIN	CIARAN WALSH	PADDY MORAN
PAUL CURRAN	KEITH BARR	MICK DEEGAN
PAUL BEALIN		BRIAN STYNES
DESSIE FARRELL	SEAN CAHILL	PAUL CLARKE
CHARLIE REDMOND	MICK GALVIN	JASON SHERLOCK

Substitutes: Jim Gavin for Mick Galvin; Vinny Murphy for Sean Cahill; Pat Gilroy for Paul Bealin

LAOIS

EMMET BURKE

ADRIAN PHELAN	MARTIN DEMPSEY	TOM CONROY
EAMON DELANEY	DENIS LALOR	GEORGE DOYLE
TONY MAHER		DAVID SWEENEY
TOM BOWE	HUGH EMERSON	MICHAEL LAWLOR
NOEL ROE	DAMIEN DELANEY	LEO TURLEY

Substitutes: Tommy Smith for Eamon Delaney; Derek O'Connell for Noel Roe

SUNDAY JULY 30

LEINSTER SENIOR FOOTBALL
CHAMPIONSHIP FINAL

DUBLIN & MEATH

CROKE PARK

REFEREE: PAT CASSERLY WESTMEATH

RESULT: DUBLIN 1-18 MEATH 1-8

Who can now beat Dublin? That was the question on the lips of the 63,000 filing out of Croke Park at about 5.30 on Sunday evening July 30th. Earlier, they had witnessed a Dublin performance of passion and commitment. The Dubs had promised to deliver such a powerpacked display for a long, long time; unfortunately for Meath, they chose to do it in the '95 Provincial decider. The 'Boys In Blue' were all heroes, but particularly Dessie Farrell, Paul Clarke, Paul Curran, Jason Sherlock and top scorer, Charlie Redmond. What would Dublin do without the Erin's Isle sharpshooter?

His young friend, Wayne McCarthy, told me before the game that Charlie had never kicked so well in training. Charlie looked confident and relaxed as he sipped water outside the dressing-room door during the minor final between Westmeath and Laois. He smiled when I told him of my conversation with his great pal. Sure enough, the fireman turned in a superlative display and kicked 7 points in the process.

The sight of Jack Sheedy, injured in the week leading up to the game, tossing water bottles from the sideline to his parched teammates, told its own story. The big Garda put his own disappointment behind him to exhort his colleagues on to greater effort. It underlined more than anything else the team spirit prevalent among the current crop of Dublin players. Manager Dr. Pat O'Neill and his three wise men, Fran Ryder, Jim Brogan and Bobby Doyle, decided to leave the right half forward position vacant and it only emerged shortly before the game that Jim Gavin would join Dessie Farrell, Paul Clarke, Charlie Redmond, Jason Sherlock and Mick Galvin in a reshuffled forward division. It was a big day for the Round Towers club man and he performed admirably.

Meath selected six players that won All-Ireland medals in 1988; Robbie O'Malley, Martin O'Connell, Colm Coyle, PJ Gillic, Brian Stafford and Colm O'Rourke. The Skyrne star was making his 62nd championship appearance in a Meath jersey and the veteran of many a battle was one of the Royal County's better players on the day. It was Dublin goalkeeper, John O'Leary's 64th game in the championship and the captain gave a faultless display.

Jack Sheedy has told me in an interview in the *RTE Guide* a week before the final that "any game between Dublin and Meath tends not to be classic football, it generally tends to be close and tight and fairly physical. The rivalry between us has built up because the lads know each other so well." Jack was right! The game was not a classic, but there were some classic scores and some wonderful passages of

Let's dance! A balancing act during the Leinster Final. Paul Curran of Dublin and Tommy Dowd of Meath.

Dublin Back row l to r: Paul Clarke, Mick Galvin, Dermot Deasy, Paul Bealin, Brian Stynes, Paddy Moran, Keith Barr. **Front row l to r:** Jason Sherlock, Jim Gavin, Dessie Farrell, John O'Leary, Paul Curran, Mick Deegan, Keith Galvin, Charlie Redmond.

Meath Back row l to r: Graham Geraghty, Colm O'Rourke, John McDermott, Cormac Murphy, Martin O'Connell, Brian Stafford, Brendan Reilly. Front row l to r: P.J. Gillic, Jody Devine, Tommy Dowd, Colm Coyle, Conor Martin, Robbie O'Malley, Trevor Giles, Evan Kelly.

play from both sides. All-Star Tommy Dowd also told me a week before the game that it was a 'do or die' situation for Meath. "There is no tighter defence in the game than Dublin's and we're going to find it very hard to get scores."

As expected, the game got off to a frantic start and referee Pat Casserly had to talk to a number of players in the opening minutes. When the game settled to a pattern, it was Dublin who dictated the pace, particulary at midfield, where Brian Stynes and Paul Bealin gave the reigning champions an advantage. Hill 16 was heaving and swaying; Charlie Redmond was kicking superbly, and none more than Dessie Farrell was causing major problems for a hard-pressed Meath defence. Jason Sherlock was revelling in the heady atmosphere and those on the Hill roared their approval when he kicked the last Dublin point of the first half. Meath opened brightly with a point from play by Jody Devine, but Dublin soon began to find their feet with 3 points from Charlie Redmond and one apiece from Mick Galvin, Dessie Farrell and Jim Gavin. Sandwiched between those scores was a Meath point from Colm O'Rourke. Further Dublin points from Farrell and Jason Sherlock, to one each for Meath from Brian Stafford and Colm O'Rourke, left Dublin ahead, double scores, 0-8 to 0-4 at half-time. It was looking bleak for Meath, who had to face the breeze in the second half.

Meath are renowned for their never-say-die spirit and Colm Brady was introduced in place of Brian Stafford at half-time. It was a totally different Meath in the early minutes after the restart as they endeavoured to break the Dublin stranglehold. And they did, if only briefly. Six minutes into the second half, left half forward Evan Kelly had the ball in John O'Leary's net and the sides were level. Dublin were rocked back on their heels! Now it was the turn of Meath to showcase their talents. Right half back, Graham Geraghty, struck over a glorious point to edge Meath in front. But inexplicably, Meath were only to score once for the remainder of the half, a point from a free by Trevor Giles. It was the day Dublin came of age. From the time Paul Clarke scored a wonderful point on 50 minutes, the Dubs were on fire. For twenty minutes, we were treated to a vintage display of Gaelic football. Redmond kicked 2 points, and the Hill sang when Clarke added another. Then came the Dublin goal. Sherlock lofted a high ball into the large rectangle and Paul Clarke fisted to the net. There was no way back for Meath as Dublin surged clear to claim their fourth successive Leinster crown. Further points from Paul Curran, Dessie, Jason and Charlie sealed a magnificent victory. Immediately after the game, I spoke with Jason Sherlock and in the course of our chat in the midst of hundreds of navy and blue clad youngsters, he turned, faced the Hill and said: 'there it is, that's what it's all about'.

Dublin manager Dr. Pat O'Neill and his backroom team had proved a point. They have assembled the best Dublin team for many a year. And judging by the Dubs performance it would be little wonder if Cork, Tyrone and Galway were quaking in their boots! GAA President, Jack Boothman was beaming when I met up with him after the game. He was a relieved man that Dublin Corporation allowed the final take place after originally seeking an injunction to prevent the use of the New Cusack Stand because of safety fears.

Everyone it appears was in a happy mood, except Meath. One of my own abiding memories of the day was the sight of a smiling Meath manager, Sean Boylan, standing in the tunnel adjoining the dressing-room, gracious as ever, offering his congratulations to the Dublin players. Truly Boylan is one of the most outstanding ambassadors in Gaelic football!

And so we return to the question: Can anyone stop the rampant Dubs. Only time will tell.

Scorers Dublin: Charlie Redmond 0-7; Paul Clarke 1-2; Dessie Farrell 0-3; Paul Curran 0-2; Jason Sherlock 0-2; Jim Gavin 0-1; Mick Galvin 0-1. **Scorers Meath:** Trevor Giles 0-3; Evan Kelly 1-0; Colm O'Rourke 0-2; Brian Stafford 0-1; Graham Geraghty 0-1; Jody Devine 0-1.

D U B L I N

	JOHN O'LEARY	
PADDY MORAN	DERMOT DEASY	KEITH GALVIN
PAUL CURRAN	KEITH BARR	MICK DEEGAN
PAUL BEALIN		BRIAN STYNES
JIM GAVIN	DESSIE FARRELL	PAUL CLARKE
CHARLIE REDMOND	JASON SHERLOCK	MICK GALVIN

Substitutes: Vinny Murphy for Mick Galvin

M E A T H

	CONOR MARTIN	
ROBBIE O'MALLEY	MARTIN O'CONNELL	COLM COYLE
GRAHAM GERAGHTY	CORMAC MURPHY	BRENDAN REILLY
PJ GILLIC		JOHN MCDERMOTT
JODY DEVINE	TREVOR GILES	EVAN KELLY
COLM O'ROURKE	BRIAN STAFFORD	TOMMY DOWD

Substitutes: Colm Brady for Brian Stafford; Enda McManus for Robbie O'Malley; Ollie Murphy for Evan Kelly

ULSTER SENIOR FOOTBALL
CHAMPIONSHIP PRELIMINARY ROUND

DONEGAL & DOWN

CLONES

REFEREE: PAT MCENEANEY MONAGHAN

RESULT: DONEGAL 1-12 DOWN 0-9

The All-Ireland Champions were well aware of what to expect! Facing Donegal at the best of times is never easy, but the Down players knew full well that taking on a Donegal team stung by their defeat at the hands of Derry in a League Final seven days previously, would present an even more difficult assignment.

No team has retained the Anglo Celt Cup since Derry in 1976 and the unpredictable nature of the Ulster championship was once again underlined at St. Tiarnach's Park in Clones. The Ulster jinx struck once more.

Defeat by Derry only served to focus the mind and strengthen resolve. But defeat by Down and the year was over! It was a crucial week for Donegal football. One of the major concerns in the Donegal camp leading up to the game was the fitness of Tony Boyle. The brilliant full forward had to retire with an ankle injury during the League Final. Would he recover in time? Noel Hegarty was also rated doubtful. He required stitches on his nose when referee Paddy Russell accidentally struck him a blow with his elbow in a bizarre incident in the League Final while signalling a free.

As the week progressed, reports from Tir Chonaill indicated that John Joe Doherty and Mark McShane were also carrying injuries. In the heel of the hunt, all the injured players were passed fit to play although captain John Cunningham, who missed the League Final through injury, was listed among the substitutes. Champions Down, relegated from Division One of the League, chose the same fifteen which defeated Dublin in the '94 All-Ireland final. It was not to be their day! It turned out to be a tough, uncompromising game. Donegal Manager PJ McGowan's tactic of moving Martin Gavigan to midfield at the start of the game worked like a dream as the Ardara clubman gave an outstanding display. Down's lack of match practice was evident and they failed to reproduce the fluency that made them the best team in the land in '94. But in fairness, Peter McGrath's men never gave up the chase and were only one point in arrears, 0-9 to 0-8, fifteen minutes into the second half. At that stage, the men from the Mourne were still very much in contention and battling for every ball.

Almost as soon as corner forward Gary Mason was sent to the line for an off the ball foul on John Joe Doherty, Down's challenge seemed to disintegrate. Donegal's style of play ensured they were well equipped to take advantage of the extra man. Once reduced to fourteen men, Down found it difficult to cope and could muster only one point in the remaining twenty minutes. Donegal displaying the determination, that brought them the Sam Maguire Cup in 1992, tacked on 1-3 in the

First round defeat of All-Ireland Champions, Down. Action from the game – J. McCartan, Down, and Matt Gallagher, Donegal.

Donegal Back row l to r: John Duffy, John Joe Doherty, Brian Murray, Gary Walsh, Mark Mc Shane, Barry McGowan, Martin Shovlin. **Front row l to r:** Noel Hegarty, Tony Boyle, Mark Crossan, Paddy Hegarty, Matt Gallagher, Manus Boyle, Martin Gavigan, James McHugh.

final sixteen minutes. Manus Boyle ended the Down challenge and underlined his class as a forward, when he palmed the ball to the net in the closing stages to bring his total to 1-5. Down substitute Ciaran McCabe had a goal disallowed near the end. Indeed, Down were out of luck on the day; earlier in the game Gregory McCartan had a goal disallowed while James McCartan hit the post. The Down attack never functioned with the same degree of style as the glory year of '94 and Donegal earned the plaudits for the way they bounced back from their League defeat to victory over the All-Ireland Champions.

Scorers Donegal: Manus Boyle 1-5; Paddy Hegarty 0-2; Tony Boyle 0-1; James McHugh 0-1; John Duffy 0-1; Brian Murray 0-1; Martin Gavigan 0-1. **Scorers Down:** Ross Carr 0-3; Gregory McCartan 0-3; Mickey Linden 0-1; Gary Mason 0-1; Aidan Farrell 0-1.

D O N E G A L

GARY WALSH

JOHN JOE DOHERTY	MATT GALLAGHER	BARRY MCGOWAN
MARK CROSSAN	MARTIN GAVIGAN	MARTIN SHOVLIN
MARK MCSHANE		BRIAN MURRAY
NOEL HEGARTY	JAMES MCHUGH	PADDY HEGARTY
JOHN DUFFY	TONY BOYLE	MANUS BOYLE

Substitutes: Declan Bonner for John Duffy; John Gildea for John Joe Doherty

D O W N

NEIL COLLINS

MICHEAL MAGILL	BRIAN BURNS	PAUL HIGGINS
EAMON BURNS	BARRY BREEN	DJ KANE
GREGORY MCCARTAN		CONOR DEEGAN
ROSS CARR	GREG BLANEY	AIDAN FARRELL
MICKEY LINDEN	JAMES MCCARTAN	GARY MASON

Substitutes: Collie Burns for Conor Deegan; Ciaran McCabe for Aidan Farrell

Down Back row l to r: Eamon Burns, Conor Deegan, Paul Higgins, Barry Breen, Brian Burns, Neil Collins, Greg Blaney, Aidan Farrell. **Front row l to r.** Ross Carr, James McCartan, Gary Mason, Mickey Linden, DJ Kane, Gregory McCartan, Micheal Magill.

SUNDAY MAY 28

ULSTER SENIOR FOOTBALL
CHAMPIONSHIP FIRST ROUND

DERRY & ARMAGH

ATHLETIC GROUNDS, ARMAGH
REFEREE: TOMMY MCDERMOTT CAVAN
RESULT: DERRY 1-17 ARMAGH 0-10

Manager Jim McCorry had sent out what appeared to be one of the fittest and best prepared team ever to represent the Orchard county, only to see them comprehensively beaten by a razor-sharp Derry side, who signalled their intentions very early on in the game. There was talk before the clash of the old rivals, that this could just be the year Armagh might mount a serious challenge in Ulster and that Derry had better tread warily. No team has ever had it easy in the Athletic Grounds, but the newly-crowned League champions imposed their authority from the throw-in and never once lost the initiative.

From the time Seamus Downey opened the scoring after two minutes, right up until corner forward Enda Gormley kicked over the last point of the game, Derry held a vice-like grip on the game and won comfortably with 10 points to spare.

The memory of their first round exit at the hands of Down at Celtic Park in '94 ensured that the Derry players were in the right frame of mind for the challenge. Manager Mickey Moran put his faith in thirteen of the team that beat Cork in the 1993 All-Ireland Final. Key forward, Joe Brolly, was forced to miss the game through injury and his place at right corner forward was taken by Declan Bateson from Ballinderry. The second member of the Derry All-Ireland winning team not

Derry Back row l to r: Dermot Heaney, Seamus Downey, Anthony Tohill, Damien Mc Cusker, Tony Scullion, Damien Barton, Declan Bateson, Brian Mc Gilligan. **Front row l to r:** Enda Gormley, Eamonn Burns, Fergal P Mc Cusker, Henry Downey, Kieran Mc Keever, Gary Coleman, Johnny Mc Gurk..

included in the starting fifteen was Damien Cassidy, who was listed among the substitutes. Eamonn Burns was the player chosen to fill the left half forward berth, but Cassidy replaced the Ballinascreen man after 59 minutes and scored a point from play. This was a fine team effort by Derry.

It looked bleak for Armagh at the interval as a determined Derry team, backboned by halfbacks, Johnny McGurk, Henry Downey and Fergal McCusker, led by double scores, 0-10 to 0-5, despite playing against a strong breeze. Armagh had failed to convert a number of good scoring opportunities in the opening half and relied far too heavily on their free taker and top scorer, Cathal O'Rourke, who had a fine game and could not be faulted for Armagh's dismal showing.

O'Rourke and Derry freetaker Enda Gormley held centre stage for some fifteen minutes after the restart and exchanged 3 points apiece from frees. Henry Downey put the game beyond the reach of Armagh when he raced through to score a splendid goal. Midfielder Anthony Tohill was involved in the build-up and the brilliant centre half back was on hand to supply the finishing touches. Downey, although hampered by injury, had a superb game for Derry and once again underlined his importance to the team, whose support play proved the key to their 10 point victory. Derry continued to dominate after the clinching goal and Seamus Downey, Dermot Heaney, Damien Cassidy and Enda Gormley scored a point apiece before the finish. Armagh could only muster a point each from Cathal O'Rourke and Diarmuid Marsden in the closing twenty minutes.

Scorers Derry: Enda Gormley 0-4; Henry Downey 1-0; Anthony Tohill 0-2; Damien Barton 0-2; Declan Bateson 0-2; Seamus Downey 0-2; Johnny McGurk 0-1; Brian McGilligan 0-1; Dermot Heaney 0-1; Damien Cassidy 0-1; Gary McGill 0-1. **Scorers Armagh:** Cathal O'Rourke 0-7; Des Mackin 0-1; Diarmuid Marsden 0-1; Martin McQuillan 0-1.

Armagh Back row l to r: Kieran Mc Geeney, Mark Grimley, Paul Mc Graine, Martin Mc Quillan, Neil Smith, Des Mackin, Cathal O'Rourke. **Front row l to r:** Ger Houlahan, Jim Mc Conville, Damien Horisk, Brendan Tierney, Diarmaid Marsden, Gerard Reid, Mark McNeill, John Rafferty.

DERRY

DAMIEN MCCUSKER

KIERAN MCKEEVER   TONY SCULLION   GARY COLEMAN

JOHN MCGURK   HENRY DOWNEY   FERGAL MCCUSKER

ANTHONY TOHILL   BRIAN MCGILLIGAN

DERMOT HEANEY   DAMIEN BARTON   EAMONN BURNS

DECLAN BATESON   SEAMUS DOWNEY   ENDA GORMLEY

Substitutes: Damien Cassidy for Eamonn Burns; Gary McGill for Henry Downey

ARMAGH

BRENDAN TIERNEY

MARK MCNEILL   GERARD REID   JOHN RAFFERTY

DAMIEN HORISK   KIERAN MCGEENEY   MARTIN MCQUILLAN

MARK GRIMLEY   PAUL MCGRANE

DIARMUID MARSDEN   NEIL SMYTH   CATHAL O'ROURKE

DES MACKIN   GER HOULAHAN   JIM MCCONVILLE

Substitutes: John Grimley for Neil Smith; Martin Toye for Des Mackin

Tyrone Back row l to r: Paul Devlin, Jody Gormley, Matt McGleenan, Seamus Mc Callan, Finbar Mc Connell, Sean McLoughlin, Danny Barr, Brendan Mallon, Paul Donnelly, Gerard Cavlan. **Middle row l to r:** Joe Cassidy, Adrian Cush, Stephen Lawn, Chris Lawn, Peter Canavan, Fay Devlin, Pascal Canavan, Fergal Logan, Ronan Mc Garrity, Damien Gormley, Paddy Muldoon. **Front row l to r:** Ciaran Corr, Adrian Nugent, Ciaran Loughran.

SUNDAY JUNE 4

ULSTER SENIOR FOOTBALL
CHAMPIONSHIP FIRST ROUND

TYRONE & FERMANAGH

ST. MOLAISE PARK, IRVINESTOWN
REFEREE: MICK MCGRATH DONEGAL
RESULT: TYRONE 1·15 FERMANAGH 1·11

Tyrone, beaten in the '94 provincial decider, were under no illusions about the difficulty of the task facing them in their opening assignment in the Ulster championship. Fermanagh, under the guidance of new manager, former Meath footballer, Terry Ferguson were always going to be a tough nut to crack, particularly in their home pitch at Irvinestown. As it transpired, Tyrone had to withstand a late, late comeback before emerging narrow winners, 1-15 to 1-11.

Fermanagh, the only county never to win an Ulster senior title, were forced to line out without injured pair, Fergal McCann and Raymond Gallagher, while Tyrone's inspirational captain Ciaran Corr suffered a heel injury in a club championship game and failed to recover in time. The Coalisland man was replaced at centre half forward by Pascal Canavan, while his brother, Peter Canavan, took over the role of captain for the day.

Fermanagh had left a vacancy at full forward and that was filled by Colm McCreesh, who scored the opening goal of the game when he lobbed goalkeeper, Finbar McConnell, much to the delight of the home supporters among the 15,000 at St. Molaise Park. Fermanagh were full value for their one point interval lead, 1-5 to 0-7, due in no small part to young Shane King , who was a constant thorn in the side of the Tyrone defence and scored 5 points in the opening half. All-star Peter

Fermanagh Back row l to r: Tommy Callaghan, Martin Greene, Colm Mc Creesh, Brian Carty, Cormac Mc Adam, Paul Brewster, Mark Gallagher, Malachy O'Rourke. **Front row l to r:** Raymond Curran, Shane King, Collie Curran, Paddy Mc Guinness, Paul Greene, Tommy Collins, Kieran Gallagher.

Canavan, a truly exceptional player, once again underlined his worth to Tyrone with some excellent points.

Fermanagh paid a heavy price for far too many basic mistakes in the second half and the more experienced Tyrone side took full advantage of their errors. Tyrone scored 1-7, without reply as the Fermanagh challenge crumbled. The loss of midfielder Paul Brewster in the second half was a big blow to Fermanagh's hopes.

Early second half points from Peter Canavan and Seamus McCallan helped nudge Tyrone in front. And then came the goal. Peter Canavan was again to the fore. He passed to the unmarked Stephen Lawn and the full forward from the Moortown club struck the ball past Conor McAdam, to push Tyrone 4 points ahead.

A further 2 points from both Canavan and Matt McGleenan, together with a point from the energetic Pascal Canavan, outstanding on the day, seemed certain to guarantee Tyrone a clearcut victory. But we reckoned without the resilience of 'Ferguson's Men'. At a stage when their supporters were despairing of their team registering even one second half score, Fermanagh fought back, scoring 6 points without reply in an eight-minute purple patch that rocked Tyrone back on their heels. During that spell, Shane King knocked over two points while Mark Gallagher, Malachy O'Rourke, Colm McCreesh and substitute Paul Coyle added one each to cut the deficit to just 3 points. Just when it appeared a shock was on the cards, Pascal Canavan finished a good Tyrone movement with the insurance point.

It was an inauspicious championship start for Tyrone and no doubt, joint team managers, Art Mc Rory and Eugene McKenna would be demanding a marked improvement for the Ulster semi-final showdown with All-Ireland favourites, Derry.

Scorers Tyrone: Peter Canavan 0-7; Pascal Canavan 0-3; Stephen Lawn 1-0; Matt McGleean 0-2; Seamus McCallan 0-1; Fergal Logan 0-1; Jody Gormley 0-1. **Scorers Fermanagh**: Shane King 0-7; Colm McCreesh 1-1; Malachy O'Rourke 0-1; Mark Gallagher 0-1; Paul Coyle 0-1.

T Y R O N E

	FINBAR MCCONNELL	
PAUL DEVLIN	CHRIS LAWN	FAY DEVLIN
RONAN MCGARRITY	SEAMUS MCCALLAN	SEAN MCLOUGHLIN
FERGAL LOGAN		JODY GORMLEY
GERARD CALVAN	PASCAL CANAVAN	ADRIAN CUSH
MATT MCGLEENAN	PETER CANAVAN	STEPHEN LAWN

Substitute: Ciaran Loughran for Adrian Cush

F E R M A N A G H

	CORMAC MCADAM	
RAYMOND CURRAN	PADDY MCGUINNESS	MARTIN GREENE
TOMMY CALLAGHAN	TOMMY COLLINS	KIERAN GALLAGHER
BRIAN CARTY		PAUL BREWSTER
COLIN CURRAN	PAUL GREENE	MALACHY O'ROURKE
MARK GALLAGHER	COLM MCCREESH	SHANE KING

Substitutes: Colm Courtney for Paul Brewster; Paul Coyle for Colin Curran; Justin Gilheaney for Tommy Callaghan

SUNDAY JUNE 11
ULSTER SENIOR FOOTBALL
CHAMPIONSHIP FIRST ROUND

CAVAN & ANTRIM

BREFFNI PARK
REFEREE: BRIAN WHITE WEXFORD
RESULT: CAVAN 2-11 ANTRIM 0-8

This was a journey into the unknown for both teams. Cavan footballers had failed to win a championship game for eight years, while Antrim's record was considerably poorer. The Glensmen had not enjoyed success in a senior championship game since 1982 when they beat Cavan at Breffni Park.

There was never any danger of a repeat victory once classy centre half forward Peter Reilly bounded through the Antrim defence to score the opening goal after just two minutes. It was the perfect start for Cavan!

There was more to follow. Mid-way through the first half, Reilly, displaying Linford Christie-like speed, ghosted past his marker to send a thunderous shot past Antrim goalkeeper, Sean McGreevey. Antrim never recovered from those early killer-blows and thereafter were always chasing the game.

Antrim defender Locky McCurdy was forced to miss the game with a broken arm and was a huge loss. Although Chris Murphy and Paul McErlean held the advantage at midfield for Antrim throughout, it was Cavan who created most of the openings and Ronan Carolan scored 2 points in the first half and was also deprived of a goal by the crossbar. At the other end, a Mickey Boyle goalbound shot was cleared off the line. Although playing against the breeze, Cavan held an 8 point advantage, 2-5 to 0-3, at half-time and the writing was on the wall for Antrim.

Cavan Back row l to r: Fintan Cahill, Peter Reilly, Dermot Mc Cabe, Paul O'Dowd, Patrick Shields, Ronan Carolan, Bernard Morris. Front row l to r: Adrian Lambe, Aidan Watters Gerry Sheridan, Finbar Reilly, Stephen King, Damien O'Reilly, Aidan Connolly, John Brady.

Ronan Carolan scored the first of his 5 second half points for Cavan two minutes after the resumption and eight minutes later he kicked over a wonderful point from a sideline ball. Joe Kennedy had opened Antrim's second half account on 42 minutes and the same player scored another point six minutes later. Sandwiched between those 2 scores was a point from play by Antrim half forward Anton Finnegan. Antrim added just 2 points for the remainder of the game, both from frees by Conal Heately, while Cavan tacked on 4 points, 3 from Carolan, and 1 from full forward John Brady.

Cavan supporters were jubilant that their team had at last ended the losing sequence and manager, Martin McHugh a former Donegal player, was delighted that his championship debut in the managerial hot-seat had ended on a happy note.

Scorers Cavan: Ronan Carolan 0-7; Peter Reilly 2-0; Adrian Lambe 0-2; Dermot McCabe 0-1; John Brady 0-1. **Scorers Antrim:** Joe Kennedy 0-4; Conal Heatley 0-2; Paul McErlean 0-1; Anton Finnegan 0-1.

CAVAN

	PAUL O'DOWD	
AIDAN WATTERS	DAMIEN O'REILLY	FINBAR REILLY
BERNARD MORRIS	AIDAN CONNOLLY	GERRY SHERIDAN
STEPHEN KING		PATRICK SHIELDS
DERMOT MCCABE	PETER REILLY	RONAN CAROLAN
ADRIAN LAMBE	JOHN BRADY	FINTAN CAHILL

Substitutes: Fergal Hartin for Patrick Shields; Raymond Cunningham for Fintan Cahill; Ray Cole for Stephen King

ANTRIM

	SEAN MCGREEVEY	
JOHN KELLY	MARTIN MULHOLLAND	CIARAN PRENTER
TERRY MCCRUDDEN	CHARLIE MCSTRAVICK	AIDAN DONNELLY
CHRIS MURPHY		PAUL MCERLEAN
FRANK WILSON	JOE KENNEDY	ANTO FINNEGAN
MICKEY BOYLE	DONAL ARMSTRONG	CONAL HEATLEY

Substitutes: Gearoid Adams for Charlie McStravick; Donagh Finnegan for Anto Finnegan; Colm McCabe for Donal Armstrong

Antrim Back row l to r: Frank Wilson, Martin Mulholland, Terry Mc Crudden, Chris Murphy, Sean Mc Greevey, Donagh Finnegan, Conal Heately, Paul McErlean. **Front row l to r.** Joe Kennedy, Anto Finnegan, Mickey Boyle, Charlie Mc Stravick, Aidan Donnelly, Donal Armstrong, John Kelly, Ciaran Prenter.

SUNDAY JUNE 18
ULSTER SENIOR FOOTBALL
CHAMPIONSHIP QUARTER FINAL

MONAGHAN & DONEGAL

BALLYBOFEY
REFEREE: JIM CURRAN TYRONE
RESULT: MONAGHAN 1-14 DONEGAL 0-8

What appeared to be nothing more than a stroll in the sunshine for Donegal in their home patch of Ballybofey turned out to be a nightmare of the worst kind. After dismissing reigning Ulster and All-Ireland Champions, Down, the 1995 League finalists were raging hot favourites to advance to a semi-final meeting with Cavan. It is not today or yesterday that we all learned not to take anything for granted in a province where no county has retained the Ulster senior title since Derry in 1976. Monaghan had spent the winter plying their trade in Division Four, not the ideal stomping ground for a team with Ulster championship ambitions. Although they performed admirably against Laois in the League Quarter Final, there was nothing to suggest they would have the measure of a fully focused Donegal.

Monaghan were forced to line out without injured centre half back, Gerard McGurk while Donegal recalled the experienced Declan Bonner at right corner forward in place of John Duffy.

Perhaps, PJ McGowan's team knew it was not going to be their day from the time Declan Bonner's well-struck penalty kick was brilliantly saved by Monaghan goalkeeper John O'Connor, barely 45 seconds into the game after James McHugh had been fouled. It was the first of many battles won by Monaghan on a day when the hotly-tipped Donegal team was dumped out of the championship in front of their own supporters at Sean Mhic Cumhaill Park.

To compound Donegal's misfortune, Declan Loughman scored a fortuitous goal for Monaghan after twelve minutes when the ball rebounded off goalkeeper Gary Walsh. It was a sign of things to come! Monaghan took advantage of the slip-up and led by 1-7 to 0-6, at half-time; still at that stage few could have envisaged what was about to unfold. Donegal scored only 2 points in the entire second half and that was due in large measure to a water-tight Monaghan back-line in which Joe Coyle was superb.

Declan Smyth increased Monaghan's lead early in the second half with a point from a free but Donegal dug deep and responded with 2 points from Manus Boyle to cut the deficit to just 3 points. That period of the game marked a Donegal revival of sorts but untypically their forwards missed a a number of chances which, if converted, could have swung the balance in their favour. Instead, Donegal were not to score for the final 25 minutes as Monaghan re-asserted themselves, particularly so in the closing quarter during which they added 5 more points to completely demoralise the opposition.

Donegal players and supporters were stunned into silence after the game as

Monaghan Back row l to r: Declan Smith, Declan Loughman, David King, Joe Coyle, John O'Connor, Noel Marron, Gregory Flanagan, John Conlon, Padraig Mc Shane. **Middle row l to r:** Michael Slowey, Peter Duffy, Martin Slowey, Frank McEneaney, Stephen Ginnity, Edwin Murphy, Ray McCarron. **Front row l to r:** Ian Larmer, Eoin Meegan, Conor Mone, Kieran Lavelle, Brian Morgan, Seamus Mullen, Colin McCaul, Glenn Murphy.

Donegal Back row l to r: Martin Shovlin, Mark Mc Shane, Paddy Hegarty, John Joe Doherty, Brian Murray, Gary Walsh, Declan Bonner, Barry Mc Gowan. **Front row l to r:** Martin Gavigan, Tony Boyle, Noel Hegarty, Manus Boyle, Matt Gallagher, Mark Crossan, James Mc Hugh.

Monaghan celebrated a thoroughly deserved, if unexpected, victory.

Scorers Monaghan: Declan Smyth 0-6; Peter Duffy 0-3; Declan Loughman 1-0; Stephen McGinnity 0-2; Padraig McShane 0-2; John Conlon 0-1. **Scorers Donegal:** Manus Boyle 0-4; Noel Hegarty 0-1; Martin Gavigan 0-1; Brian Murray 0-1; Declan Bonner 0-1.

MONAGHAN

JOHN O'CONNOR

EDWIN MURPHY	DAVID KING	NOEL MARRON
MARTIN SLOWEY	JOE COYLE	JOHN CONLON
PADRAIG MCSHANE		FRANK MCENEANEY
PETER DUFFY	MICHAEL SLOWEY	GREGORY FLANAGAN
STEPHEN MCGINNITY	DECLAN LOUGHMAN	DECLAN SMYTH

Substitute: Ray McCarron for Gregory Flanagan

DONEGAL

GARY WALSH

JOHN JOE O'DOHERTY	MATT GALLAGHER	BARRY MCGOWAN
MARK CROSSAN	NOEL HEGARTY	MARTIN SHOVLIN
MARTIN GAVIGAN		BRIAN MURRAY
MARK MCSHANE	JAMES MCHUGH	PADDY HEGARTY
DECLAN BONNER	TONY BOYLE	MANUS BOYLE

Substitutes: John Duffy for Mark McShane; John Gildea for Declan Bonner

SUNDAY JUNE 25

ULSTER SENIOR FOOTBALL
CHAMPIONSHIP SEMI-FINAL

TYRONE & DERRY

CLONES

REFEREE: TOMMY MCDERMOTT CAVAN

RESULT: TYRONE 0-11 DERRY 0-10

The warning bells had been ringing loudly in Ulster but nobody appeared to take any heed. Nearly everyone expected Derry, not only to win the provincial title, but also to claim the Sam Maguire Cup for the second time. But the signs were ominous. Reigning All-Ireland Champions Down had fallen at the first hurdle to Donegal and then the 1992 Champions were in turn dumped out of the championship by complete outsiders, Monaghan. It could never happen to Derry, or so we thought! We were wrong. The League Champions and the 1993 All-Ireland title holders succumbed to the Tyrone challenge in front of over 30,000 at Clones. In a show of confidence, Derry named the same team that defeated Armagh in the opening round, while Tyrone made two changes from the side that had a first round victory over Fermanagh.

Inspirational captain Ciaran Corr returned from injury to take his place in the half forward line along with Ciaran Loughran, with Adrian Cush and Gerard Cavlan the players to lose out. It was a day of extreme emotion for players and supporters, with enough incidents to keep Ulster football men and women in conversation through the long winter months.

On a sun-scorched day, All-Star Peter Canavan, operating at full forward, turned in a superlative display scoring 8 points as Tyrone fought back from near disaster at half-time to clinch an Ulster Final spot with a display of raw courage.

Few gave Tyrone a ghost of a chance of winning at the break when they trailed by 0-8 to 0-5 and had to face the second half with only thirteen players after Seamus McCallan and Pascal Canavan were both sent off in separate incidents. Tyrone joint managers, Art McRory and Eugene McKenna, deserve great credit for this victory as their side benefitted enormously from many shrewd sideline decisions, including the introduction of Paul Donnelly and Adrian Cush at half-time. Perhaps Derry felt victory was theirs at that stage but whatever the reason it was Tyrone, displaying commitment and passion beyond the call of duty, who rallied to the cause and took the game . Eleven minutes into the second half and with the sides level 0-8 all, Derry left half back, Fergal McCusker became the third player to be dismissed by Cavan referee, Tommy McDermott after Peter Canavan was floored in an off-the-ball incident. Derry scored just twice in the second half through frees from Anthony Tohill and Enda Gormley, whose pointed free edged Derry in front with seventeen minutes left to play. But then Peter Canavan levelled the game and the clinching score came seven minutes from time when Jody Gormley floated the ball over Damien McCusker's crossbar. Clones was painted red and white!

Both sides missed chances in the closing tension-filled minutes but Derry supporters must have known it was not to be their day when a shot from substitute Jeoffrey McGonigle struck the post. The victory compensated for Tyrone's disappointing performance in last year's Ulster Final defeat by the All-Ireland champions to be, Down.

Only three players scored for Derry, Anthony Tohill and Enda Gormley finished with 9 points between them, all from frees, while Eamon Burns was the only Derry player to score from play. The summer was only beginning in earnest and already, Down, Donegal and Derry had bit the dust. Tyrone were now installed as favourites to win a first Ulster title since 1989!

Scorers Tyrone: Peter Canavan 0-8; Ciaran Corr 0-1; Sean McLoughlin 0-1; Jody Gormley 0-1. **Scorers Derry:** Anthony Tohill 0-5; Enda Gormley 0-4; Eamonn Burns 0-1.

T Y R O N E

	FINBAR MCCONNELL	
PAUL DEVLIN	CHRIS LAWN	FAY DEVLIN
RONAN MCGARRITY	SEAMUS MCCALLAN	SEAN MCLOUGHLIN
FERGAL LOGAN		JODY GORMLEY
CIARAN CORR	PASCAL CANAVAN	CIARAN LOUGHRAN
MATT MCGLEENAN	PETER CANAVAN	STEPHEN LAWN

Substitutes: Paul Donnelly for Ciaran Corr; Adrian Cush for Matt McGleenan; Gerard Cavlan for Ciaran Loughran

D E R R Y

	DAMIEN MCCUSKER	
KIERAN MCKEEVER	TONY SCULLION	GARY COLEMAN
JOHNNY MCGURK	HENRY DOWNEY	FERGAL MCCUSKER
ANTHONY TOHILL		BRIAN MCGILLIGAN
DERMOT HEANEY	DAMIEN BARTON	EAMON BURNS
DECLAN BATESON	SEAMUS DOWNEY	ENDA GORMLEY

Substitutes: Oliver Collins for Brian McGilligan; Damien Cassidy for Declan Bateson; Geoffrey McGonigle for Damien Barton

Tyrone Back row l to r: Paul Devlin, Jody Gormley, Seamus McCallan, Brendan Mallon, Sean McLoughlin, Finbar McConnell, Matt McGleenan, Ciaran McBride, Pascal Canavan, Paul Donnelly, Gerard Cavlan, Stephen Conway. **Front row l to r:** Joe Cassidy, Adrian Cush, Chris Lawn, Stephen Lawn, Ciaran Corr, Peter Canavan, Ciaran Loughran, Fay Devlin, Fergal Logan, Ronan McGarrity, Damien Gormley, Damien Loughran (on ground).

Derry Back row l to r: Dermot Heaney, Anthony Tohill, Damien Mc Cusker, Seamus Downey, Tony Scullion, Damien Barton, Brian Mc Gilligan. **Front row l to r:** Enda Gormley, Fergal P Mc Cusker, Gary Coleman, Johnny Mc Gurk, Henry Downey, Kieran Mc Keever, Eamonn Burns, Declan Bateson.

Cavan Back row l to r: Peter Reilly, Dermot Mc Cabe, Ronan Carolan, Paul O'Dowd, Patrick Shields, Bernard Morris, Aidan Watters. **Front row l to r:** Adrian Lambe, Gerry Sheridan, Stephen King, Aidan Connolly, Damien O'Reilly, John Brady, John Donnellan, Fintan Cahill.

SUNDAY JULY 2
ULSTER SENIOR FOOTBALL
SEMI-FINAL

CAVAN & MONAGHAN

CLONES
REFEREE: MICK MC GRATH DONEGAL
RESULT: CAVAN 1-9 MONAGHAN 0-10

Donegal man Martin McHugh was the centre of attention at Clones on a day when Cavan booked their place in the Ulster Final for the first time since 1983. McHugh took charge of Cavan after failing to land the Donegal job, and immediately set about the task of leading his side out of Division Three. After achieving that first objective with something to spare, McHugh and his team then set their sights on the first round of the Ulster championship where Cavan overcame the Antrim challenge to register a first win in the championship for eight years. The talk around Cavan was 'Martin has what it takes'. Nearly everyone expected Donegal to be Cavan's opponents in the Ulster semi-final and I even heard it suggested more than once that Martin McHugh would re-join Donegal as a player once Cavan were beaten. With the 'Big Three' out of the reckoning the Ulster championship took on a whole new perspective.

There has always been intense rivalry between Cavan and Monaghan and so it proved once again in this game. Monaghan, not surprisingly, named the same team that shocked Donegal, while Cavan made just one change to the side that beat Antrim. Bailieboro club man, John Donnellan, was drafted in at corner back in place of Finbar Reilly.

Pre-match favourites, Monaghan had more than a sufficient share of scoring opportunities to have won, but they were guilty of some appalling misses and ultimately paid the price. It was a sad end to their football journey, particulary after such an accomplished dismissal of Donegal.

Cavan led by 4 points 1-6 to 0-5, at half-time after Paul O'Dowd brilliantly saved a penalty from Declan Smyth, while at the other end, Fintan Cahill made no mistake with a splendid goal after twelve minutes to put his side 1-1 to 0-3 ahead. Cavan had stretched their lead to 5 points, 1-8 to 0-6, fifteen minutes into the second half, and at that stage looked reasonably assured of a place in the Ulster Final against Tyrone.

It was then that Monaghan began their fightback as the Cavan defence came under intense pressure but they stubbornly refused to yield, none more so than wing back, Bernard Morris. Monaghan were also the architechts of their own downfall by missing a number of good scoring chances. Poor markmanship ultimately ended Monaghan's summer dream. Cavan could only manage one score in the closing twenty minutes, a point from star forward Fintan Cahill, as Monaghan agonisingly closed the gap with 2 points from Peter Duffy, one from Frank McEneaney and the final point of the afternoon from Declan Smyth.

Cavan's second half return amounted to a meagre 3 points and even amid the celebrations that followed the semi-final win, one would not be at all surprised if manager Martin McHugh had already begun planning ways to bring about a marked improvement in scoring returns in time for the provincial decider. But one step at a time. For the moment at least Cavan players had every right to feel pleased. Job well done!

Scorers Cavan: Fintan Cahill 1-2; Ronan Carolan 0-3; Peter Reilly 0-2; Adrian Lambe 0-1; Dermot McCabe 0-1. **Scorers Monaghan:** Peter Duffy 0-4; Declan Smyth 0-3; Michael Slowey 0-1; Declan Loughman 0-1; Frank McEneaney 0-1.

C A V A N
PAUL O'DOWD

AIDAN WATTERS	DAMIEN O'REILLY	JOHN DONNELLAN
GERRY SHERIDAN	AIDAN CONNOLLY	BERNARD MORRIS
STEPHEN KING		PATRICK SHEILS
DERMOT MCCABE	PETER REILLY	FINTAN CAHILL
ADRIAN LAMBE	RONAN CAROLAN	JOHN BRADY

Substitutes: Fergal Harton for Patrick Shiels

M O N A G H A N
JOHN O'CONNOR

EDWIN MURPHY	DAVID KING	NOEL MARRON
MARTIN SLOWEY	JOE COYLE	JOHN CONLON
PAURIC MCSHANE		FRANK MCENEANEY
PETER DUFFY	MICHAEL SLOWEY	GREGORY FLANAGAN
STEPHEN MCGINNITY	DECLAN LOUGHMAN	DECLAN SMYTH

Substitutes: Gerard McGuirk for Joe Conlon; Ray McCarron for Declan Loughman; Eoin Meegan for Pauric McShane

Monaghan Back row l to r:. Declan Smith, Declan Loughman, Gregory Flanagan, David King, John O'Connor, Joe Coyle, Padraig Mc Shane, Noel Marron. **Middle row l to r:** Ian Larmer, Michael Slowey, Stephan Mc Ginnity, Frank Mc Eneaney, Peter Duffy, John Conlon, Martin Slowey, Edwin Murphy. **Front row l to r:** Ray Mc Carron, Conor Mone, Eoin Meegan, Colin Mc Caul, Glen Murphy, Kieran Lavelle, Brian Morgan, Gerard Mc Gurk.

SUNDAY JULY 23
ULSTER SENIOR FOOTBALL
CHAMPIONSHIP FINAL

TYRONE & CAVAN

ST. TIGHEARNACH'S PARK, CLONES
REFEREE: PAT MCENEANEY MONAGHAN
RESULT: TYRONE 2-13 CAVAN 0-10

The formbook had been turned upside down in Ulster! Reigning champions, Down, league finalists, Donegal, and their conquerors in that final, and the side tipped by many to win the Sam Maguire Cup, Derry, surprisingly were all just onlookers for the biggest day of the year in the province. Instead, it was the footballers of Tyrone and Cavan who marched behind the Artane Boys Band as all around the ground, the white and red flags intertwined with the blue and white of Cavan. The atmosphere certainly did justice to any Ulster Final of the past.

The game itself was by no means a classic, but Cavan's courageous second half fightback ensured no one was too anxious to leave the friendly town of Clones early. But the dream died for Cavan when Matt Gleenan punched the ball to the net eight minutes from time. Tyrone's other substitute, Adrian Cush, scored Tyrone's second goal in injury time to set up an All-Ireland semi-final meeting with Connacht Champions, Galway.

It was the first meeting of the teams in an Ulster Final since 1956, the day Tyrone recorded their first ever victory over Cavan in the Ulster championship. Some of the household names on that history making Tyrone team were Iggy Jones, Jody O'Neill and Patsy Devlin; among the players lining out for Cavan that day were Victor Sherlock, Phil Brady, Paddy Carolan, Jim McDonnell and Charlie Gallagher.

Now, thirty-nine years on, it was the turn of players like Damien O'Reilly, Stephen King, Peter Reilly, Ronan Carolan, Fintan Cahill and John Brady to wear the Cavan jersey. While favourites, Tyrone, also fielded a quality team with players of the calibre of Fay Devlin, twins Chris and Stephen Lawn, Paul Devlin, Fergal Logan, inspirational captain Ciaran Corr, Pascal Canavan and, of course, his brother, Peter, regarded by many as the best full forward in the country.

Tyrone had been well beaten in the '94 final by eventual All-Ireland winners, Down, but they bounced back in style and deservedly reached their second successive provincial decider with victory over Fermanagh and Derry. Pascal Canavan and Seamus McCallan were sent off against Derry, but the thirteen men of Tyrone performed magnificently in the second half to beat their close rivals by one point. McCallan and Canavan each received a one-month suspension and that allowed themto line out against Cavan. Tyrone decided to make one change from the Derry game, calling in debutant Ciaran McBride in place of Matt McGleenan.

Cavan had won their first game in the championship for eight years when they disposed of the Antrim challenge in the opening round and then pulled off a famous victory over Monaghan, shock winners over Donegal in the previous round. Cavan made one change from the team that disposed of Monaghan; Tommy Smith was drafted in to midfield in place of Patrick Shiels.

Cavan manager, Martin McHugh, was the centre of attention in the football mad county. Writing in the official programme, McHugh had this to say: "I have been associated with Cavan football since September '94. The commitment and enthusiasm of the senior panel has been exceptional. To date they have completed over 120 training sessions. It has given us great encouragement to be promoted to Division Two of the National League and to reach today's Ulster Final. Tyrone go into today's match as firm favourites after their great victory over Derry. We know we have to improve on previous performances to win today."

Tyrone joint-manager Art McRory wrote: "It's great to be back in the Ulster Final and the fact that we are playing Cavan will bring back memories of the famous day in 1956 when Tyrone beat Cavan to win our first senior interprovincial title. Eugene (McKenna) and myself consider it a privilege to work with the present panel of players and it is as a result of their hard work that we are in Clones today. I want to thank the players for their commitment and I also want to thank all the many people who have helped us since the start of the year."

The scene was set. Cavan grabbed the initative immediately. Peter Reilly blasted over a point after just 25 seconds. Tyrone promptly replied with a point from Ciaran McBride. Tyrone goalkeeper, Finbar McConnell quickly came to his side's rescue with a top class save from Dermot McCabe. Cavan had a number of good chances early on and a point each from Ronan Carolan and Tommy Smyth edged them ahead 0-3 to 0-1, after six minutes. Inexplicably, Cavan's challenge faltered for the remainder of the half and it was over thirty minutes later, in fact in injury time, before they got their next score, a point from Reilly. Tyrone scored 8 points without

Tyrone Back row l to r: Paul Devlin, Jody Gormley, Danny Barr, Matt Mc Gleenan, Gerard Cavlan, Brendan Mallon, Sean McLoughlin, Finbar McConnell, Seamus Mc Callan, Ciaran McBride, Paul Donnelly, Damian Loughran, Joe Cassidy. **Front row l to r:** Ronan McGarrity, Chris Lawn, Ciaran Loughran, Peter Canavan, Ciaran Corr, Fay Devlin, Stephen Lawn, Fergal Logan, Pascal Canavan, Damien Gormley. **Ground l to r:** Adrian Cush, Adrian Nugent, Paddy Tully.

reply in a purple patch; Peter Canavan scored 3, with one each from Ciaran McBride, captain Ciaran Corr, Stephan Lawn, and half backs, Sean McLoughlin and Seamus McCallan. It was Tyrone's best period of the game.

Trailing 0-9 to 0-4 at half-time, it appeared a lost cause for Cavan. We reckoned without their true grit and determination. What happened after the restart, followed along similar lines to the opening minutes of the first half. Cavan desperately came in search of scores and Dermot McCabe kicked a point after just 12 seconds. Then Peter Canavan underlined his awesome ability with a point from play. During the next 18 minutes, Cavan absorbed the pressure and outscored Tyrone by 0-4 to 0-2. Suddenly, the margin was down to just 3 point, and 13 minutes still remained. Tyrone had introduced Adrian Cush for Ciaran McBride after 48 minutes and then sprung Matt McGleenan from the substitutes bench with ten minutes to go. It proved a master stroke for joint managers, Art McRory and Eugene McKenna. Cush sent in a high ball and 'Big Matt' fisted past Paul O'Dowd. The smile on the face of the popular Eiglish club man told its own story. Next it was the turn of Cush to stake a claim for a place in the All-Ireland semi-final line-up.

Allowed far too much space, the Donaghmore player punished Cavan with a well taken goal. Large numbers of Tyrone followers, in absolute delight, raced on to the Clones pitch. The game was still not over. Eventually, everyone returned to their place and the match resumed. But it was now only a matter of playing out time and Tyrone were crowned champions for the first time since 1989!

Even the most ardent of Tyrone followers will have to agree that their side were flattered by a 9 point winning margin. After the game Martin McHugh, although conceding Tyrone deserved to win, summed it up when he said: "Remember, we were only 3 points behind with seven minutes left in the game."

Rarely have I witnessed such an outpouring of emotion as when referee, Pat

Cavan Back row l to r: Gerry Sheridan, Dermot Mc Cabe, Ronan Carolan, Paul O'Dowd, Bernard Morris, Tommy Smyth, Fintan Cahill. **Front row l to r.** Aidan Watters, Peter Reilly, Adrian Lambe, Aidan Connolly, Damien O'Reilly, Stephen King, John Brady, John Donnellan.

McEneaney, blew the full-time whistle. Deliriously happy Tyrone supporters once again coverged on the pitch in their thousands. There was a sea of red and white as the players were congratulated for their supreme effort. Ulster Finals are special and that was underlined emphatically when a delighted Ciaran Corr raised the Anglo Celt Cup. The cheering was loud enough to be heard in Ardboe and beyond. Cavan players and supporters joined in the occasion, perhaps looking forward to a day when the blue and white flags would swap places with the red and white.

After the game, an emotionally drained Ciaran Corr joined me in the RTE commentary box and surrounded by well wishers told me he felt 'honoured and privileged to be the man chosen to lift the Anglo Celt Cup for the people of Tyrone."

Scorers Tyrone: Peter Canavan 0-5; Adrian Cush 1-0; Matt McGleenan 1-0; Ciaran McBride 0-2; Stephen Lawn 0-2; Sean McLouglin 0-1; Ciaran Corr 0-1; Seamus McCallan 0-1; Ciaran Loughran 0-1. **Scorers Cavan:** Ronan Carolan 0-5; Dermot McCabe 0-2; Peter Reilly 0-2; Tommy Smyth 0-1.

T Y R O N E

	FINBAR MCCONNELL	
PAUL DEVLIN	CHRIS LAWN	FAY DEVLIN
RONAN MCGARRITY	SEAMUS MCCALLAN	SEAN MCLOUGHLIN
FERGAL LOGAN		JODY GORMLEY
CIARAN CORR	PASCAL CANAVAN	CIARAN LOUGHRAN
CIARAN MCBRIDE	PETER CANAVAN	STEPHEN LAWN

Substitutes: Adrian Cush for Ciaran McBride; Matt McGleenan for Jody Gormley

C A V A N

	PAUL O'DOWD	
AIDAN WATTERS	DAMIEN O'REILLY	JOHN DONNELLAN
GERRY SHERIDAN	AIDAN CONNOLLY	BERNARD MORRIS
STEPHEN KING		TOMMY SMYTH
DERMOT MCCABE	PETER REILLY	RONAN CAROLAN
ADRIAN LAMBE	FINTAN CAHILL	JOHN BRADY

Substitutes: Fergal Hartin for Adrian Lambe; Anthony Forde for John Brady

Ulster Final Action– Fay Devlin, Tyrone, and Peter Reilly, Cavan.

MUNSTER SENIOR FOOTBALL
CHAMPIONSHIP FIRST ROUND

KERRY & LIMERICK

GAELIC GROUNDS, LIMERICK
REFEREE: SEAN O'CAOIMH CORK
RESULT: KERRY 3-17 LIMERICK 0-8

Maurice Fitzgerald was the scoring hero as Kerry trounced Limerick by 18 points in an all too one-sided encounter. The brilliant full forward scored 2-10, and not for the first time emphatically underlined just why he is rated one of the most outstanding players of the present era. Fitzgerald was the jewel in Kerry's crown and the St. Mary's club man exuded class in every facet of play. Limerick manager, Ger Power and his Kerry counterpart, Ogie Moran, were key members of the Kerry team that won eight All-Ireland titles between 1975 and 1986.

Red-hot favourites, Kerry made sweeping changes from the side that lost to Tyrone in the League quarter final, due in part to the unavailability through injury of Sean Burke, Pa Laide, Sean Geaney and Pa Dennehy. Newcomer Darren Aherne was chosen at centre half forward and as the only representative from county champions, Austin Stacks, he was also named as captain.

Aherne had a fine game and his opening goal after 27 minutes increased Kerry's lead to 8 points, 1-7 to 0-2.

Despite Kerry's overall dominance, it was a none too happy outing for midfielders, Liam Flaherty and Conor Kearney, who were forced to play second fiddle to John Quane and Donal Fitzgibbon throughout the first half. Dara O'Se replaced an out of sorts Flaherty at the interval and matters improved in the second

Kerry Back row l to r: Barry O'Shea, Liam Flaherty, Eamon Breen, Conor Kearney, Gene 'Bingo' Driscoll, Peter O'Leary, Maurice Fitzgerald, Mike Hassett. **Front row l to r:** Seamus Moynihan, Bernard McElligott, Billy O'Shea, Darren Aherne, Anthony Gleeson, Dara O'Cinneide, John Crowley.

half for the Kerry men in the troublesome midfield sector. Limerick failed to take advantage of their midfield supremacy in the opening half and wasted far too much good possession to make an impact. Kerry led by, 1-9 to 0-4, at half-time and the Limerick challenge totally disintegrated ten minutes after the restart when Fitzgerald completed a slick Kerry move, fisting the ball past goalkeeper, Richard Bowles. Thereafter, it was a case of damage limitation for an outclassed Limerick team.

Fitzgerald had a few more aces up his sleeve and his second goal six minutes from time sealed a magnificent individual display.

Scorers Kerry: Maurice Fitzgerald 2-10; Darren Aherne 1-1; Dara O'Cinneide 0-2; Dara O'Se 0-1; Bingo Driscoll 0-1; Billy O'Shea 0-1; John Crowley 0-1. **Scorers Limerick:** Timmy Cummins 0-2; Tom Fitzgerald 0-2; Chris McGill 0-2; John Power 0-1; Donal Fitzgibbon 0-1.

K E R R Y
PETER O'LEARY

MIKE HASSETT	ANTHONY GLEESON	BARRY O'SHEA
SEAMUS MOYNIHAN	BERNARD MCELLIGOTT	EAMON BREEN

LIAM FLAHERTY   CONOR KEARNEY

BINGO DRISCOLL	DARREN AHERNE	JOHN CROWLEY
BILLY O'SHEA	MAURICE FITZGERALD	DARA O'CINNEIDE

Substitutes: Dara O'Se for Liam Flaherty; Morgan Nix for Eamon Breen

L I M E R I C K
RICHARD BOWLES

JOHN STOKES	JOHN KEANE	PADDY BARRETT
DONAL MULLIGAN	CON KELLY	LIAM SHEEDY

JOHN QUANE   DONAL FITZGIBBON

JOHN POWER	JOE REDDINGTON	MUIRIS GAVIN
TIMMY CUMMINS	TOM FITZGERALD	CHRIS MCGILL

Substitutes: Kieran Power for Donal Mulligan; Derek Ryan for Joe Reddington; Ger O'Connor for Tom Fitzgerald

Limerick Back row l to r: Donal Fitzgibbon, Joe Reddington, John Quane, Con Kelly, Richard Bowles, John Power, Muiris Gavin. **Front row l to r:** Chris McGill, Tom Fitzgerald, John Stokes, Liam Sheedy, John Keane, Donal Mulligan, Paddy Barrett, Timmy Cummins.

SUNDAY MAY 28
MUNSTER SENIOR FOOTBALL
CHAMPIONSHIP FIRST ROUND

CORK & WATERFORD

PAIRC UI CHAOIMH,CORK
REFEREE: MAURICE O'SULLIVAN KERRY
RESULT: CORK 0-23 WATERFORD 0-9

There was not even the remotest possibilty of an inexperienced Waterford team upsetting the odds against a very accomplished Cork line-up for whom corner forward, Colin Corkery, scored a massive 12 points. It was perhaps just as well that club commitments had restricted Cork's preparations because the Champions had far and away too much firepower for the battling Decies men. Still, Waterford produced one of the game's heroes in goalkeeper, Tom Brennan, who brought off a number of outstanding saves throughout the game and should be well satisfied to have kept a clean sheet against a rampant Cork forward division.

Ciaran O'Sullivan, who had to sit out the entire championship in 1994 because of a ligament injury, was selected at right half back on the Cork team. He marked his comeback with a fine display. Stephen O'Brien and Mark O'Connor also returned to the Cork colours after missing the League campaign. O'Brien had surgery on a groin injury while Army man O'Connor was on UN peace keeping duties.

Neither former All-Ireland winning captain, Larry Tompkins, the Waterford under-21 trainer, or Niall Cahalane were considered for selection, both were recovering from injuries. With an eye to the future, manager Billy Morgan gave senior championship debuts to Paudie Dorgan, Kevin Cowhie, Paudie O'Mahony and goalkeeper, Kevin O'Dwyer.

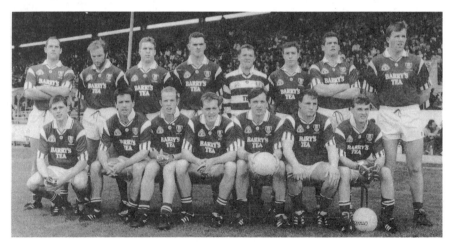

Cork Back row l to r: Mark O'Connor, Brian Corcoran, Padraig O'Mahony, Pat Hegarty, Kevin O'Dwyer, Joe Kavanagh, Liam Honohan, Colin Corkery. **Front row l to r:** Don Davis, Stephen Calnan, Paudie Dorgan, Ciaran O'Sullivan, Danny Culloty, Stephen O'Brien, Kevin Cowhie.

Waterford named a largely inexperienced team and the loss of team captain, Ger Walsh, through injury, and midfielder Owen Cunningham because of suspension, significantly undermined their slim chances.

Cork, aided by the breeze, led at half-time by 0-11 to 0-1. Waterford's solitary first half point came from a free by Brian Arrigan less that three minutes before the interval. Corkery scored 5 points for Cork in the opening half; Stephen Calnan added two points while Ciaran O'Sullivan, Joe Kavanagh, Liam Honohan and Paudie O'Mahony contributed one point each.

It was a case of from the fire into the furnace for Waterford when corner back Don McMahon was sent off shortly after the resumption. But they fought back to reduce the deficit with 2 points from Brian Arrigan and one from Peter Ferncombe.

Cork's play became a little disjointed in the early stages of the second half but they recovered their composure after Liam Honohan opened their second half scoring with an excellent point. Corkery scored 7 points for Cork in the second half. To compound Waterford's misfortune, corner back Alan Reynolds was sent off near the end for a foul on Stephen Calnan.

Brian Arrigan turned in a fine display for Waterford and scored 6 points, quite an achievement in the circumstances.

Scorers Cork: Colin Corkery 0-12; Stephen Calnan 0-3; Ciaran O'Sullivan 0-3; Joe Kavanagh 0-2; Liam Honohan 0-2; Paudie O'Mahony 0-1. **Scorers Waterford:** Brian Arrigan 0-6; Peter Ferncombe 0-1; Richie Power 0-1; Kieran Whelan 0-1.

Waterford Back row l to r: Richard Power, Michael O'Brien, Mattie Kiely, Tom Brennan, Kieran Whelan, Darrell Donnelly, Liam Dalton, Michael Fenton, Don Mc Mahon. **Front row l to r:** Michael Fitzgerald, Joe Murray, John Power, Peter Ferncombe, Alan Reynolds, Brian Arrigan.

C O R K

KEVIN O'DWYER

MARK O'CONNOR	BRIAN CORCORAN	PAUDIE DORGAN
CIARAN O'SULLIVAN	STEPHEN O'BRIEN	KEVIN COWHIE

DANNY CULLOTY   LIAM HONOHAN

DON DAVIS	JOE KAVANAGH	PADRAIG O'MAHONY
STEPHEN CALNAN	PAT HEGARTY	COLIN CORKERY

Substitutes: Mark Farr for Mark O'Connor; John O'Driscoll for Padraig O'Mahony; Paul Coleman for Liam Honohan

W A T E R F O R D

Tom Brennan

Alan Reynolds	Michael Fitzgerald	Don McMahon
Michael O'Brien	Darrell Donnelly	Mattie Kiely

Michael Fenton   Richie Power

JOE MURRAY	LIAM DALTON	JOHN POWER
PETER FERNCOMBE	KIERAN WHELAN	BRIAN ARRIGAN

Substitute: Dermot O'Callaghan for John Power

SUNDAY JUNE 25

MUNSTER SENIOR FOOTBALL
CHAMPIONSHIP SEMI-FINAL

CORK & CLARE

PAIRC UI CHAOIMH
REFEREE: TOMMY HOWARD KILDARE
RESULT: CORK 0-17 CLARE 0-11

On the same day that Tyrone forward Peter Canavan destroyed Derry's hopes with a scoring return of 8 points, and Maurice Fitzgerald accounted for 2-6, as Kerry easily defeated Tipperary, a young Cork man was creating havoc in the sweltering heat of Pairc Ui Chaoimh. Colin Corkery struck over 11 points, one less than his contribution against Waterford in the first round, as Cork overcame the challenge of Clare in the Munster Semi-Final in convincing fashion. Even though 9 of Corkery's tally came from frees, it should in no way detract from what was a prolific display of point scoring. Right corner forward Ger Keane, finished top scorer for Clare with 5 points, underlining his value to a forward line that sparkled on occasions until Cork defenders tightened their grip as the game progressed.

The Cork selectors were able to call on the services of one of their most experienced players Niall Cahalane, but John O'Driscoll, although chosen at full forward, was unable to play and his place was taken by Pat Hegarty. Carl Walsh was handed the Clare goalkeeper's jersey ahead of the more experienced James Hanrahan.

Clare, favoured by the breeze, began in sprightly fashion and had moved 4 points clear after twelve minutes as Cork struggled to find their rhythm. It took Billy Morgan's team fourteen minutes to register their first score through a pointed free from Padraig O'Mahony, but Clare still held a 4 point advantage, 0-7 to 0-3, after 25 minutes. Cork dominated the remainder of the first half with centre half back Stephen O'Brien getting his name on the scoresheet and dangerman Corkery punishing indiscretions by the Clare back line by landing four points to edge Cork in front,

Cork Back row l to r: Brian Corcoran, Liam Honohan, Niall Cahalane, Danny Culloty, Pat Hegarty, Kevin O'Dwyer, Joe Kavanagh, Colin Corkery, Stephen Calnan, Mark O'Connor. **Front row l to r:** Padraig O'Mahony, Don Davis, Kevin Cowhie, Stephen O'Brien, Ciaran O'Sullivan.

0-8 to 0-7, at half-time.

Try as they might in the second half there was no way back for Clare. Although they trailed by only two points, 0-11 to 0-9, fifteen minutes after the restart, it was becoming more and more evident that Cork had the upperhand and so it proved, as they outscored Clare by 6 points to 2 in the closing twenty minutes. Perhaps not as polished a performance as some Leeside supporters would have desired, but nevertheless there were some positive aspects of Cork's game to enthuse about.

Scorers Cork: Colin Corkery 0-11; Padraig O'Mahony 0-2; Stephen O'Brien 0-1; Joe Kavanagh 0-1; Stephen Calnan 0-1; Mark O'Sullivan 0-1. **Scorers Clare:** Ger Keane 0-5; Francis McInerney 0-3; Odran O'Dwyer 0-1; Michael Hynes 0-1; Martin Daly 0-1.

Clare Back row l to r: Michael Hynes, Colm Clancy, Francis Mc Inerney, Aidan Moloney, Carl Walsh, Tom Morrissey, Ger Keane, Brendan Rouine. **Front row l to r:** Kieran Mahony, Odran O'Dwyer, Martin Keavey, Padraic Gallagher, Seamus Clancy, Frankie Griffin, Martin Daly.

C O R K

KEVIN O' DWYER

M ARK O'CONNOR	BRIAN CORCORAN	KEVIN COWHIE
C IARAN O'SULLIVAN	STEPHEN O'BRIEN	NIAL CAHALANE

DANNY CULLOTY   LIAM HONOHAN

DON DAVIS	JOE KAVANAGH	PADRAIG O'MAHONY
STEPHEN CALNAN	PAT HEGARTY	COLIN CORKERY

Substitute: Mark O'Sullivan for Pat Hegarty

C L A R E

CARL WALSH

SEAMUS CLANCY	BRENDAN ROUINE	KIERAN MAHONY
PADRAIC GALLAGHER	FRANKIE GRIFFIN	MARTIN KEAVEY

TOM MORRISSEY   AIDAN MOLONEY

ODRAN O'DWYER	COLM CLANCY	MICHAEL HYNES
GER KEANE	MARTIN DALY	FRANCIS MCINERNEY

Substitutes: Donal O'Sullivan for Aidan Moloney; John Leahy for Michael Hynes; Peter Cosgrove for Tom Morrissey

Kerry Back row l to r: Dara O'Se, Barry O'Shea, Dara O'Cineide, Maurice Fitzgerald, Sean Burke, Liam Hassett, Mike Hassett, Eamon Breen. **Front row l to r:** John Crowley, Liam Flaherty, Billy O'Shea, Anthony Gleeson, Peter O'Brien, Gene 'Bingo' Driscoll, Seamus Moynihan.

SUNDAY JUNE 25
MUNSTER SENIOR FOOTBALL
CHAMPIONSHIP SEMI-FINAL

KERRY & TIPPERARY

TRALEE
REFEREE: KEVIN WALSH CLARE
RESULT: KERRY 7-12 TIPPERARY 1-13

Five goals in an incredible five minute spell early in the first half earned Kerry a Munster Final place in an extraordinary game at Tralee. Kerry were raging hot favourites to dismiss a Tipperary team whose abysmal League form resulted in demotion to Division Four.

Brendan Cummins was chosen at left corner forward on the Tipperary team and that decision by the selectors went some way towards easing the disappointment of the Ardfinnan dual star, who was goalkeeper the previous Sunday when the hurlers lost by a point to Limerick in an enthralling Munster Semi-Final. But there was bad news concerning Cummins' hurling colleague, Anthony Crosse, who was forced to miss the game through injury. Crosse accidentally suffered a facial injury in the game against Limerick and had to undergo an operation in the Cork Regional Hospital.

Kerry made a number of changes from the side that registered an 18 point victory over Limerick in the first round, the most notable being the demotion of team captain and Austin Stacks club man, Darren Aherne, whose place at centre half forward was taken by senior championship debutant, Liam Hassett. Dara O'Se returned to the team to partner Liam Flaherty at midfield.

What occured in the opening ten minutes gave not even the briefest hint of the Kerry onslaught about to unfold. Tipperary began confidently and were leading by three points to one when the floodgates opened. Bingo Driscoll scored the first goal and in the twinkling of an eye Maurice Fitzgerald added two more. Ace marksman Fitzgerald accounted for 2-6 of his side's total as he once again underlined his importance to Kerry with an all-star display.

Tipperary's bemused defence could only watch in horror as Kerry's scoring madness continued unabated and resulted in 2 further goals from Sean Crowley and Liam Hassett. Trailing by 5-2 to 0-3, barely midway through the first half, it was a lost cause for Tipperary. They refused to accept the inevitable and began a spirited fightback to attempt to retrieve the situation. Centre half forward, Pat Maguire scored a goal approaching half-time and were it not for some fine saves from goalkeeper, Peter O'Brien, a replacement before the start for the injured Peter O'Leary, Kerry's 8 point lead at half-time would have been considerably less significant. As it was, Tipperary outscored Kerry by 1-4 to one point in the second quarter.

Peter O'Brien also came to Kerry's aid on a number of occasions in the second half as Tipperary fought tooth and nail to rescue the game. Four unanswered points early in the second half from Brendan Cummins left Tipperary just 4 points in arrears. No doubt Kerry manager Ogie Moran was concerned with the statistic which revealed that Tipperary scored 1-8, to a solitary Kerry point before his team regained the initiative and ran out comfortable winners.

The old order had been restored. Kerry's total of 7-12, was the highest recorded in the 1995 football championship.

Scorers Kerry: Maurice Fitzgerald 2-6; John Crowley 2-1;Liam Hassett 1-2; Darragh O'Cinneide 1-0; Bingo Driscoll 1-0; Eamon Breen 0-2; Gene Farrell 0-1. **Scorers Tipperary:** Brendan Cummins 0-7; Peter Lambert 0-5; Pat Maguire 1-0; Mark Sheahan 0-1.

K E R R Y

PETER O'BRIEN

BARRY O'SHEA	ANTHONY GLEESON	MIKE HASSETT
SEAMUS MOYNIHAN	SEAN BURKE	EAMONN BREEN

LIAM FLAHERTY   DARA O'SE

BINGO DRISCOLL	LIAM HASSETT	JOHN CROWLEY
BILLY O'SHEA	MAURICE FITZGERALD	DARRAGH O'CINNEIDE

Substitutes: Gene Farrell for Dara O'Se; Morgan Nix for Anthony Gleeson

---

T I P P E R A R Y

PHILLY RYAN

TOM MACKEN	PETER GLEESON	BRIAN LACEY
JOHN OWENS	JOHN COSTELLO	TOM ANGLIM

BRIAN BURKE   DERRY FOLEY

DAVY HOGAN	PAT MAGUIRE	MARK SHEAHAN
PETER LAMBERT	CRISTOR MCGRATH	BRENDAN CUMMINS

Substitutes: Liam Cronin for Tom Anglim; Ger Maguire for John Costello

Tipperary Back row l to r: Christoir Mc Grath, Brian Lacey, Derry Foley, Brendan Cummins, Brian Burke, John Costello, Pat Maguire, Mark Sheahan. **Front row l to r:** Tom Anglim, Peter Gleeson, Philly Ryan, Tom Macken, Davy Hogan, Peter Lambert, John Owens.

SUNDAY JULY 23
MUNSTER SENIOR FOOTBALL
CHAMPIONSHIP FINAL

CORK & KERRY

FITZGERALD STADIUM, KILLARNEY
REFEREE: PADDY RUSSELL TIPPERARY
RESULT: CORK 0-15 KERRY 1-9

Yet another championship defeat for Kerry! Even a very early goal from left half back Eamon Breen could not produce the desired result for the Kingdom supporters, now well and truly frustrated at Cork's continued dominance in the southern province.

Since Tommy Doyle raised the Sam Maguire Cup in the Hogan Stand in 1986, Kerry have failed to contest an All-Ireland Final and incredibly have succeeded in winning just one Munster senior title of the nine on offer. In sharp contrast, Cork have enjoyed a rich harvest during that same period and their two All-Irelands and seven Munster crowns is testimony of their controlling influence in Munster.

Although this was a team effort, it is difficult not to single out the immense contribution of Cork midfielders Danny Culloty and Liam Honohan, whose dominance proved the launching pad for a well-merited victory.

Up front, Colin Corkery scored 7 points for Cork and one of those scores in the second half underlined his genius as a free taker. From a very acute angle, close to the sideline he sent over an inspirational point that had both sets of supporters still talking long after the game was over. Larry Tompkins returned after a lengthy absence through injury and although chosen at centre half forward, instead lined out at full forward in a direct switch with Joe Kavanagh. The 1990 All-Ireland winning captain was clearly lacking in match fitness, but still made a valuable contribution, particularly in the closing quarter. Maurice Fitzgerald, with limited possession, proved a handful for the Cork defence and he finished the day with 4 points, 3 from frees. The entire Cork back line gave little away on the day.

Kerry had a dream start after two minutes when Fizgerald passed to Breen who flicked the ball past Kevin O'Dwyer. Cork had moved ahead by the twelfth minute with a point apiece from corner back and captain, Niall Cahalane and half back Ciaran O'Sullivan, and 2 pointed frees from Corkery. Kerry appeared to have settled to their task with vigour and had again opened up a 3 point lead by the 28th minute, through points from Gene Farrell, Mike Hassett and 2 from Fitzgerald, only to lose the advantage and allow Cork come back and level the scores by half-time. Cork finished the half in confident mood with a point each from Joe Kavanagh, Don Davis, and that man Corkery.

Kerry had the breeze at their backs in the second half and Fitzgerald edged them in front with a point. The St. Mary's player had a big part in the next score, a point from play by corner forward, Farrell. But Cork were soon back on level terms with a

1995 Munster Final tussle between Cork and Kerry. Kerry's Dara O' Sé has the ball.

Cork Back row 1 to r: Larry Tompkins, Brian Corcoran, Liam Honohan, Danny Culloty, Kevin O'Dwyer, Colin Corkery, Niall Cahalane, Mark Farr, Mark O'Connor. **Front row 1 to r:** Stephen Calnan, Padraig O'Mahony, Ciaran O'Sullivan, Stephen O'Brien, Joe Kavanagh, Don Davis.

point each from Mark O'Sullivan and Corkery. Bingo Driscoll and Fitzgerald restored Kerry's 2 point lead, but it was then we saw the true character of this Cork team. Six unanswered points from Morgan's men in a blistering seven-minute spell, including 3 from Corkery and 2 from Davis, and Kerry's championship ambitions were in ruins.

Scorers Cork: Colin Corkery 0-7; Don Davis 0-3; Ciaran O'Sullivan 0-2; Niall Cahalane 0-1; Joe Kavanagh 0-1; Mark O'Sullivan 0-1. **Scorers Kerry:** Maurice Fitzgerald 0-4; Eamon Breen 1-0; Gene Farrell 0-2; Mike Hassett 0-1; Bingo Driscoll 0-1; Pa Dennehy 0-1.

C O R K
KEVIN O'DWYER

MARK FARR	MARK O'CONNOR	NIALL CAHALANE
CIARAN O'SULLIVAN	STEPHEN O'BRIEN	BRIAN CORCORAN
DANNY CULLOTY		LIAM HONOHAN
DON DAVIS	LARRY TOMPKINS	PADRAIG O'MAHONY
STEPHEN CALNAN	JOE KAVANAGH	COLIN CORKERY

Substitutes: Mark O'Sullivan for Stephen Calnan; Teddy McCarthy for Larry Tompkins; John O'Driscoll for Padraig O'Mahony

K E R R Y
PETER O'BRIEN

MIKE HASETT	SEAN BURKE	MORGAN NIX
DARA O'CINNEIDE	SEAMUS MOYNIHAN	EAMON BREEN
CONOR KEARNEY		LIAM FLAHERTY
GENE 'BINGO' DRISCOLL	LIAM HASSETT	JOHN CROWLEY
BILLY O'SHEA	MAURICE FITZGERALD	GENE FARRELL

Substitutes: Pa Dennehy for John Crowley; Dara O'Sé for Conor Kearney; Anthony Gleeson for Mike Hassett

Kerry Back row l to r: John Crowley, Liam Flaherty, Sean Burke, Conor Kearney, Maurice Fitzgerald, Liam Hassett, Mike Hassett, Leo Griffin (Team attendant). **Front row l to r:** Eamon Breen, Seamus Moynihan, Dara O'Cinneide, Morgan Nix, Peter O'Brien, Billy O'Shea, Gene Farrell, Gene 'Bingo' Driscoll.

CONNACHT SENIOR FOOTBALL
CHAMPIONSHIP FIRST ROUND

GALWAY & SLIGO

MARKIEVICZ PARK
REFEREE: SEAN MAC EIL MAYO
RESULT: GALWAY 0-11 SLIGO 0-11

Half forward Declan McGoldrick made amends for a first half penalty miss
when he calmly struck over the levelling point in injury time to earn Sligo a
replay a week later at Tuam Stadium. Favourites Galway appeared in trouble when
Eamon O'Hara edged Sligo one point in front with seven minutes left to play, but
Niall Finnegan replied with 2 points for Galway to set up a grandstand finish. A
courageous Sligo team refused to accept defeat and when referee Sean Mac Eil
awarded a free from an acute angle, McGoldrick once again assumed responsiblity.
It was a difficult kick against the breeze, but the St. Mary's man put all thoughts of
that first half penalty miss out of his mind to convert the free with a commendable
degree of authority.

It was a fitting climax to a hugely entertaining game and a draw was no more than
Sligo deserved. PJ Carroll's young team, backed by a strong breeze, took control of
the game early on and Paul Taylor opened the scoring in the third minute with a
point from play. Further points from McGoldrick and Bernard Mulhern left Sligo in
front, 0-3 to no score, after ten minutes. And then soon after came the penalty!
Goalkeeper, Cathal McGinley could only parry a goalbound shot from Sligo half
forward, Eamon O'Hara, and Galway corner back, Mark Kelly handled the ball on
the ground. Mc Goldrick's well-struck penalty came off the upright and was cleared
to safety. Galway availed of their good fortune and a point each from Niall Finnegan,
Brendan Duffy and Tommy Wilson levelled the game after 23 minutes.

By the half-time break, Galway had moved one point in front, 0-5 to 0-4, and
Finnegan stretched the Tribesmen lead with 2 quick points early in the second half.
The expected Galway dominance never materialised. Instead, Sligo took up the
challenge and a point each from Ken Killeen and Fintan Feeney was the signal for a
revival. Jarlath Fallon extended Galway's lead only for Eamon O'Hara and
McGoldrick to level the game with a point each.

Paul Seevers edged Sligo a point in front; substitute Austin Leonard levelled
matters once again; O'Hara restored Sligo's slender lead only for Finnegan to land
two points in quick succession. Galway appeared to have weathered the storm, but
McGoldrick had the final say and his pointed free earned Sligo a replay.

Both teams deserve great credit for displaying such commitment throughout.
Sligo had five players new to championship football: Colin White, David Durcan,
Nigel Clancy, Paul Taylor, and Wicklow-born Ciaran Shannon, while captain Tom
Breheny returned after injury to line out at centre half back. A long-term injury ruled

Galway Back row l to r: Kevin Fallon, Tomas Mannion, Gary Fahy, Cathal Mc Ginley, Kevin Walsh, Mark Kelly, Val Daly. **Front row l to r:** Fergal Gavin, Sean Og De Paor, John Kilraine, Jarlath Fallon, Ray Silke, Tommy Wilson, Niall Finnegan, Brendan Duffy.

Sligo Back row l to r: Nigel Clancy, Paul Durcan, Eamonn Sweeney, Pat Kilcoyne, Colin White, Paul Severs, Ciaran Shannon. **Front row l to r:** Declan Mc Goldrick, Paul Taylor, Eamonn O'Hara, Tom Breheny, David Durkin, Bernard Mulhern, Kenneth Killeen, Fintan Feeney.

out the experienced Brendan Kilcoyne.

Former basketball international, Kevin Walsh was recalled to the Galway side at centre half forward for his first competitive game in the maroon and white jersey since last year's championship. There were three newcomers chosen in the starting fifteen; goalkeeper Cathal McGinley and defenders Ray Silke and Mark Kelly. Galway's Damien Mitchell was unable to take his place at centre half back due to injury. He was replaced by Kevin Fallon.

Scorers Galway: Niall Finnegan 0-6; Jarlath Fallon 0-2; Brendan Duffy 0-1; Austin Leonard 0-1; Tommy Wilson 0-1. **Scorers Sligo:** Declan McGoldrick 0-3; Eamon O'Hara 0-2; Paul Seevers 0-2; Bernard Mulhern 0-1; Paul Taylor 0-1; Ken Killeen 0-1; Fintan Feeney 0-1.

GALWAY

CATHAL MCGINLEY

| JOHN KILRAINE | GARY FAHY | MARK KELLY |
| RAY SILKE | KEVIN FALLON | TOMAS MANNION |

JARLATH FALLON   FERGAL GAVIN

| BRENDAN DUFFY | KEVIN WALSH | TOMMY WILSON |
| NIALL FINNEGAN | VAL DALY | SEAN OG DE PAOR |

Substitutes: Fergal O'Neill for Brendan Duffy; Austin Leonard for Fergal Gavin; Ollie Hynes for Val Daly

SLIGO

PAT KILCOYNE

| NIGEL CLANCY | EAMON SWEENEY | COLIN WHITE |
| DAVID DURKIN | TOM BREHENY | BERNARD MULHERN |

PAUL DURCAN   CIARAN SHANNON

| DECLAN MCGOLDRICK | PAUL TAYLOR | EAMON O'HARA |
| KEN KILLEEN | FINTAN FEENEY | PAUL SEEVERS |

Substitutes: Karl Kearins for Ken Killeen; Liam Filan for Nigel Clancy

Galway Back row l to r: Val Daly, Gary Fahy, Kevin Walsh, Cathal Mc Ginley, Ray Silke, Mark Kelly, Fergal Gavin, Tomas Mannion. **Front row l to r:** Damien Mitchell, Sean Og De Paor, John Kilraine, Brendan Duffy, Jarlath Fallon, Tommy Wilson, Niall Finnegan.

SUNDAY JUNE 4

CONNACHT SENIOR FOOTBALL
CHAMPIONSHIP FIRST ROUND
REPLAY

GALWAY & SLIGO

TUAM STADIUM

REFEREE: SEAN MAC EIL MAYO

RESULT: GALWAY 1-12 SLIGO 0-8

The drawn game emphatically underlined just how much football standards have levelled off in Connacht in recent years. The character of the Galway team was severely tested the first day out and they were somewhat fortunate to escape with a draw, although in the end it took a late point from Sligo half forward Declan McGoldrick to force a replay.

In the 1994 championship, Galway drew with Leitrim at Carrick-On-Shannon, but John O'Mahony's team defied the odds to win the replay at Tuam. With that defeat still fresh in their minds, Galway players made it abundantly clear in the build-up to the re-match with Sligo that they were in no mood to allow lightning to strike twice in successive championships.

Galway decided to reshuffle their team and moved Sigerson Cup-winning captain, Seán Óg de Paor, from corner forward to left half back, a position occupied by Tomas Mannion at Markievicz Park. Manager Bosco McDermott and his selectors switched Mannion to midfield in place of captain, Jarlath Fallon, who was chosen instead at right half forward. Damien Mitchell returned to replace Kevin Fallon at centre half back after missing the drawn game due to a hamstring injury. Sligo manager, PJ Carroll, not surprisingly, gave a vote of confidence to the same fifteen that started the first day. Ballymote club man Nigel Clancy, who suffered bruised ribs in the drawn game, recovered sufficiently to take his place at right corner back.

Sligo started promisingly with points from Declan McGoldrick and Paul Taylor as Galway struggled to come to terms with the early onslaught. This replay could have taken an entirely different route early on had Sligo goalkeeer, Pat Kilcoyne, not deprived Niall Finnegan a certain goal, with the game little more than a minute old. Instead, Mc Goldrick and Ken Killeen copperfastened Sligo's grip on the game with further points as their supporters roared approval. Kilcoyne saved from Finnegan again shortly before Galway registered their first score, a point from a free after 21 minutes. Galway then took control and despite missing a number of scoring opportunites were in front, 1-4 to 0-4, at half-time, thanks to a goal from Brendan Duffy.

After Sligo failed to convert a number of good scoring opportunities early in the second half, Galway took control of affairs with Gary Fahy outstanding at full back. A point each from Tommy Wilson, Damien Mitchell, Niall Finnegan, Val Daly, Jarlath Fallon, and 2 points from Gavin put Galway into an unassailable lead. Sligo

Sligo Back row l to r: Paul Durcan, Paul Severs, David Durkin, Ciaran Shannon, Pat Kilcoyne, Eamonn Sweeney, Nigel Clancy, Colin White. **Front row l to r:** Declan Mc Goldrick, Ken Killeen, Eamonn O'Hara, Tom Breheny, Bernard Mulhern, Paul Taylor, Fintan Feeney.

failed to score from the 13th minute of the first half until eight minutes from time, when substitute Karl Kearins, son of former Sligo great, Mickey, kicked over a point. By that stage, Galway, clearly the better team, had built up a 1-11 to 0-5 lead. Ken Killeen and Karl Kearins added another point apiece for Sligo before Galway captain, Jarlath Fallon, wrapped up the scoring with a point from a free.

Scorers Galway: Jarlath Fallon 0-3; Brendan Duffy 1-0; Niall Finnegan 0-2; Kevin Walsh 0-2; Fergal Gavin 0-2; Damien Mitchell 0-1; Tommy Wilson 0-1; Val Daly 0-1. **Scorers Sligo:** Ken Killeen 0-2; Karl Kearins 0-2; Declan McGoldrick 0-2; Paul Taylor 0-1; Paul Seevers 0-1.

<table>
<tr><td colspan="3" align="center">G A L W A Y</td></tr>
<tr><td></td><td align="center">CATHAL MCGINLEY</td><td></td></tr>
<tr><td>JOHN KILRAINE</td><td align="center">GARY FAHY</td><td align="right">MARK KELLY</td></tr>
<tr><td>RAY SILKE</td><td align="center">DAMIEN MITCHELL</td><td align="right">SEAN OG DE PAOR</td></tr>
<tr><td></td><td align="center">FERGAL GAVIN</td><td align="right">TOMAS MANNION</td></tr>
<tr><td>JARLATH FALLON</td><td align="center">KEVIN WALSH</td><td align="right">TOMMY WILSON</td></tr>
<tr><td>NIALL FINNEGAN</td><td align="center">VAL DALY</td><td align="right">BRENDAN DUFFY</td></tr>
</table>

Substitutes: Seamus Fallon for John Kilraine; Fergal O'Neill for Tommy Wilson; Conor McGauran for Val Daly

<table>
<tr><td colspan="3" align="center">S L I G O</td></tr>
<tr><td></td><td align="center">PAT KILCOYNE</td><td></td></tr>
<tr><td>NIGEL CLANCY</td><td align="center">EAMON SWEENEY</td><td align="right">COLIN WHITE</td></tr>
<tr><td>DAVID DURKIN</td><td align="center">TOM BREHENY</td><td align="right">BERNARD MULHERN</td></tr>
<tr><td></td><td align="center">PAUL DURCAN</td><td align="right">CIARAN SHANNON</td></tr>
<tr><td>DECLAN MCGOLDRICK</td><td align="center">PAUL TAYLOR</td><td align="right">EAMON O'HARA</td></tr>
<tr><td>KEN KILLEEN</td><td align="center">FINTAN FEENEY</td><td align="right">PAUL SEVERS</td></tr>
</table>

Substitutes: Karl Kearins for Paul Taylor; Fintan Kennedy for Eamon Sweeney; Martin McGrath for Declan McGoldrick

SUNDAY JUNE 4
CONNACHT SENIOR FOOTBALL
CHAMPIONSHIP FIRST ROUND

ROSCOMMON & LONDON

RUISLIP, LONDON
REFEREE: SEAMUS PRIOR LEITRIM
RESULT: ROSCOMMON 0-19 LONDON 1-7

Roscommon qualified for a Connacht semi-final meeting against Mayo after brushing aside the London challenge with a degree of authority, if not altogether consummate ease. Yet in defeat, London, on the back of a disastrous League campaign, deservedly won many admirers among the attendance of over 2,000 for their sheer grit and determination. They struggled to cope with a more physically endowed Roscommon side, whose approach work was also much superior. There was never any danger of this courageous London side pulling off a shock victory against an understrength Roscommon side, minus key players, Pat Doorey and John Newton, but neither did they capitulate against overwhelming odds. Despite the assistance of a stiff breeze, the Exiles trailed by 6 points at the interval, but to their credit they still refused to lose heart.

Roscommon midfielders, Don Connellan and Nigel Dineen, ruled their patch with total authority while Derek Duggan in particular provided the finishing touches with clinical precision. The Castlerea club man scored 5 points in the opening half, and a point each from, Luke Dolan, Conor Connelly, Tom Grehan and Vincent Glennon, ensured Roscommon held a commanding, 0-9 to 0-3, interval lead. London's first half points came from Niall Magee, centre half back Barry McDonagh and corner forward Kevin Blaney.

London's performance improved considerably in the second half, but they failed to take advantage of the opportunities that presented themselves. Roscommon were much more economical and decisive, with Luke Dolan displaying his undoubted skill with some well-taken points. London, too, had their heroes; none more than Joe Darcy at full back who epitomised the spirit of the Exiles with an outstanding display.

Gabriel O'Neill scored the only goal of the game for London four minutes from the end, but Roscommon replied with a point each from Conor Connelly and Tommy Grehan to underline their superiority. When the teams last met in the championship in 1990, Roscommon had 23 points to spare over London; the margin of victory on this occasion was 9 points. Any improvement, however marginal, is welcome news for London, who deserve every credit for their tremendous work in promoting the game.

Scorers Roscommon: Derek Duggan 0-6; Luke Dolan 0-4; Tommy Grehan 0-3; Conor Connelly 0-2; Vincent Glennon 0-2; Lorcan Dowd 0-2. **Scorers London:** Gabriel O'Neill 1-0; Eamon Prenter 0-2; Niall Magee 0-1; Barry McDonagh 0-1; Kevin Blaney 0-1; Sean Doherty 0-1; Tommy Maguire 0-1.

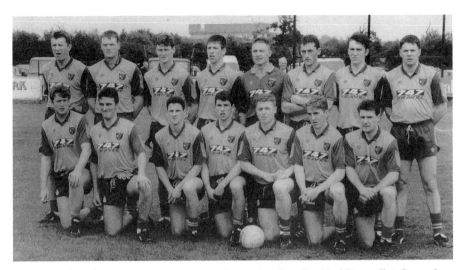

Roscommon Back row l to r: David O'Connor, Derek Duggan, Don Connellan, Nigel Dineen, Chris Grogan, Sean Staunton, Conor Connelly, Tommy Grehan. **Front row l to r:** Luke Dolan, Joey Connaughton, Lorcan Dowd, Damien Donlon, Enon Gavin, Bernard Butler, Vincent Glennon.

R O S C O M M O N

	CHRIS GROGAN	
SEAN STAUNTON	DAVID O'CONNOR	ENON GAVIN
JOEY CONNAUGHTON	DAMIEN DONLON	BERNARD BUTLER
NIGEL DINEEN		DON CONNELLAN
VINCENT GLENNON	CONOR CONNELLY	TOMMY GREHAN
LUKE DOLAN	LORCAN DOWD	DEREK DUGGAN

Substitute: Tom Ryan for Vincent Glennon

L O N D O N

	JOHN COLLINS	
PEARSE O'REILLY	JOE DARCY	PADDY TINNELLY
PAUL HEGARTY	BARRY MCDONAGH	PASCAL CULLEN
NIALL MAGEE		GABRIEL O'NEILL
SEAN DOHERTY	TOMMY MAGUIRE	AIDAN CREAMER
KEVIN BLANEY	SEAN WOODS	EAMON PRENTER

Substitutes: Jack Harnan for Paul Hegarty; Senan Hehir for Sean Woods; Richie Harnan for Eamon Prenter

London Back row l to r: Paul Hegarty, Niall Mc Gee, Joe Darcy, Aidan Creamer, Eamon Prenter, Paddy Tinnelly, Sean Woods. **Front row l to r:** Kevin Blaney, Sean Doherty, Gabriel O'Neill, John Collins, Barry Mc Donagh, Pascal Cullen, Tommy Maguire, Pearse O'Reilly.

SUNDAY JUNE 11
CONNACHT SENIOR FOOTBALL
CHAMPIONSHIP SEMI-FINAL

GALWAY & LEITRIM

PAIRC SEAN MAC DIARMADA
REFEREE: PAT CASSERLY WESTMEATH
RESULT: GALWAY 0-12 LEITRIM 0-11

Leitrim footballers first defence of a Connacht title since 1928 ended in misery when Galway corner forward, Niall Finnegan, sensationally kicked over the winning point from a free with the game in injury time. It was cruel luck on a Leitrim team that had built up a 2 points lead with just three minutes remaining. Galway, displaying tremendous courage, stormed back to score 3 points without reply to snatch victory and stun the home following into silence. Leitrim's achievement in winning the Connacht Final after a lapse of 67 years was one of the major highpoints of the '94 football championship. The whole country celebrated. The fact that Leitrim were beaten by Dublin in the All-Ireland semi-final failed to dampen the enthusiasm of the players and supporters alike. A Connacht title had been secured and Croke Park had provided valuable experience. Next year promised to be even better still!

John O'Mahony's gallant heroes were widely tipped to retain the provincial crown and return to Croke Park older, wiser and much more formidable. Galway tore the script to shreds and scattered it around Pairc Sean Mac Diarmada on a late Sunday evening in June. Leitrim appeared to have booked a place in the Connacht final when Paul Kieran and substitute Ciaran McGovern scored a point each to put their team two points in front after 63 minutes.

No one, least of all their tiny band of supporters, was prepared for Galway's dramatic comeback. First, captain Jarlath Fallon kicked over a superb point, then left half back, Seán Óg de Paor, levelled the sides for the seventh time. Before the home supporters could grasp what was happening, up popped corner forward Finnegan to float a free kick over the bar. It was a game Leitrim should have won, but credit Galway for their late, late rally which resulted in a dramatic victory.

Although favoured by a stiff breeze, Leitrim held a slender one point lead, 0-7 to 0-6, at the interval. Galway began in brisk fashion and 2 points from Val Daly and one from Fallon had the Tribesmen three points to one in front after seven minutes play. Leitrim half forward, Brian Breen got the opening score of the game in the third minute and 2 points apiece from Padraig McLoughlin and Colin McGlynn, plus one each from Liam Conlon and Declan Darcy, accounted for Leitrim's first half total.

Seán Óg de Paor and Niall Finnegan got Galway's last 2 points of the opening half to supplement the earlier contribution of 4 points, evenly shared between Daly and Fallon. Galway star Kevin Walsh had to retire injured after twenty-five minutes

Galway Back row l to r: Val Daly, Niall Finnegan, Seamus Fallon, Cathal Mc Ginley, Ray Silke, Gary Fahy, Kevin Walsh. Front row l to r: Damien Mitchell, Tomas Mannion, Fergal Gavin, Jarlath Fallon, John Kilraine, Brendan Duffy, Sean Og De Paor, Tommy Wilson.

of the first half and early in the second half corner back, John Kilraine was also forced to succumb to injury.

Half forward Tommy Wilson, got the equalising score for Galway immediately after the restart; McGlynn restored Leitrim's lead; Finnegan replied for Galway; McGlynn edged Leitrim a point ahead, but Fallon levelled the match once again after 57 minutes. Mickey Quinn was now ruling the roost at midfield for Leitrim and when Paul Kieran and substitute Ciaran McGovern found the target it appeared the champions would survive. The drama was only just beginning. Galway scored 3 points without reply to advance to their first Connacht Football Final since 1990.

Leitrim Back row l to r: Mickey Quinn, Seamus Quinn, Brian Breen, Martin Mc Hugh, Liam Conlon, Colin Mc Glynn, Ciaran Murray, Noel Moran. Front row l to r: Joe Honeyman, Gerry Flanagan, Pat Donohoe, Declan Darcy, Padraig McLoughlin, Paul Kieran, Padraig Kenny.

One has to sympathise with the losers, Leitrim controlled the game for long periods in the second half but they failed to take advantage of an abundance of possession and their forwards were altogether too wayward with their scoring attempts.

Scorers Galway: Jarlath Fallon 0-4; Niall Finnegan 0-3; Seán Óg de Paor 0-2; Val Daly 0-2; Tommy Wilson 0-1. **Scorers Leitrim:** Colin McGlynn 0-4; Padraig McLoughlin 0-2; Brian Breen 0-1; Liam Conlon 0-1; Paul Kieran 0-1; Ciaran McGovern 0-1; Declan Darcy 0-1.

G A L W A Y
CATHAL MCGINLEY

| JOHN KILRAINE | GARY FAHY | SEAMUS FALLON |
| RAY SILKE | DAMIEN MITCHELL | SEAN OG DE PAOR |

FERGAL GAVIN   TOMAS MANNION

| JARLATH FALLON | KEVIN WALSH | TOMMY WILSON |
| NIALL FINNEGAN | VAL DALY | BRENDAN DUFFY |

Substitutes: Conor McGauran for Kevin Walsh; Kevin Fallon for John Kilraine; Fergal O'Neill for Brendan Duffy

L E I T R I M
MARTIN MCHUGH

| JOE HONEYMAN | SEAMUS QUINN | CIARAN MURRAY |
| NOEL MORAN | DECLAN DARCY | GERRY FLANAGAN |

MICKEY QUINN   PAT DONOHOE

| BRIAN BREEN | PAUL KIERAN | PADRAIG KENNY |
| PADRAIG MCLOUGHLIN | COLIN MCGLYNN | LIAM CONLON |

Substitutes: Ciaran McGovern for Noel Moran; Aidan Rooney for Padraig Kenny; Jason Ward for Pat Donoghue

Mayo Back row l to r: Ray Dempsey, James Nallen, Colm McMenamon, Barry Heffernan, Liam Niland, Kevin Cahill, Kevin O'Neill. **Front row l to r:** John Casey, Peter Butler, Tony Corcoran, Paul Cunney, Pat Fallon, Kenneth Mortimer, Gary Ruane, Padraig Brogan.

SUNDAY JUNE 25

CONNACHT SENIOR FOOTBALL
CHAMPIONSHIP SEMI-FINAL

MAYO & ROSCOMMON

MCHALE PARK, CASTLEBAR
REFEREE: MICK CURLEY GALWAY
RESULT: MAYO 2-11 ROSCOMMON 1-10

Changed times as Mayo and Roscommon faced each other in McHale Park. There was no Jack O'Shea and no Dermot Earley to issue instructions from the sidelines. New Mayo manager, Anthony Egan, was the man chosen to succeed former Kerry great, 'Jacko', while Donie Shine was entrusted with the task of guiding the fortunes of Roscommon after Earley, the county's favourite son, took over from Mick O'Dwyer in Kildare. Changed times indeed. Egan and Shine may not be household names, but both are astute football men with one shared ambition, to restore pride and achieve success with their native counties.

The Connacht Semi-final meeting represented a journey into the unknown for two counties that had disappointed somewhat in the League; Roscommon failed to gain promotion from Division Three, while Mayo joined their near neighbours after a most unhappy winter sojourn in Division Two ended in relegation.

Roscommon started out as slight favourites to advance to a Connacht Final meeting with Galway after it emerged midweek that high-fielding John Newton would partner Don Connellan at midfield with long serving Pat Doorey returning to his customary full back position.

It appeared Roscommon would have too much strength and experience to be unduly troubled by a young Mayo side. That was not the case. The 'Boys From The County Mayo' defied the odds and, aided by the breeze, dictated the pace right from the start and despite kicking 9 wides, led by 1-7 to 0-4 at half-time. Full forward John Casey scored the Mayo goal after 34 minutes, and when pacey right half back, Tony Corcoran crashed the ball past goalkeeper Chris Grogan, nine minutes after the restart, Mayo had moved 8 points clear, 2-8 to 0-6. Mayo's confidence was sky high at that juncture whereas Roscommon appeared bereft of ideas. As they have proved so often in the past, Roscommon are most dangerous when they appear most vulnerable. Centre half forward, Fergal O'Donnell kicked a point and Donie Shine's men were handed a lifeline when Tommy Grehan converted a penalty to cut the deficit to just 4 points with more than twenty minutes still left to play.

Strokestown's Damien Donlon was unlucky a few moments later when his shot rebounded off the upright and the chance was lost. Both teams scored three points apiece in the closing quarter as Mayo put their miserable league campaign behind them to fashion a deserved victory.

Roscommon Back row l to r: Derek Duggan, Enon Gavin, Don Connellan, Chris Grogan, John Newton, Damien Donlon, Fergal O'Donnell, Tommy Grehan. **Front row l to r:** Nigel Dineen, Bernard Butler, Lorcan Dowd, Pat Doorey, Luke Dolan, Joey Connaughton, Sean Staunton.

Scorers Mayo: Tony Corcoran 1-0; John Casey 1-0; Padraig Brogan 0-2; Colm McMenamon 0-2; Paul Cunney 0-2; Ray Dempsey 0-2; Peter Butler 0-1; Pat Fallon 0-1; Kevin O'Neill 0-1. **Scorers Roscommon:** Luke Dolan 0-5; Fergal O'Donnell 0-3; Tommy Grehan 1-0; Derek Duggan 0-1; John Newton 0-1.

	M A Y O	
	BARRY HEFFERNAN	
KENNETH MORTIMER	KEVIN CAHILL	GARY RUANE
TONY CORCORAN	JAMES NALLEN	PETER BUTLER
PAT FALLON		COLM MCMENAMON
PAUL CUNNEY	RAY DEMPSEY	LIAM NILAND
KEVIN O'NEILL	JOHN CASEY	PADRAIG BROGAN

Substitutes: Anthony McGarry for Peter Butler; Diarmuid Byrne for Padraig Brogan; Jarlath Jennings for Liam Niland

	R O S C O M M O N	
	CHRIS GROGAN	
SEAN STAUNTON	PAT DOOREY	ENON GAVIN
JOEY CONNAUGHTON	DAMIEN DONLON	BERNARD BUTLER
JOHN NEWTON		DON CONNELLAN
NIGEL DINEEN	FERGAL O'DONNELL	TOMMY GREHAN
LUKE DOLAN	LORCAN DOWD	DEREK DUGGAN

Substitues: David O'Connor for Nigel Dineen; Conor Connelly for Derek Duggan; Alan Nolan for Don Connellan

SUNDAY JULY 23
CONNACHT SENIOR FOOTBALL
CHAMPIONSHIP FINAL

GALWAY & MAYO

TUAM STADIUM
REFEREE: FRANCIS FINAN SLIGO
RESULT: GALWAY 0-17 MAYO 1-7

Galway had a comprehensive 7 point victory over old rivals Mayo to reclaim the JJ Nestor Cup after a lapse of eight years. Bosco McDermott's team, conquerors of Leitrim in the semi-final, courtesy of an injury-time point from Niall Finnegan, had no reason to leave it as late on this occasion against a strangely subdued Mayo side.

Galway were clearly the better team on the day, but Mayo were their own worst enemies. That they wasted an inordinate amount of possession and in the process kicked 18 wides. Although Pat Fallon and Colm McMenamon controlled midfield for long periods, the Mayo forwards were far too wasteful for any benefits to accrue from that dominance. In fairness, credit must be given to an extremely vigilant Galway defence that gave little away and hustled and harried the Mayo forwards at every opportunity. Galway, too, were guilty of poor marksmanship on far too many occasions, but overall the Tribesmen made considerably better use of their opportunities.

Mayo left out the experienced Padraig Brogan, who had played against Roscommon, and instead opted for Diarmuid Byrne from the Castlebar Mitchels club in a reshuffled full forward line. Galway made two changes from the team that beat Leitrim. Kevin Fallon replaced his injured brother Seamus at left corner back, and Galway United soccer player Fergal O'Neill was chosen ahead of Brendan Duffy at left corner forward.

Niall Finnegan got scoring underway with a point for Galway after just two minutes. A minute later, Mayo right half forward Paul Cunney levelled the game. Mayo failed to score again for the next twenty minutes, during which time Galway tacked on 5 points, with 2 of those coming from full forward Val Daly and one each from Kevin Walsh, Finnegan, Tommy Wilson and wing back Sean Og de Paor. The steadying influence of Peter Butler was sorely missed in the Mayo backline. The Knockmore man failed a late fitness test and his place at left half back was taken by Tony Corcoran, who himself had to retire injured after just fifteen minutes. It was a setback Mayo could have done without.

Hard-working midfielder Colm McMenamon scored Mayo's second point after 23 minutes, and nine minutes later corner back, Kenneth Mortimer reduced the deficit to 4 points. Daly had the final say before the half-time whistle with a good point from play to make it, Galway 0-8 Mayo 0-3 at the interval. It was Galway's first score for seventeen minutes.

Galway Back row l to r: Val Daly, Fergal O'Neill, Fergal Gavin, Kevin Fallon, Ray Silke, Cathal Mc Ginley, Niall Finnegan, Kevin Walsh, Gary Fahy. **Front row l to r:** Damien Mitchell, Tomas Manion, Jarlath Fallon, John Kilraine, Tommy Wilson, Sean Og De Paor.

Mid-air challenge between John Kilraine, Galway, and Diarmuid Byrne, Mayo during the Connacht Final 1995.

Tommy Wilson increased Galway's lead with a point immediately after the restart, but Mayo responded with a point each from Kevin O'Neill and substitute Padraig Brogan. Any chances of a Mayo revival were well and truly dashed when the home side scored 3 unanswered points. While Mayo's misery continued in front of goal, Galway piled on the scores and they had moved into a commanding 10 point lead, 0-17 to 0-7, when Ray Dempsey broke through their ranks to score a consolation goal.

Scorers Galway: Val Daly 0-4; Niall Finnegan 0-4; Tommy Wilson 0-3;Fergal O'Neill 0-3; Sean Og de Paor 0-1; Fergal Gavin 0-1; Kevin Walsh 0-1. **Scorers Mayo:** Ray Dempsey 1-1; Padraig Brogan 0-2; Kenneth Mortimer 0-1; Colm McMenamon 0-1; Paul Cunney 0-1; Kevin O'Neill 0-1.

GALWAY

CATHAL MCGINLEY

JOHN KILRAINE	GARY FAHY	KEVIN FALLON
RAY SILKE	DAMIEN MITCHELL	SEAN OG DE PAOR
FERGAL GAVIN		TOMAS MANNION
JARLATH FALLON	KEVIN WALSH	TOMMY WILSON
NIALL FINNEGAN	VAL DALY	FERGAL O'NEILL

Substitute: Alan Mulholland for Tomas Mannion

MAYO

BARRY HEFFERNAN

KENNETH MORTIMER	KEVIN CAHILL	GARY RUANE
ANTHONY MCGARRY	JAMES NALLEN	TONY CORCORAN
PAT FALLON		COLM MCMENAMON
PAUL CUNNEY	RAY DEMPSEY	LIAM NILAND
DIARMUID BYRNE	JOHN CASEY	KEVIN O'NEILL

Substitutes: Michael Coleman for Tony Corcoran; Padraig Brogan for Liam Niland; Maurice Sheridan for Diarmuid Byrne

Mayo Back row l to r: John Casey, Colm McMenamon, Raymond Dempsey, Barry Heffernan, James Nallen, Liam Niland, Kevin Cahill, Kevin O'Neill. **Front row l to r:** Diarmuid Byrne, Paul Cunney, Kenneth Mortimer, Pat Fallon, Gary Ruane, Anthony McGarry, Tony Corcoran.

ALL-IRELAND SENIOR FOOTBALL SEMI-FINAL

TYRONE & GALWAY

CROKE PARK
REFEREE: BRIAN WHITE WEXFORD
RESULT: TYRONE 1-13 GALWAY 0-13

Joint team manager, Art McRory, once said that Peter Canavan was the icing on the cake for Tyrone. And that was never more in evidence than in the second half when the brilliant all-star turned in a performance of sheer class to sink the Connacht Champions and send Tyrone into their first All-Ireland final since 1986.

Tyrone can count their lucky stars that Canavan, with a personal tally of 1-7, was on top of his game, for this was a day when a skilful Galway team came to Croke Park and rubbished the claims that Connacht football is a lost cause. The odds were stacked againt Galway right from the start. Tomas Mannion had to withdraw because of injury before the game and the Monivea/Abbey man was replaced at centre half forward by Alan Mulholland, who turned in a fine display.

Tyrone approached their first semi-final since 1989 brimming with confidence after emerging tops in Ulster, a province that had produced the last four Sam Maguire Cup winners. Expectations were high!

In contrast, only the most optimistic of their true blue supporters gave Galway a ghost of a chance of disposing of the Tyrone challenge. Indeed, only a small number of maroon and white flags greeted Galway's return to Croke Park after a gap of eight years and that in itself told its own story. The sceptics had once again decided to stay away. Galway supporters in the 37,000 plus attendance were well and truly outnumbered, perhaps three to one on the day, but those that went to the trouble of making the journey were made to feel proud of their team's battling performance. And justifiably so! 'Bosco's Men' are made of stern stuff and can take great encouragment from their performance.

It was never going to be easy for Tyrone: they had beaten All-Ireland favourites, Derry in Ulster and had trounced Galway in the League. Their fanatical supporters had already convinced themselves that the Connacht champions would be easy prey. Although the players did their level best to avoid listening to those who suggested an easy semi-final win, it proved no simple task in a football-mad county. When players continually listen to supporters saying things like, 'no bother Sunday', it becomes difficult to counteract and causes its own problems.

Tyrone corner back, Paul Devlin, told me on the eve of the game that Galway were not renowned for their short game and would likely rely on the high ball into their forwards. Instead, Galway closed Tyrone down in the opening half and proceeded to take them on at their own short passing game. The Ulster champions had to work hard for their opening scores which came inside six minutes, courtesy of

Ciaran McBride and midfielder Fergal Logan. If the opening exchanges proved anything, it was that Galway meant business and were in Croke Park to restore pride to their county and their province.

Corner forward Niall Finnegan opened Galway's account after seven minutes and wing back Ray Silke kicked the equaliser five minutes later. The Connacht champions were now playing with the type of fervour not associated with Galway football of recent years. Further points from Finnegan, Jarlath Fallon and Tommy Wilson left Galway, 0-5 to 0-2, ahead after 20 minutes. Tyrone appeared leaderless and it suddenly dawned on them that this was a game they could lose. Then Peter Canavan settled their nerves with a point, their first for eighteen minutes, and the classy full forward steered them clear of stormy waters with the only goal of the game. A high ball from Ronan McGarritty landed between Peter Canavan and Galway goalkeeper, Cathal McGinley. Somehow, Canavan made contact and the ball ended up behind the goal line. Galway responded and registered the final 3 scores of the half, 2 points from Finnegan and one from midfielder, Fergal Gavin.

It was, Galway 0-8 Tyrone 1-3, at half-time and former great Sean Purcell told me as he made his way to the dressing-room, that Galway with the breeze at their backs in the second half had the ability to win. Hopes were high among the Galway supporters and an upset appeared likely.

Although Peter Canavan scored 1-1 in the opening half, the Errigal Ciarain man was feeding on crumbs. Within two minutes of the restart, Canavan had kicked 2 points to level the scores. Points from Fallon and Finnegan again edged Galway 2 points ahead, but by now Canavan was in top gear. He scored 2 points from play; then half back Sean McLoughlin and substitute, Matt McGleenan, added 2 more before Canavan again found the target with a pointed free. Yet again, Galway fought back and points from Finnegan and Daly reduced the deficit to the minimum, but guess what, that man again, Peter 'The Great' Canavan, kicked a free to put Tyrone back in front. It was an absorbing contest. Substitutes, Adrian Cush and Mattie McGleenan, what a difference both players made when introduced, scored Tyrone's final 2 points while Niall Finnegan brought his tally to 7 points with the last score of the game, a point from a free. The Ulster bandwagon rolls on, but Galway won many admirers for their heart-warming display.

Afterwards Tyrone joint team manager, Art McRory, told me: "We don't reach All-Ireland finals very often and it doesn't matter how we get there, front door, back door, any door, we're there and that's all that matters at the moment. I was pleased we had the character to come back. In the first half we were nothing but dreadful. We came in at half-time two points down, we should have been more down, except that Peter Canavan conjured a goal. That was the lifeline. At that stage we had dug ourselves a very deep hole, but we climbed out of it and away we went. I think it shows a lot of character in the side that we were able to do that. But if the All-Ireland final was played today our display wouldn't win it, but it's not played today, it's played on the 17th of September."

Tyrone Back row l to r: Paul Devlin, Jody Gormley, Ronan Mc Garrity, Sean McLaughlin, Finbar Mc Connell, Seamus McCallan, Ciaran McBride. **Front row l to r:** Peter Canavan, Ciaran Loughran, Chris Lawn, Pascal Canavan, Ciaran Corr, Stephen Lawn, Fay Devlin, Fergal Logan.

Galway Back row l to r: Val Daly, Fergal Gavin, Cathal Mc Ginley, Ray Silke, Gary Fahy, Kevin Fallon, Fergal O'Neill, Kevin Walsh. **Front row l to r:** Damien Mitchell, Niall Finnegan, Alan Mulholland, Jarlath Fallon, John Kilraine, Tommy Wilson, Sean Og De Paor.

Scorers Tyrone: Peter Canavan 1-7; Matt McGleenan 0-2; Ciaran McBride 0-1; Fergal Logan 0-1; Sean McLoughlin 0-1; Adrian Cush 0-1. **Scorers Galway:** Niall Finnegan 0-7; Jarlath Fallon 0-2; Ray Silke 0-1; Tommy Wilson 0-1; Fergal Gavin 0-1; Val Daly 0-1.

TYRONE

FINBAR MCCONNELL

PAUL DEVLIN	CHRIS LAWN	FAY DEVLIN
RONAN MCGARRITY	SEAMUS MCCALLAN	SEAN MCLOUGLIN

FERGAL LOGAN JODY GORMLEY

CIARAN CORR	PASCAL CANAVAN	CIARAN LOUGHRAN
CIARAN MCBRIDE	PETER CANAVAN	STEPHEN LAWN

Substitutes: Matt McGleenan for Stephen Lawn; Adrian Cush for Fergal Logan; Brian Gormley for Ciaran Loughran

GALWAY

CATHAL MCGINLEY

JOHN KILRAINE	GARY FAHY	KEVIN FALLON
RAY SILKE	DAMIEN MITCHELL	SEAN OG DE PAOR

KEVIN WALSH FERGAL GAVIN

JARLATH FALLON	ALAN MULHOLLAND	TOMMY WILSON
NIALL FINNEGAN	VAL DALY	FERGAL O'NEILL

Substitutes: None

Great action from the All-Ireland semi-final! Peter Canavan, Tyrone, and Gary Fahy, Galway, struggling for possession.

SUNDAY AUGUST 20

ALL-IRELAND SENIOR FOOTBALL
SEMI-FINAL

DUBLIN & CORK

CROKE PARK
REFEREE: PAT MCENEANEY MONAGHAN
RESULT: DUBLIN 1-12 CORK 0-12

Jason Sherlock once again emphatically underlined his importance to Dublin with a first half goal of the highest quality that altered the course of the game. Jason found himself in a one-to-one situation with Mark O'Connor. The Cork full back slipped at precisely the wrong moment and Sherlock glided away and sent a thundering shot past goalkeeper, Kevin O'Dwyer. The goal breathed life into a Dublin team that had been forced to play second fiddle to a swift-moving Cork side up to then. All changed from the time Jason found the target. Rarely has a goal so early on in a major championship game had such a dramatic impact.

Afterwards Charlie Redmond heaped praise on the hugely popular Finglas man, easily the most talked about sportsman in the country.

"Jason has added pace to our forward line, the kind of pace we probably hadn't before. The fact that Jason is so small and quick, it's hard for defenders to cope with him. Jason is lethal one-to-one!"

Dublin had many heroes. Midfielder Brian Stynes never played a greater game in the navy and blue jersey and few could argue with Dublin manager Dr. Pat O'Neill's comments after the game: "Brian is the best midfielder in the country at the moment." The former Aussie Rules star revelled in his role. His fielding was near immaculate and his work-rate and distribution was second to none. Much was expected of Liam Honohan and Danny Culloty but despite dominating early on, the much vaunted Cork midfield pairing were never allowed to display their undoubted skills thereafter. The loss through injury of Stynes midfield partner Paul Bealin ,after just 27 minutes was a big blow to Dublin, but towering St. Vincent's man Pat Gilroy proved a very able replacement.

Dublin reshuffled their forces early on, most notably Dessie Farrell moved to centre halfforward and Paddy Moran and Keith Galvin switched corners in the last line of defence.

It all began so well for the Munster champions. Four points from frees by Colin Corkery and one from play by Mark O'Sullivan against 2 pointed frees from Charlie Redmond left Cork in front, 0-5 to 0-2, after twenty minutes. Jason's goal transformed the Dubs and ace place kicker Redmond landed 3 further points from frees as the Cork challenge faded somewhat. The Dublin defence, which earlier on had appeared very porous, now closed ranks with a vengeance and the Cork forwards, with the exception of the brilliant Mark O'Sullivan, found it extremely difficult to make any inroads. O'Sullivan wreaked havoc most everytime he got the

Dublin Back row l to r: Paul Clarke, Mick Galvin, Dermot Deasy, Paul Bealin, John O'Leary, Brian Stynes, Paddy Moran, Keith Barr. **Front row l to r:** Jason Sherlock, Jim Gavin, Dessie Farrell, Paul Curran, Keith Galvin, Mick Deegan, Charlie Redmond.

ball in the first half and consistently had the measure of Keith Galvin.

The young St. Sylvester's club man was replaced early in the second half by the experienced Ciaran Walsh, who turned in a commanding display. But at that juncture, the supply to O'Sullivan from outfield was not as plentiful. Keith Barr was outstanding at centre half back for the Dubs throughout.

Dublin held a 2 point advantage 1-5 to 0-6, at half-time and had increased that lead to 5 points after 39 minutes with a point each from Mick Galvin, Paul Clarke and Redmond. The supporters on the Hill were in jubilant mood. Their team had failed to score even a single point from play in the entire first half, but now they watched in admiration as the Dubs well oiled-machine moved into top gear with 3 points from play within the space of four minutes. Time to celebrate. Cork's demise appeared imminent. But mighty Larry Tompkins kicked a great point to raise the hopes of the Rebel county supporters and when full forward Joe Kavanagh added another, just 3 points separated the sides.

Tompkins battled bravely throughout and at times showed flashes of his old brilliance. Corner forward Mick Galvin had an outstanding game for the Dubs and scored 4 points from play at vital stages in the second half. Cork fought the good fight to the finish and Corkery and Tompkins had the final 2 points of the game, but the elusive goal never came. In fact, Cork failed to score a goal in their entire championship campaign and that in itself speaks volumes. Disappointed Cork supporters streaming out of Croke Park after the game needed no reminding of the fact that Dublin's goal-scoring hero, Jason Sherlock, learned his football in Ballyhea, near Charleville. Surely, a case of what might have been!

Scorers Dublin: Charlie Redmond 0-7; Mick Galvin 0-4; Jason Sherlock 1-0; Paul Clarke 0-1.
Scorers Cork: Colin Corkery 0-7; Mark O'Sullivan 0-2; Larry Tompkins 0-2; Joe Kavanagh 0-1

Images & Action
From the 1995 All-Ireland Football Final

The ball is in, the game is on. Centre stage, Croke Park, 17 September 1995.

Dublin – **Back row l to r:** Paul Clarke, Mick Galvin, Ciarán Walsh, Paul Bealin, Brian Stynes, Paddy Moran, Keith Barr. **Front row l to r:**

Ciaran Corr, Tyrone, and Mick Deegan, Dublin.

ason Sherlock and Chris Lawn.

Peter Canavan, Tyrone.

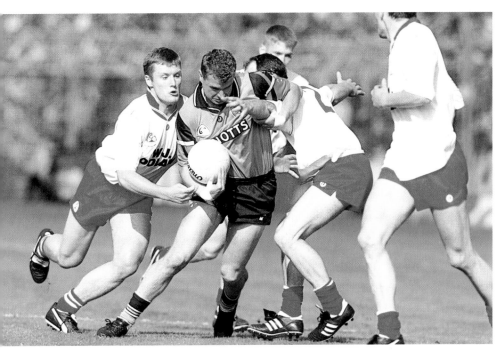

Charlie Redmond/ Seamus McCallan/ Paul Devlin.

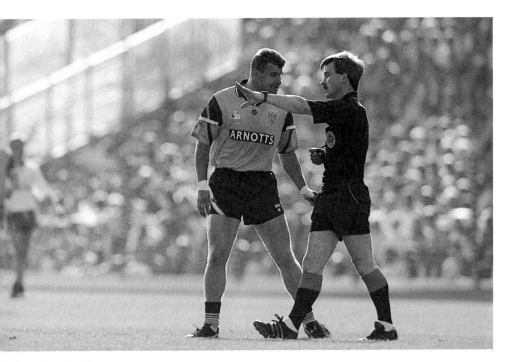

Redmond on the line.

Winning the battle – Fergal Logan eludes Dublin's Jim Gavin.

A famous victory! Dublin's captain John O'Leary and team-mate Paul Curran, triumphant at last. Sam Maguire returns to Dublin after a 'barren' 12 years.

Images & Action
from the 1995 All-Ireland Hurling Final

For the first time in 83 years a Clare captain, Anthony Daly, raises the McCarthy Cup.

Eamonn Cregan, Offaly's manager, watches the game intensely.

Ger Loughnane, Clare's manager, celebrates after the All-Ireland semi-final victory over Galway.

Johnny Dooley, Offaly, and Brian and Frank Lohan, Clare, battling for the sliotair.

Cyril Lyons of Clare and Kevin Kinahan of Offaly in a tussle for possession.

P.J. O'Connell, Clare, and Johnny Pilkington, Offaly.

Michael Duignan, Offaly, and Brian Lohan, Clare.

ergus Tuohy of Clare racing clear.

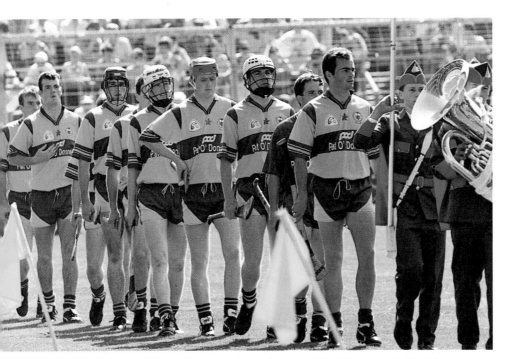

ack to the beginning — expectant, ready to march, ready to win! The Clare team behind the
rtane Boys Band.

Clare – Back row l to r: Brian Lohan, Michael O'Halloran, Frank Lohan, Conor Clancy, David Fitzgerald, Sean McMahon, Ger 'Sparrow' O'Loughlin. **Front row l to r:** Liam Doyle, P. J. O'Connell, Ollie Baker, Anthony Daly, Jamesie O' Connor, Fergal Hegarty, Fergus Tuohy,

Cork Back row l to r: Mark O'Sullivan, Danny Culloty, Colin Corkery, Liam Honohan, Mark Farr, Niall Cahalane, Larry Tompkins, Mark O'Connor. **Front row l to r:** Brian Corcoran, Ciaran O'Sullivan, Kevin O'Dwyer, Stephen O'Brien, Don Davis, Joe Kavanagh, Padraig O'Mahony.

DUBLIN

	JOHN O'LEARY	
KEITH GALVIN	DERMOT DEASY	PADDY MORAN
PAUL CURRAN	KEITH BARR	MICK DEEGAN
PAUL BEALIN		BRIAN STYNES
JIM GAVIN	PAUL CLARKE	DESSIE FARRELL
CHARLIE REDMOND	JASON SHERLOCK	MICK GALVIN

Substitutes: Pat Gilroy for Paul Bealin; Ciaran Walsh for Keith Galvin; Vinny Murphy for Paul Clarke

CORK

	KEVIN O'DWYER	
MARK FARR	MARK O'CONNOR	NIALL CAHALANE
CIARAN O'SULLIVAN	STEPHEN O'BRIEN	BRIAN CORCORAN
LIAM HONOHAN		DANNY CULLOTY
DON DAVIS	LARRY TOMPKINS	PADRAIG O'MAHONY
MARK O'SULLIVAN	JOE KAVANAGH	COLIN CORKERY

Substitutes: Stephen Calnan for Padraig O'Mahony; Shay Fahy for Don Davis; Padraig O'Regan for Stephen Calnan

Dublin's Dessie Farrell and Cork's Brian Corcoran in All-Ireland semi-final action.

DUBLIN v TYRONE — BEFORE THE FINAL

In the hectic week leading up the Final, I talked to Jason Sherlock, Peter Canavan and some of the other key players involved in the showdown.

Back in the Sixties, a cub reporter in the Old Trafford press box watched as superstar George Best scored a wonderful goal. Turning to his colleagues he asked: "What was the time of that goal?" Quick as a flash an older journalist replied: "Never mind the time, son, just write down the date."

Roll the clock forward over three decades. Never mind the time, the date is Sunday, August 20, 1995, All-Ireland Football semi-final day in Croke Park. Jason Sherlock finds himself in a one-to-one situation with Mark O'Connor. The Cork full-back slips at precisely the wrong moment, and Sherlock glides away and sends a thundering shot past Kevin O'Dwyer. One chance, one Dublin goal. The supporters on the Hill roar their approval; "Jayo, Jayo."

Take heed! Jason Sherlock is on the high road to stardom. He is the most talked-about sportsman in the country, and easily the most marketable. The nineteen-year-old Dublin Gaelic footballer is now vying with international pop stars like Boyzone in the popularity stakes. Young boys and girls adore him, and many of their parents are also caught up in the new craze called Jasonmania.

Jason's rise to fame has been nothing short of meteoric. He was on Hill 16 last year when Dublin lost to Down. He was unable to see Charlie Redmond taking the penalty, but knew the outcome from the crowd's reaction. He vividly recalls the utter sense of despondency among the navy and blue supporters after the game. But how times have changed! Next Sunday in the Dublin forward line, Jason will line out alongside Charlie, one of the game's most outstanding and most popular players of the past decade. A dream come true for the youngster.

"I don't think the whole campaign has sunk in yet," Jason tells me. "Here I am in my first year in senior championship football and I'm playing in an All-Ireland Final with Dublin. I don't think it's something I'll appreciate until maybe a few years down the road when I can look back on it all. Obviously last year was disappointing. I suppose in a way it was probably more frustrating than anything else. Dublin had so much possession but didn't use it properly. But this is another year and so far things have gone well and hopefully it will all come together again on Sunday."

He is eagerly anticipating the challenge ahead. The attitude is right in the Dublin camp and the direct focus is on winning. But the Ulster champions are formidable opposition.

"I didn't know much about Tyrone before the championship, but since they've reached the final we've been well briefed on them," Jason says. "They look a very serious team. They have a great attitude and hunt in packs. Obviously, they're going to be hungry for victory and they'll have a big support coming down to Croke Park. Hopefully, we'll be able to match them in every way and get the breaks on the day."

How does Charlie Redmond rate the Dubs newest acquisition?

"Jason has added pace to our full forward line, the kind of pace we probably didn't have before now. The fact that he is so small and quick makes it very hard for defenders to cope. Obviously, there's no point in kicking in a high ball to him, or in asking him to shoulder defenders or knock them off the ball. That's not his game. It's a 'horses for courses' scenario. Jason is lethal one-to-one, possibly the best I've ever seen. The only one I'd compare with him in those situations would be Barney Rock. Hopefully, Jason will get a few chances on Sunday."

Jason has spent a hectic summer visiting GAA camps, mostly around Dublin. Everyone wants to shake his hand and get his autograph. Through it all, the friendly Finglas man remains calm and unruffled. Here is a level-headed young man with a perceptiveness beyond his years. His long-term ambition is to play Premiership football in England, but right now his main priority is to help the Dubs win their first All-Ireland football crown since 1983!

"At the moment all I have is one ambition and that is to win an All-Ireland medal with Dublin," says Jason. "My career is for another day. When the final is over then I can sit down and think out what I'm going to do. But at the moment, all the focus is on Tyrone. I'll only think about my future when the final is over."

There are ever-increasing pressures on inter-county players, but those who wear the navy and blue of Dublin come under the most intense scrutiny of all. Even by Dublin standards, Jason is attracting phenomenal attention. Unperturbed, he takes all the adulation in his stride.

"I'm just enjoying it all. I know it's not going to last forever. It's just the way things have worked out. I also know how lucky and privileged I am to play in an All-Ireland Final with Dublin. Being so young myself, I just seem to appeal to children."

"Hopefully some kids who have not played Gaelic football before might now try it out. That's all you can ask for. I seem to have struck a chord with everyone and being involved in the GAA summer camps has helped an awful lot with the kids. I got to know a lot of them and it was very enjoyable. Every game to me is a great occasion and I just go out to enjoy it."

The Dubs supporters have had to endure more than their fair share of setbacks in recent years and another defeat on Sunday would be almost unbearable. After last year's bitter disappointment, the players and management had to endure some harsh criticism for their failure to see off the challenge of the Ulster Champions, Down.

Particularly talked about was the radical decision to switch Paul Curran from his best position as an attacking half back to corner back in order to counter the threat of footballer-of-the-year, Mickey Linden. Despite the mistake of playing Curran out of position and Charlie missing a penalty, Dublin still had ample opportunity to win the game. Down failed to register a score in the final twenty minutes, but the Dubs, despite an abundance of possession, were unable to get the vital scores.

Charlie Redmond advises caution. His message is straight and to the point. Underestimate Tyrone and the Dubs will pay a heavy price.

"Everyone seems to be writing off Tyrone, although they've come through what is the toughest province, and they've come through it with aplomb. I think if we were playing Derry in the final they'd be favourites, but the truth of the matter is that Tyrone beat Derry with thirteen men. So obviously, Tyrone will be a very formidable team; a team full of confidence and talent."

Charlie is happy with the manner in which Dublin has progressed to the final. He believes that Meath let their guard down in the closing stages of the Leinster Final and that helped put a lopsided look on the scoreboard. He considers the games against Louth, Laois and Cork to be a more accurate indicator of Dublin's worth. Charlie himself has had what he considers his best year in a Dublin jersey.

"I probably haven't scored as much as last year, but I've been asked to do a different job and forage a little deeper. I think it has worked out very well and I've been able to open up a lot of avenues for others. People say that Dublin deserve to win an All-Ireland, but you don't always get what you deserve. Tyrone will also tell you that they deserve to win the title. There's a lot of sympathy out there for Dublin, but sympathy won't put scores on the board. It's going to be a matter of Dublin getting down to hard work for seventy minutes no matter what the conditions, and forcing our game on Tyrone."

Will this year end on a happy note for Dublin? One could not but be impressed by their swaggering performance in the Leinster Final and particularly the manner in which they stormed back after Meath edged a point in front in the second half. The Dubs appear to have learned from past experiences and they will be in the right frame of mind for the Tyrone challenge. They struggled a little early on against Cork in the semi-final, but confidence soon returned once Jason put the ball in the net.

Tyrone footballers would relish the opportunity to shatter the notion that this is the year the Sam Maguire Cup returns to the capital after an absence of twelve years. If the Dubs need any reminding of the inherent dangers of being cast in the role of favourites, then a visit to Clare should help put everything in perspective. Few outside the Banner County gave Ger Loughnane's team any chance of causing an upset against defending champions, Offaly, but at the end of a gruelling seventy minutes it was captain Anthony Daly from Clarecastle who raised the Liam McCarthy Cup. The 81-year famine had ended. Maybe this is going to be the year of the underdog after all!

Outsiders Tyrone are attempting to win their first All-Ireland title and make it five-in-a-row for Ulster counties. Joint team manager Art McRory once said that Peter Canavan is "the icing on the cake", but that Tyrone had to have the cake in the first place.

Canavan has been wreaking havoc among some of the best defences in the country for many years now. He is equally balanced on either side, and his fluidity of movement and sheer skill and craft as a forward mark him out as an exceptional player. Off the field he prefers to shun the limelight. He is an extremely modest man who offers frankness and demands nothing less in return. Few outside the county expected Tyrone to emerge as kingpins of Ulster this year, but their appearance in an

All-Ireland Final owes much to the free-scoring All-Star. The man himself typically plays down his own very signigicant contribution.

"There'll be fifteen of us going out on Sunday and we all know we have a big job ahead of us. I think it's only fair that Dublin are favourites because they've been the most consistent team in the country this year and have played the best football. Tyrone would have matched them maybe for twenty minutes against Derry, but we've been unable to lift it since then. We're hoping to reproduce that type of performance against Dublin."

Most of the Tyrone players will be conceding height and weight to a Dublin team with an abundance of physical power. There is a huge burden on the shoulders of Peter Canavan. Can it all be too much at times?

"I try not to let the pressure affect me. At the end of the day, you can only go out and give your best and as long as I content myself that I've given my best, then I can do more," Peter tells me. "It's always great to play for Tyrone, but to pull on the jersey before an All-Ireland Final will be something special. We want to have something to show for all our effort over the past few years and we don't want to be the team to break the winning sequence of Ulster counties."

Tyrone midfielder Fergal Logan believes that Dublin have been the most consistent team in the country over the past four years.

"They've developed great strength and physical condition, together with ball work and certainly we would be the new kids on the block in this regard. Dublin are a very tight-knit unit; their midfield and half back line are very strong; they have a phenomenal free-taker in Charlie Redmond and they have the unpredictable in Jason Sherlock," Fergal says. "Dublin are a very strong team. Maybe we've suffered a bit from our semi-final performance against Galway in terms of people saying that Tyrone aren't up to it, but I would like to think that the players will look back on the day we beat Derry. Without a doubt, that was the performance that indicated the arrival of this Tyrone team. There's been an upward curve with this team over the past two or three years and we realised in advance of the Derry game that it was the day we had to stand up and be counted. We've managed to produce the goods when it counted most this summer, and I'm hopeful we can do that again on Sunday."

The county of Tyrone has gone football crazy. Anyone familiar with its friendly people knows of their great passion for the game. Tyrone has never won an All-Ireland senior football title. They led Kerry by 7 points early in the second half of the 1986 final, only to lose in the end by 8 points. It was a hard blow for players and supporters alike. If Dublin could be beaten then rest assured the scenes witnessed in Clare would be repeated all around the county, from Omagh to Dungannon, Cookstown to Ardboe and all places in between.

What would it mean to Dublin? Last words to Charlie Redmond. "If we could win on Sunday, it would be the highpoint for all the players. It would be the culmination of a dream for all of us. But anything that's worth winning, doesn't come easy. It's a matter of total work-rate on the day." The game was a strange final clouded by controversy. Before a capacity crowd of 65,092 in Croke Park, Dublin beat Tyrone by a single point, 1-10 to 0-12.

For my report on the Final see above pages 11 to 15.

After the Final – celebrations in O'Connell Street.

Talking to the Players

Jason Sherlock

Nineteen-year-old Jason Sherlock is the most talked-about sportsmen on these islands, recognised as an immense talent at both Gaelic football, soccer and basketball. He was fullforward on the Dublin team that won this year's All-Ireland title and his ambition now is to make it as a full-time soccer professional in England. No other player in the history of Gaelic games has attracted so much attention. He has an inherent magic called 'star quality.'

He won numerous All-Ireland medals at basketball, by his own admission his favourite sport. He also played an important part in helping Dr. Tony O'Neill's and Theo Dunne's side win promotion to the Premier Division of the league this year.

Jason Sherlock is a level-headed and friendly young man of substance. He uses his words with intelligent care and has a firm sense of identity and a lively sense of humour. He offers directness in a gently unobtrusive manner and is perceptive beyond his years.

Earlier this year, Roy Evans approached Jason after a friendly between the Merseysiders and UCD, and expressed interest in bringing him to Anfield for a trial. Evans was greatly impressed with the level of skill and athleticism displayed by the Finglas youngster against the professionals from Liverpool. Jason was mightily pleased that someone of the stature of Evans expressed an interest.

But Jason made it clear very early on that his main priority was to win an All-Ireland medal with the Dubs. That dream came true on Sunday September 17. There is no doubt that Jason added an extra dimension to Dublin's play all through the '95 championship and make no mistake his piercing runs and crucial goals made all the difference. He was delighted to be part of the team that delivered a long overdue success to the capital. He was on Hill Sixteen last year when Dublin lost to Down in the final, and remembers the devastation among the navy and blue supporters.

It is always difficult for players to combine a number of sports. The commitment to club and county generally takes its toll, and players suffer from exhaustion and lose their form. Jason Sherlock considers himself too young to be bothered with occupational hazards like burn-out but agrees it would be wise to trim down his heavy schedule before fatigue sets in.

"It wasn't until I was twelve or thirteen that I began to play soccer competitively with Rivermount Soccer Club, and later on with St Kevin's. When I began to play three sports competitively, I was lucky to be on good teams and have good managers." Jason told me. "I played a different sport every night. When you think about it, I was thirteen or fourteen and too young to realise what I was doing and how much it took out of the body. I was only there for the love of the game and I

suppose I could run all day. I know a lot of dual sportsmen suffer from burn-out, but thankfully it doesn't seem to affect me at the moment."

Jason Sherlock has a wisdom beyond his nineteen years. His philosophy on life, as with sport, is more advanced than one would expect from one so young. He pays tribute to his mother, Alice, his grandmother Kathleen and his uncle Brian Sherlock for all their help and encouragement. His stepfather Bill and Uncle Eddie also come in for special mention.

From the time he could walk, Jason had a football in his hand all day every day. He would kick the ball until late in the evening with his neighbours in Carigallen Park in Finglas South.

"I started playing with Rivermount when I was eight, and began playing Gaelic football at primary school in St Vincent's CBS in Glasnevin. My interest in basketball was developed in St Vincent's Secondary School. I didn't have a preferred sport at the time, I loved playing all of them. It wasn't until I got a little older that I appreciated the games for what they were and realised that every game had its good points and bad. I tried to play them all because I liked them so much."

"My main sport was basketball. I was lucky to play with a very successful team at St Vincent's under a great coach, Joey Boylan, who guided us to numerous Leinster and All-Ireland titles at school and club level. I also played soccer with St Kevins boys in Whitehall where I won an Under-15 All-Ireland and an Under-17 Dublin League. During my summer holidays in Cork with my uncle Eddie in Ballyhea near Charleville, I won numerous North Cork Medals in hurling and football. I also won a County hurling medal."

When pressed for a preference in sport, he opts for basketball. The fact that every player has a specific job appeals to him, and he believes there's much more camaraderie and team spirit because of the smaller number of players on a team. The most appealing aspects of soccer he finds are the skills and techniques. Gaelic football is special for many varying reasons.

"Everyone has grown up with Gaelic and everyone is passionate about it in this country. There's a great spirit in it and especially with crowds you can feel the passion in the game. It is probably the most passionate sport in the country and it should be like that. It's part of our culture and is unique."

Gaelic football was always bound to appeal to Jason Sherlock. Although he has a light physique he compensates for it with blinding pace, and he can kick equally well with either foot. "It's such a wonderful game and has so much prestige attached to it. I'm lucky to have the education behind me. Children should think more about their education these days and avoid going over at a young age to English clubs. Instead they should concentrate on getting an education before they travel, and have something to fall back on if the soccer doesn't work out."

Interestingly for a young man with such a remarkable flair for all sports, one of the major high points in Jason's life so far was not on the playing field but meeting the legendary Magic Johnson. The Irish Basketball team were on their way to Estonia to play in the European Championship qualifier in '93, and while stopping off in Helsinki Airport they spotted the American mega-star relaxing in a coffee bar. "Life is all about great experiences and meeting Magic was special," Jason told me. "We couldn't believe our eyes. We were on a buzz for hours afterwards. It's one of the things I'll always cherish."

On the night of the All-Ireland final, Jason took time out to talk with me about 'the greatest day of his life'.

"Keith (Galvin) and myself must be two of the luckiest people in the world. It's our first year on the Dublin team and we have an All-Ireland medal to show for it. No matter what happens in the future, today's All-Ireland Final will always be special to me. My future career is for another day."

Anthony Daly

Anthony Daly has made front page headlines like few other sportsman in this country throughout the past six months. Everyone still talks about his riveting speech in Semple Stadium in Thurles after Clare had won their first Munster title for 63 years. That impassioned delivery was well and truly matched in Croke Park on the first Sunday in September when the Clarecastle man addressed thousands of delirious saffron and blue-clad supporters moments after Clare had claimed their first All-Ireland senior hurling titles in eighty years. His year was not all about speech making. He proved an inspirational captain on the field of play and never once shirked his responsibility, no matter how tough the going. Here is a proud Clare man who has worn the saffron and blue jersey with pride and distinction for many years. He knew the hard times and that made him appreciate more fully the significance of 1995 for Clare hurling.

"Every young fellow's dream from the time he starts playing hurling is to win an All-Ireland medal and I was no different." Anthony tells me. "To captain an All-Ireland winning team is an extra bonus it was very emotional to look down from the Hogan Stand and see the absolute delight on the faces of the Clare supporters. I

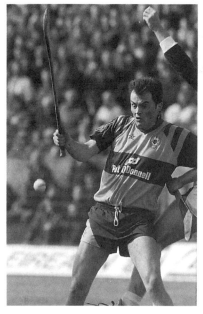

knew my family was there among them and that made it even more special. I couldn't help thinking of all the bad days and that was reflected in my speech. Our supporters had endured a lot of disappointment over the years and it was wonderful to see them savour our greatest moment."

The memory that stands out in Anthony's mind above all others, after the Munster Final win, is of the night when the victorious Clare team arrived in his native village of Clarecastle. He will never forget the feeling as he got off the bus and carried the Cup though the village with the four of his club colleagues on the county team. The famous five had done the little village proud.

"It was an unbelievable feeling. All my family and friends and all the fellows who hurled with Clarecastle were there. There are six of us from Clarecastle on the panel; Stephen Sheedy was injured so he wasn't actually with the party that day, but he was there to support us. We were carried shoulder high through the village. I suppose arriving with the Cup to their native place was the ultimate for all the fellows. The Munster Final was way more emotional than the All-Ireland Final. It was the one we always dreamed of winning and we never even spoke of an All-Ireland. As far as most of us would be concerned the Munster Final was nearly a better day; we were outnumbered by Limerick supporters, which wouldn't normally be the case, so it was great to win for those die-hard supporters who never lost faith in us. There was something more down-to-earth and more satisfying about the Munster Final."

He will never forget the moment Jamesie O'Connor struck the ball over the bar coming near the end of the All-Ireland Final against Offaly to edge Clare 2 points ahead. At that precise moment he knew his team had answered all the questions.

"I was certain we would win it after Jamesie scored the point. I think Johnny Dooley turned around and shook hands with me even before the referee blew the whistle. He knew it was over as well. It was wonderful to hear the sound of the final whistle. I thought nothing could match the welcome home we received after winning the Munster Final, but the reception given to the players on the Monday following the All-Ireland certainly surpassed everything gone before. There was an unbelievable wash of colour all over the county."

Anthony Daly's heart skipped a beat when Offaly captain, Johnny Pilkington sent the ball to the net in the second half of the All-Ireland Final. Did he feel the defending champions might win it at that stage?

"For a few seconds after Johnny scored the goal, I must say, I thought it was going away from us, but even running back out after the goal, I was consoling myself that there was still plenty of time left in the game. I was fairly confident all through that we'd win it. Ger Loughnane had it buried in us that we were going to beat Offaly and that was that. Nothing was going to stop us. He had instilled a great belief in us. There was always a doubt about whether we could win Munster because of the hoodoo attached to it, but once we came out of the province and beat Galway in the semi-final, we knew it would take a great team to beat us in the final." Anthony Daly is well aware of his roots. Clarecastle is steeped in hurling tradition. He is deeply grateful to all the people who guided him on the path to hurling fame. His father, Pad Joe, a keen hurler, sadly died when Anthony was just eight years old. He pays tribute to his mother, Mary, for all her help and encouragement. His school teacher, John Hanly, is another who comes in for special mention for his work with the young hurlers in the area.

"Since our school-days there are people from Clarecastle who have trained us and looked after us and they were all there to see us bringing the Munster Cup and Liam McCarthy Cup into the village. It meant a lot to us. That's when it all hit home."

In 1987, Anthony won an All-Ireland Colleges medal in his fifth year at St. Flannan's in Ennis, the famous hurling nursery. Despite enduring many heartbreaks on the playing field, including two Munster Final defeats and a League Final loss to Kilkenny earlier in the year, Anthony has garnered many awards during his career. He was chosen as an All-Star in '94 and won an interprovincial winners medal with Munster in '95. He has also three county senior championship medals. And now a Munster and All-Ireland medal. Dreams after all do come true!

No matter what happens in the future, Anthony Daly's name will live forever in the hearts and minds of Clare people everywhere. His place in the history books is secure!

Charlie Redmond

The smile said it all. Charlie Redmond was sent off in the second half of this year's All-Ireland Final against Tyrone, but he was a relieved and happy man when he raised the Sam Maguire Cup in front of thousands of adoring Dublin supporters. It was a far cry from the previous year when he missed a penalty against Down and had left Croke Park even before DJ Kane was presented with the Cup. A few weeks after that shattering All-Ireland defeat, I met Charlie at home for an exclusive interview for the RTE Guide.

It is Sunday, September 18, 1994. Are our eyes deceiving us? Could it be that the big clock at the back of the Canal End, near the scoreboard, is getting carried away with all the excitement? Safer to check the old reliable stopwatch. Sure enough, only eight minutes left. The Dubs on the Hill are tense and soaked to the skin. Worse still, their footballing heroes are trailing by 3 points. Eight minutes! But surely sufficient

Sarah Rose Redmond smiles contently as her dad celebrates his All-Ireland medal.

time for the Dubs to claw their way back and win that first title in eleven years. Clearly, Dublin are enjoying a monopoly of possession, but from their point of view the scoreboard still has an unfavourable look about it. And then out of the blue comes the penalty!

"When the penalty was given my immediate thought was, 'Oh, no, it's Dessie (Farrell) who's been fouled'," Charlie Redmond tells me. "The penalty I missed in the 1992 All-Ireland also came about as a result of a foul on Dessie. That was my immediate reaction."

Over 58,000 pairs of eyes peer through the rain in Croke Park and focus on Charlie and then on the greasy white leather ball placed on the thirteen-metre line. Millions more watch on television. Charlie is once again the centre of attention. He knows the moment has arrived. He failed to score from a penalty against Donegal in the final only two years before. But, like all great sportsmen, he accepts the responsibility. Lightning would never strike twice. Or would it?

Charlie would normally be expected to rattle the net with consummate ease. Down goalkeeper Neil Collins admitted afterwards he had studied Charlie's penalty-taking and had decided to dive to his right. He guessed correctly, and luck was again on his side when the rebound was driven wide.

Sitting next to Charlie in the sitting-room of his County Meath home, with his baby daughter Sarah Rose smiling contently, it is impossible not to feel a wave of sympathy towards this brave footballer as he relives the moment. He is still clearly very upset.

"When I put the ball down I had no doubt in my own mind but that I'd score," Charlie tells me. "Unfortunately, Neil Collins had different things on his mind and his power of thought succeeded and he made a good save. The rebound came straight back to me and it was quite a simple shot. All I had to do was tap the ball in. I was trying to make up my mind whether to tap the ball or pick it up and hit it from the hand. And of course, as I was just about to kick it, Johnny (Barr) came in and hit the ball wide!"

The record will show that Down won the 1994 All-Ireland Final, defeating Dublin by 2 points, 1-12 to 0-13. What it will not reveal is that while captain DJ Kane and all the Down players and supporters celebrated in Croke Park, a devastated Charlie Redmond was wandering aimlessly around a car park adjacent to the famous ground.

At the end of the game, Charlie shook hands with Down corner back Michael Magill and then disappeared into the dressing-room like a flash. Engulfed by sadness, he was changed and on his way out of Croke Park before any of the Dublin team or officials had even made it in from the pitch. Charlie met a tearful young friend of his, 13-year-old Wayne McCarthy, at the dressing-room door, and asked him to take his kit-bag so as to avoid being recognised.

Outside, it was raining heavily. He had no coat and had to wait some time in the rain before his wife joined him. A few people recognised him but left him alone with his thoughts. One man did an about-turn when he realised the identity of the forlorn figure with the rain and tears streaming down his face. Charlie pretended it was his brother but the man noticed the strapping on his hand and smiled sympathetically.

Eventually, a kind stranger allowed Charlie sit in his car until his wife, Grainne, arrived with the keys of their car. Charlie was back in his home a short time later and spent over two hours alone in the semi-darkness, his thoughts in a turmoil. Why me, Lord, why me! After a drink and a bath, he retired to bed early, but after some phone calls from his team-mates he was eventually persuaded to attend the post-match function. Two weeks after that traumatic day in Croke Park, Charlie Redmond is still devastated. Everyone tells him not to worry but it is no use. He is weighed down by it all.

"I still feel as if everyone is looking at me and talking about me. Paranoid, I suppose, is the word. I'm trying to keep as low a profile as I can, but it's not that easy. I'll try and keep out of circulation for a few weeks and see how I feel then." He is very grateful to the local community for their concern and support.

Every sport needs its heroes. Charlie Redmond has deservedly been in that category for some time now. Few can argue that the Erin's Isle man is one of the finest footballers in the country, a man who has worn the navy and blue with pride and distinction for many years. Football has long been the centre of his world. His earliest memories are of kicking a ball in his home in Charles Street, near the Four Courts. The kindly neighbours nick-named him 'Little Johnny Giles'.

His childhood consisted of a diet of football, football, and more football. The Redmonds moved to Finglas when Charlie was two years of age, and it was there his love for Gaelic games was nurtured, first in St Canice's National School, then De La Salle in Finglas, and, of course, the Erin's Isle club. His father was a keen soccer supporter and often brought young Charlie to Tolka Park to watch League of Ireland games. He could kick the rubber ball a good distance by the time he was four.

It must be said that Dublin would never have reached the 1994 All-Ireland Final but for the brillance of Charlie Redmond. Watching him now run his hand over his face and through his hair, it is clear that no matter how well-intentioned, in this instance, sympathy is not what the doctor ordered. He has played some outstanding football in the Dublin colours over the past decade, but accepts his whole career could now be unfairly measured by 2 missed penalties.

"It's a fact of life and I'm sure no matter how much football I've played or will continue to play, I'll always be remembered as the man who missed the penalty. There's nothing I can do now or in the future to rectify that, because I've made up my mind that I won't be taking any more penalties. I don't think the penalties are for me."

On the positive side, he has words of encouragement for long-suffering Dublin followers. He has no intention of retiring and is convinced the present side is capable of winning that elusive All-Ireland title.

Charlie Redmond made his senior inter-county debut in 1982 in an O'Byrne Cup game against Meath. He lost his place for the championship the following year but was unlucky not to get a run-out against Cork in the All-Ireland semi-final at Pairc Ui Chaoimh.

"Everyone who was there that day will remember it. There was an electric atmosphere," Charlie recalls. "Previous to the game a lot of people had been expecting trouble, but there's seldom crowd trouble at a GAA game. In the latter stages of the second half, Tommy Conroy came over to the sideline and said he was injured and I was told to warm up. Kevin Heffernan deemed him not to be injured and sent him back on. Some time later, Tommy came back again, insisting he was injured and I was warming up again when Mr Heffernan, in all his wisdom, said Mr Conroy was not coming off. With seven or eight minutes to go, Kevin Heffernan told me to warm up, and this was different bacause Tommy Conroy was playing very well. He handed me a piece of paper and it had on it, 'Charlie Redmond for Barney Rock'. Just as he handed me the piece of paper, Barney got the ball and buried it in the back of the net. I just handed the paper back to Lorcan Redmond and sat down on the bench."

Charlie Redmond spent ten months in America during '84, but returned in early '85 and has since been a regular on the Dublin team.

Charlie smiles when he relates the circumstances surrounding his first meeting with his London-born wife, Grainne. He was involved in ambulance training with Dublin Fire Brigade and part of the procedure was a visit to the Rotunda Maternity Hospital to witness some births.

Charlie takes up the story: "As it happened, the woman giving birth was a Mrs Redmond and Grainne was the mid-wife delivering the child. We got chatting afterwards and I asked Grainne for a date and she was shocked as she thought I was the father of the child she had just delivered! I can tell you she gave me a funny look, but after some quick explaining she agreed to go out with me. I always say to her that our eyes met across an umbilical cord!"

They married in 1989 and are the proud parents of a beautiful daughter, Sarah Rose. He jokes about finding it difficult to get enough sleep, but then, in a serious moment, wonders what Grainne and himself did with their time before Sarah Rose was born. Clearly a doting dad.

Grainne had no interest in Gaelic games when Charlie first met her. But all that has now changed and she loves going to matches.

"She was in tears when we met after the 1994 Final. Her first words to me were, 'Why do you take them! Why do you take them?'"

Charlie shakes his head and winces. He has asked himself the same question over and over again. He adds: "She has been very philosophical about it all and keeps telling me to put the experience behind me and come back stronger next year. She has always maintained that missing the penalty against Donegal has made me a better footballer and the miss against Down might make me an even better one."

Nearly two hours in the company of Charlie Redmond, and it is easy to see why so many people from all over the country had such an overwhelming goodwill towards Dublin the 1994. Pressed for an explanation, most people admitted that Charlie Redmond was the reason, saying things like "He's a wonderful ambassador for the game and no-one more deserves to enjoy success on All-Ireland Final day in Croke Park."

It is time to take my leave, but not before we discuss Charlie's golf handicap and the huge demands placed on inter-country players.

Outside, it is a bright and warm evening. Happy young boys and girls play hurling and football on the green in front of his house without a care in the world, like 'Little Johnny Giles' in Charles Street nearly 30 years ago.

PETER CANAVAN

Peter Canavan is widely acclaimed to be the finest forward in present day Gaelic football. The twenty-four year old school teacher from the Errigal Ciaran club had another outstanding year in the white and red of Tyrone and emerged the premier marksman in the championship with one goal and 38 points. His remarkable tally of 11 points in the final against Dublin edged him clear of Colin Corkery, Charlie Redmond and Maurice Fitzgerald at the top of the Championship scoring charts.

Canavan brings to the game the highest essence of silken skills and defenders find it extremely difficult to curb his genius. There are many dimensions to his play: he is equally balanced on either side and is deadly accurate from both frees and play.

Despite his extraordinary scoring display against Dublin in the All-Ireland Final, the All-Star still ended up on the losing side. It was one of the most controversial

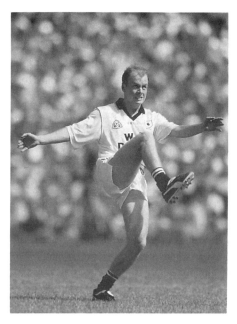

deciders in recent years. Dublin finished the game with fourteen men after Charlie Redmond was ordered off after 14 minutes of the second half. Confusion reigned. Charlie continued to play on for another two minutes or so, until the referee approached him a second time and sent him to the line. There was further drama near the end. Tyrone half back Sean McLoughlin kicked what appeared to be the levelling point in injury time, but the referee adjudged Canavan had handled the ball on the ground before delivering the pass to his colleague. Typically, Peter Canavan makes no excuses! "We didn't click as a team on the day and it could well be that Dublin never allowed us to settle. To me, the strongest part of the Dublin game was the way their forward line was able to tackle. They made some great tackles and never allowed our defence time to come out with the ball. It was the same around the middle of the field. I said after the game that Dublin didn't play well, but that we played even worse. We gave a performance that was well below par and the fact that we didn't do ourselves justice is annoying. It's hard to know how big of a bearing Charlie Redmond's sending off had on the game, but it was not a deciding factor. We didn't get the last decision, but there were some fifty/fifty decisions during the game where we got frees close to the goals and scored from them. Dublin might have felt hard done by on those occasions. It was a very empty feeling after the game and that turned to anger when we realised just how close we came to winning an All-Ireland title. There's a hurt that might never go away and the only way to get rid of that is to come back and win an All-Ireland. It's now a matter of keeping our heads up and putting our minds to it. There's no reason to stop us getting back to a final again."

Tyrone began their 1995 Ulster senior championship with a none too impressive victory over Fermanagh and then shocked Derry in the second round, despite having Seamus McCallan and Peter's brother, Pascal, sent off in separate incidents in the first half. The Ulster Final against Cavan was by no means a classic as Tyrone won by a flattering margin of 9 points. Connacht champions Galway changed their 'long ball' game in the All-Ireland semi-final and Tyrone were somewhat fortunate to escape with a 3 point victory. Peter was captain for the day against Fermanagh as Ciaran Corr was out with an injury.

"We played some great football in the first ten or fifteen minutes against Fermanagh, but we just couldn't score. we wasted a number of goal chances and

Fermanagh came back into the game and were in with a shout up to the last five or ten minutes. We had a particularly good second half against Derry and played our best football of the year in that period. Our performance was very inconsistent against Cavan in the Ulster Final and again we had difficulty in finishing them off. It took 'Big Matt' and Adrian Cush to come on and settle the issue. We were in an awkward position against Galway in the All-Ireland semi-final; Connacht football was dismissed out of hand while Ulster football was reputed to be as strong as ever. We had beaten Galway very easily in their own backyard in the League and that was brought up time and time again, even though it counted for nothing. We went into the game with everything to lose and nothing to gain. We were sure they would mainly play a catch and kick game and get the ball in as early as possible, but instead they came out and played great possession football from the backs out. As well as that their forwards moved the ball about very well and that caught us by surprise. It was a good performance by Galway."

Peter Canavan was greatly influenced by his father and mother, Sean and Sara, who encouraged him at every opportunity. His father attended most of the games and was never slow to offer advice while his mother mostly stayed in the background and in Peter's own words: "would have agreed with whatever Sean said about our football." His five older brothers all played the game so it was only natural that Peter took up the sport at a very early age. There was also a strong Gaelic tradition in the area.

"I went to Glencull Primary School and later to St. Kieran's High School in Ballygawley. We had a lot of success at St. Kiernan's and won county titles at under-14 and under-15 as well as an Ulster under-14 title. I would like to think that I played my part in those victories and likewise at secondary school. There was huge emphasis on coaching at St. Kieran's and my football would have come on a long way at that school."

His curriculum vitae makes impressive reading: two All-Ireland Vocational Schools medals with Tyrone; one Ulster minor championship medal; three Ulster and two All-Ireland under-21 medals; four Railway Cup medals; one All-Star Award and one Ulster senior medal in '95. He prefers to steer clear of publicity as much as possible. He learned some valuable lessons during Tyrone's successful campaigns in the under-21 championship and is now a much more experienced campaigner.

"I was under the spotlight quite a lot when the under-21's were doing well, maybe to such to such an extent that when it came to the senior championship I was placing myself higher than I should have and that brought me down to reality. I also found that some aspects of the media were quick to build me up and equally as quick to knock me down again. It was a tough way to learn. It's not wise to bring a lot of attention to yourself as a player, because it only serves to motivate your next opponent. Looking at it from my point of view, you'd love to be going in against a player that's getting a lot of hype and a lot of attention. You'll raise your game to play better against that person, so that's why I try not to bring attention on myself."

In my book *Football Captains, The All-Ireland Winners*, 1982 Offaly captain, Richie Connor, spoke about his younger brother Matt, considered to be one of the most outstanding forwards ever.

"I once heard some one comparing other well known quality players to Matt and he put it like this: Some top-class players do the expected brilliantly, but Matt Connor does the expected brilliantly and the unexpected ever more brilliantly."

Those exact same sentiments could be applied to Peter Canavan, the only player to captain two All-Ireland winning under-21 teams.

DJ CAREY

S anta Claus paid a visit to the Carey household in the little townland of Demesne near Gowran on Christmas even 1974. Next morning four-year-old DJ was up bright and early and, after rummaging through the various wrappings, he located the hurling helmet. Santa was as good as his word!

DJ Carey has worn that helmet ever since. He would never contemplate taking the field without it. It is as much as part of him as the hurley, only considerably more durable. He mislaid the helmet while studying as St Kieran's College in Kilkenny and spent a miserable few days before it was located. All those years later and it still fits like a glove! The helmet was perched on his head when he starred on the Kilkenny team that won the All-Ireland minor hurling title in 1988, the Under-21 title in 1990 and the senior crowns in 1992 and again in 1993.

DJ Carey is widely acclaimed the most outstanding forward in the present-day game. A hurling wizard who often makes what appears the impossible happen on the field of play.

The eldest in a family of seven, DJ has never felt the need to move away from his homeplace. All his brothers and sisters are into sport. Catriona, the oldest of the girls, was a member of the Irish Under-18 hockey team that won the Home Countries International in Scotland. His brother, Martin is an outstanding goalkeeper and was on the Kilkenny team beaten in this year's All-Ireland Under-21 Final.

The family home borders on Gowran Park Racecourse under the shadow of the Blackstairs mountains. One of DJ's earliest memories was watching his Aunt Peggy Carey playing camogie for Kilkenny. He also attended many matches with his uncle Martin Carey who hurled with Gowran. His parents John and Maura were always a wonderful support.

"My parents had to make a lot of sacrifices to accommodate our sports needs. It wasn't always easy for them to bring us to matches as my father was very much involved in farm hire work," DJ tells me. "The four lads in the family were all with the same team around the one time so there was a lot of travelling to games. We were often late but somehow always got there. My father and mother were constantly there to support and encourage me. I suppose every sportsperson goes through a stage where they have a 'stinker' and entertain thoughts of giving it all up; in moments like that my parents would always give me encouragement and confidence."

DJ's granduncle on his father's side, Paddy Phelan, was chosen at wing back on 'Team Of The Century'.

He remembers his days at national school in Gowran as special. There he came under the influence of John Knox and Dick O'Neill. He retains happy memories of the days he made his way home along the country roads. The family lived two miles from school and, depending on the time of year and what game was getting most coverage, DJ would trot home either kicking a ball from toe to hand or else soloing with the hurley and sliothar. As soon as he arrived home, DJ would throw the schoolbag in the corner and spend the rest of the evening practising his skills against the gable wall which regularly needed a coat of paint to offset the damage of the sliothar. It was not unusual to have up to twenty fellows hurling in the local fields at weekends.

He attended secondary school in St Kieran's College, the famed hurling nursery. He pays tribute to all his teachers, great men like Fr Paddy Bollard, Fr Fergus Farrell, Nicky Cashin, Seamus Knox, Tommy Lannigan and Denis Philpott. It was an out-and-out sports school and during his time there, DJ was involved in hurling, football, handball, basketball, soccer and athletics. His Kilkenny team mate, Adrian Ronan, maintains that DJ was never in school except when there was a match on. DJ himself laughs and agrees that Adrian's observations were not too far off the mark. DJ Carey is twice winner of the Under-23 World Handball Championship.

A near neighbour, Richie Bryan, now sadly deceased, first introduced him to the game he still loves. He had become All-Ireland Under-12 Champion before Richie passed away. Tommy O'Brien was another man who guided his handball career. He would like to see more youngsters taking up the game.

He considers hurling to be the best field game in the world and is glad to see non-traditional counties like Kerry and Down making considerable progress on the hurling front. The game is very expensive to run and, though a non-drinker himself, he welcomes the decision of the GAA to clear the way for an alcoholic drinks company to sponsor the game.

DJ is very much in favour of youngsters using all the protection available to them in hurling. He feels it should be made compulsory for children to wear helmets, face guards, gloves and shin guards.

"Hurling is such a fast and skilful game, players have to pull on a ball overhead and on the ground and there's always the danger of getting hit on the face or hands by a hurley," DJ says. "It's important to become accustomed to wearing the safety gear from the start because when you get to a certain age it is very difficult to begin wearing a helmet. I can use a helmet fine, but I wouldn't be able to wear a face guard helmet because I never got used to it. It may be psychological but I tried it a number of times but couldn't get used to it. It could be that I didn't give it fair enough trial."

DJ Carey's childhood hero was the former Kilkenny star, Ger Henderson. One of the

greatest thrills in his career was the day he played alongside Henderson on the team.

"I played in goal that day in a league game and Ger was centre back. He made a mistake out in the field and his man got clean through and I made a pretty good save. Ger came in and said 'well done' and gave me a box in the chest and because I was real small he knocked me back into the goal. That will be a memory that will stick with me for the rest of my life. It was one of my proudest moments."

Of the present day crop, he rates Offaly's Brian Whelehan as an outstanding exponent of the game. Tipperary's Nicky English and Galway's Joe Cooney were two great heroes over the past decade.

Apart from winning two world handball titles, DJ Carey has a staggering collection of souvenirs and trophies. He is the holder of twenty-six All-Ireland medals covering hurling and handball. He also has two All-Ireland senior hurling medals and rates winning the 1992 final against Cork as a major highlight.

DJ married Christine O'Keeffe from Mooneenroe, near Castlecomer in early October this year and they plan to travel to Australia in December on a belated honeymoon.

BRIAN CARTHY' S CHAMPIONSHIP QUIZ

ANSWERS PAGE 189

1. Noel Cooney from Offaly refereed the first game between Laois and Carlow in the 1995 Leinster Senior Football Championship in which substitute Michael Turley scored a hotly disputed point near the end. Who took charge of the re-fixture a week later?

2. What player took the penalty for the Dubs which was well saved by Louth goalkeeper Niall O'Donnell in this year's Leinster Senior Championship Quarter Final?

3. Who is the only man to captain two All-Ireland winning under-21 teams?

4. The year 1988 saw the first appearance of Tipperary in an All-Ireland Hurling Final for seventeen years. Who captained the Munster Champions in the 1988 decider against Galway?

5. Who put the ball in John O'Leary's net early in the second half of the Leinster Senior Football Championship Final between Dublin and Meath?

6. Who scored the goals for Cavan in their, 2-11 to 0-8, victory over Antrim in the first round of this year's Ulster Senior Football Championship tie at Breffni Park?

7. Name the new sponsors of the GAA All-Star Awards?

8. Who is the present manager of the Kerry hurling team?

9. Name the last county to retain the Anglo Celt Cup?

10. Who captained Tyrone to victory over Fermanagh in the first round of the 1995 Ulster Senior Football Championship?

11. Name the former Meath player who is now manager of the Fermanagh team?

12. What player collected the Sam Maguire Cup when Kerry won the All-Ireland senior football title in 1975?

13. Who is the PRO of the Limerick County Board?

14. In which county would you find Sean Mhic Cumhaill Park?

15. Richard Bowles was goalkeeper for which county in this year's Football Championship?

16. Who captained Offaly to win their first ever All-Ireland senior hurling title in 1981?

17. Who is the new manager of the Longford senior football team?

18. Who is the only player to win 8 All-Ireland senior football medals playing in one position?

19. Name the player that scored the last-gasp winning goal for Clare in their Munster Senior Hurling Championship semi-final clash against Cork at the Gaelic Grounds in June?

20. Who were the two defenders suspended by the Munster Council for their part in a fracas during the Tipperary/Waterford Munster Senior Hurling Championship first round match at Pairc Ui Chaoimh?

21. With which team did John Gorry line out with in this year's All-Ireland Senior Hurling Championship?

22. Who was captain of the Laois hurlers that lost to Kilkenny by just 2 points in this year's Leinster Senior Hurling Championship?

23. Who was the first Westmeath player to win an All-Star hurling award?

24. Who was centre half forward on the Dublin team that lost to Kilkenny in the 1995 Leinster Senior Hurling Championship?

25. Why was Liam Dunne stripped of the captaincy of the Wexford team that lost to Offaly in

the 1995 Leinster Senior Hurling Championship semi-final?

26. Name the Offaly player that struck the ball which came off the chest of Kilkenny goalkeeper, Michael Walsh and dropped behind the goal line to completely alter the course of the 1995 Leinster Senior Hurling Final?

27. What is the name of the Cup presented to the winners of the Ulster Senior Hurling Championship?

28. With which county did John Small line out with in the 1995 All-Ireland Hurling Championship series?

29. With which county did Sean Paul McKillop line out with in the 1995 All-Ireland Hurling Championship series?

30. Who captained Kerry to win the last of their All-Ireland Senior Football titles in 1986?

31. Who captained Down to win the 1995 Ulster Senior Hurling Championship?

32. With which county would you associate the following hurling goalkeepers? (a) Adrian Tully, (b) Michael Neary and (c) Ray Barry

33. In what year did current Offaly hurling manager, Eamon Cregan, win an All-Ireland senior hurling medal with Limerick?

34. What Offaly player won an All-Ireland senior hurling and football medals in the eighties?

35. Who is the manager of the Wexford senior hurling team?

36. Name the club of Offaly full back Kevin Kinahan?

37. In what years did Clare manager Ger Loughnane win his two League medals?

38. What county registered the highest scored in the 1995 All-Ireland Senior Hurling Championship?

39. What county registered the highest score in the 1995 All-Ireland Senior Football Championship?

40. With which county did John James Reilly line out at midfield in the 1995 All-Ireland Senior Football Championship?

41. With which county did Muiris Gavin line out for in the 1995 All-Ireland Senior Football Championship?

42. With which county did Darrell Donnelly line out for in the 1995 All-Ireland Senior Football Championship?

43. In what position did Johnny Culloty play when he won an All-Ireland Senior Football medal with Kerry in 1955?

44. How many All-Ireland Senior Football medals did Galway footballer Mattie McDonagh win?

45. Who is the first Kerry footballer to be honoured with an All-Star Award?

46. Who is the only player to win six All-Ireland senior medals in a row?

47. Name the three Connacht men who have captained back-to-back All-Ireland winning senior footballs teams?

48. Who captained Meath to success in the 1967 All-Senior Football Final?

49. Who was captain of the Cork Hurlers in the 1995 Munster Championship?

50. What Connacht player had the honour of being chosen as goalkeeper on the first All-Star football selection in 1971?

Clare & Offaly

CROKE PARK
REFEREE: DICKIE MURPHY WEXFORD
RESULT: CLARE 1-13 OFFALY 2-8

A re our eyes deceiving us? Could that really be Anthony Daly on the Hogan Stand raising the Liam McCarthy Cup to the heavens? It was a fairytale ending to the most momentous year ever in the history of Clare hurling. Eighty-one years of heartbreak and misery were wiped away by the sight of a Clarecastle man clutching the most famous prize in hurling in the heart of the most famous sporting venue in the land. The thousands of delirious saffron and blue clad supporters directly below him cheered his every word as if he were the Lotto man handing out big cheques. Something stirred from deep within the soul of Clare people on that glorious September day in Croke Park that would change their lives forever. FOREVER!

All those unhappy memories of the 'long road back from Thurles and Limerick' were banished for good. And how they celebrated! They embraced each other, then they danced, sang, waved flags, banners, and beat bodhrans to their heart's content in a show of emotion perhaps never before seen even in the 'theatre' Croke Park. We thought we had witnessed everything, and then along came Clare to crown it all. There was magic in the air as men and women surprised even themselves by the intensity of their emotions. There was no place to hide.

Through it all, Clare manager, Ger Loughnane, as he had done all year, smiled and smiled and smiled. Loughnane is a proud Clare man who epitomises everything positive, everything enriching in the ancient game. No one man was more deserving of success as a hurler, but yet cruelly he was deprived of even a Munster medal for his collection. Now here he was, the school teacher, watching on as Anthony Daly paid tribute to him for his single-minded determination, his will to win and his love of Clare.

I had visited the Clare training sessions on a few occasions during the league and championship and had interviewed Ger on many occasions for RTE Sport. I remember earlier in the year saying to him before the League final against Kilkenny, "How can you prepare against a collapse, Ger?" He laughed that hearty laugh and then his answer was straight and to the point; "I can assure you, Brian, there will be no collapse, no collapse." He repeated it once more to drive the message home! Clare were well beaten by Kilkenny in that final, but true enough, Clare did not collapse. In the dressing-room in Thurles immediately after the game, Loughnane boldly proclaimed, that Clare would win the Munster title. They did! And better still, they went 'two' better and won the All-Ireland!

The game itself may not have been a classic, but there were many classic moments perhaps the most vivid of all, because of its significance, was Anthony Daly sending over a '65 near the very end to edge the Banner County one point in front. Croke Park was enveloped in saffron and blue. And what about the moment substitute Eamon Taffe cracked the ball to the net to level the game with four minutes left to play; and the moment Jamesie O'Connor sent over the last point of the game in injury time to seal a magnificent victory, a victory that will be talked about as long as fires remain burning in the hills Of Clare!

There were many Clare heroes. The six backs hurled like never before, but none more than fullback Frank Lohan, who was quite simply magnificent throughout. Offaly showed flashes of brilliance but never seemed to be able to sustain the pressure long enough to stamp their authority on proceedings. Kevin Kinahan proved the doubters terribly wrong once again; Martin Hanamy was tight-marking as ever and Brian Whelehan underlined why he is the finest defender in the land.

Overall Offaly's performance was too inconsistent and even a fortuitous goal from Michael Duignan coming up to half-time failed to inspire the Leinster champions. Clare goalkeeper David Fitzgerald attempted to control the sliothar and got the shock of his life when it dropped behind the line. A goal for Offaly. We waited for the avalanche. It never came. Instead, it was Clare who responded with a point apiece from Fergal Hegarty and Ger 'Sparrow' O'Loughlin. It was that kind of a day!

Offaly led at half-time by 2 points, 1-6 to 0-7, but the defending champions had to face the breeze in the second half.

Clare had drawn level by the thirteenth minute of the second half but all their hard work was wiped out in an instant when Johnny Pilkinton first-timed a ground shot to the net. Offaly were now 3 points in front and appeared likely winners. It was then we saw the true character of this Clare team. Ollie Baker was now playing superbly at midfield, but the Munster champions were still 2 points in arrears with only four minutes left to play. Substitute Eamonn Taaffe plagued by injury all year, rescued Clare with a goal. Offaly levelled with a point from Johnny Dooley, but the game turned Clare's way when Captain Anthony Daly sent over a '65 and Jamesie O'Connor wrapped up the scoring with a point from a free.

Anthony Daly told me the week before the game that Clare had modelled themselves on Offaly. "It was their success that inspired us. Offaly showed us the way, we felt if Offaly could beat the traditional counties, why not Clare also."

It was ironic then that Clare should beat Offaly in the final. The Offaly men, although bitterly disappointed, were gracious in defeat and paid tribute to Clare for the manner in which they achieved victory.

Clare won their first All-Ireland title in 81 years because they played as a team for the duration of the game; it never came together for Offaly who relied far too much on individuals.

All-Ireland Hurling Final action– Brian Lohan, Clare, and Pat O'Connor, Offaly.
See colour section for winning Clare team

Offaly Back row l to r: Gary Cahill, Liam Coughlan, P.J. Martin, Daithi Regan, Shane McGuckin, Kevin Kinahan, David Hughes, Kevin Martin, Michael Duignan, Hubert Rigney, Brian Whelehan, Paudie Mulhare, Kevin Flynn, Joe Errity. **Front row l to r:** Brendan Kelly, David O'Meara, John Miller, Billy Dooley, John Troy, Martin Hanamy, Johnny Pilkington, Pat O'Connor, Joe Dooley, Johnny Dooley, Jim Troy, Brian Hennessy, Declan Pilkington.

As soon as the referee blew the final whistle and Clare were crowned champions for the first time in eighty-one years, I made my way on to the pitch to get an interview for RTE Radio Sport. It was an unwise move!

Producer Pat O'Donovan, and myself, were swallowed up by thousands of wildly-cheering Clare supporters that poured on to the pitch. Eventually, I made my way to the presentation area and met up with Ger Loughnane on the steps of the stand. He talked to me about the game and what the win would mean to the people of Clare. He was dragged about like a rag doll, but yet he stood his ground and talked to me. He need not have done it. But he did. And I thank him for it.

Anthony Daly's speech matched his masterpiece in Thurles on Munster Final Day. Enough said! And where would we be without a song? Selector Tony Considine, like he did in Thurles, gave a rousing rendition of the Banner Anthem, 'My Lovely Rose Of Clare.' Tony told me a few days before the All-Ireland that someone had said to him after the Munster final; 'stick to the hurling, Tony.'

That was the most appealing aspect of Clare's run through the championship. Good humour was in evidence throughout. The camaraderie was second to none. It was almost as if the Clare players, manager and selectors knew the outcome and were laughing in that certain knowledge. After the Munster Final victory, every one of the Clare players attained celebrity status within the county. The footballers had shown the way in '92 and now it was the turn of the hurling men from the Banner County to taste sweet success! Anthony Daly told me during the year that, 'to a lot of other counties, Clare are nobodies in the hurling world, and they would always be seen as a soft touch to the traditional powers in Munster.'

But '95 was different; super-sub, Ollie Baker, scored the winning goal late in the game against Cork in the opening round; last year's beaten All-Ireland finalists; Limerick succumbed to the Clare onslaught in the Munster Final; Galway were next on the Clare hit-list in the All-Ireland semi-final and the Banner men won with 5 points to spare. Then the stiffest test of all in the All-Ireland Final against defending champions and favourites, Offaly.

Few gave Clare a ghost of a chance of beating the team with all the talents; a team that could proudly boast players of the calibre of Brian Whelehan, Martin Hanamy, Johnny Pilkington, John Troy, and of course, the three Dooley brothers, Johnny, Billy and Joe! Reading the newspapers in the week leading up to the game, it appeared most everyone expected Offaly to retain the crown. I was reminded of what Tony Hanahoe said to me in my book, *Football Captains, The All-Ireland Winners*, when recalling Dublin's victory in the 1974 All-Ireland Final against overwhelming favourites, Cork.

"One of the Sunday newspapers was callous enough to put the names and faces and say, 'on an individual basis, how could Dublin be expected to beat Cork? We never stopped running and playing that day and Cork were totally rocked back on their heels. We were young, vibrant, enthusiastic and psyched up and things ran for us that day."

It was much the same 21 years later for the men of Clare. On an individual basis, journalists, broadcasters, present players, past players and neutral supporters, all questioned: 'whether Clare could be expected to beat Offaly?' But they did and deservedly so. Not too many would have allowed for Clare's utter determination and the fact that they played like men possessed.

The long famine was at an end. It was time to celebrate. The following Monday night tens of thousands converged in Ennis to welcome home the Liam McCarthy Cup. Earlier, Anthony Daly and his team were given a heroes welcome on arrival at Shannon Airport before they began their very emotional journey to Ennis. It was never-to-be-forgotten occasion. There was magic in the air and an extra spring in the step of Clare people everywhere. And rightly so! But spare a thought, for the beaten finalists, Offaly, who only narrowly failed to become the first team from the Faithful County to retain the Liam Mc Carthy Cup. Unfortunately, only one team can win the ultimate prize in hurling and in 1995 that team was Clare!

Scorers Clare: Fergus Tuohy 0-4; Sean Mc Mahon 0-3; Eamon Taaffe 1-0; Jamesie O'Connor 0-2; Anthony Daly 0-1; Ollie Baker 0-1; Fergal Hegarty 0-1; Ger O'Loughlin 0-1. **Scorers Offaly:** Johnny Dooley 0-5; Michael Duignan 1-0; Johnny Pilkington 1-0; John Troy 0-1; Daithi Regan 0-1; Billy Dooley 0-1.

CLARE

DAVID FITZGERALD

MICHAEL O'HALLORAN	BRIRAN LOHAN	FRANK LOHAN
LIAM DOYLE	SEAN MC MAHON	ANTHONY DALY
JAMESIE O'CONNOR		OLLIE BAKER
FERGUS TUOHY	P.J. O'CONNELL	FERGAL HEGARTY
STEPHEN MCNAMARA	CONOR CLANCY	GER O'LOUGHLIN

Substitutes: Eamon Taaffe for Stephen Mc Namara; Cyril Lyons for Conor Clancy; Alan Neville for Eamon Taaffe

OFFALY

DAVID HUGHES

SHANE MC GUCKIN	KEVIN KINAHAN	MARTIN HANAMY
BRIAN WHELEHAN	HUBERT RIGNEY	KEVIN MARTIN
JOHNNY PILKINGTON		DAITHI REGAN
JOHNNY DOOLEY	JOHN TROY	MICHAEL DUIGNAN
BILLY DOOLEY	PAT O'CONNOR	JOE DOOLEY

Substitutes: Declan Pilkington for Pat O'Connor; Brendan Kelly for Joe Dooley

Ger O'Loughlin of Clare and Brian Whelehan of Offaly chasing the ball.

CORK & KERRY

AUSTIN STACK PARK, TRALEE
REFEREE: JOHNNY MCDONNELL TIPPERARY
RESULT: CORK 1-22 KERRY 0-12

Cork had made it clear in the week leading up to the game that nothing would be taken for granted against a confident Kerry team buoyed by their promotion to Division One. There was a feeling in the Kingdom that at last they had assembled a team eminently capable of despatching their more distinguished rivals. It came as no surprise to see Cork approach the game at Austin Stacks Park in a cautious mood.

Tony O'Sullivan was recalled to the Cork team at left half forward and justified his selection by scoring 4 points. It was a game Cork deserved to win ,although their impressive 13 point winning margin certainly flattered them and did little justice to Kerry's brave display. Full forward Alan Browne scored the only goal of the game in injury time to give the final scoreline a lopsided look in Cork's favour.

Kerry goalkeeper John Healy was unfortunate to drop a high shot and Browne struck the ball to the net. It was cruel luck on Healy who otherwise had an outstanding game. It was an evening when Kerry players learned of the chasm that exists between winter hurling and the cut and thrust of championship. It is a game that should help prepare them for life in the higher echelons of the League.

Kerry only trailed by 4 points at half-time, 0-10 to 0-6, and that despite playing against the breeze and hitting a number of wides from scorable positions. Furthermore, Kerry full forward Liam O'Connor failed to put away a gilt-edged goal opportunity.

Darren O'Donoghue came on as a substitute early in the second half and made an immense contribution scoring 4 points from play. When Barry Egan, Cork's top scorer with 7 points, was moved to midfield in the second half, the visitors strengthened their grip on the game. Kerry showed great commitment throughout and Pa O'Rourke was outstanding at midfield. Two points apiece in the second half from captain Mike Hennessy, Christy Walsh and Pat O'Connell allowed Kerry to sustain their challenge. Cork always had the edge at crucial stages and scored, 1-4, in the final quarter to seal a Munster Semi-Final meeting with Clare.

Kerry manager, John Meyler was naturally disappointed to lose, but predicted a bright future for his team. He was confident Kerry would benefit enormously from playing in Division One and that a championship breakthrough was imminent. And what of Cork? Manager Johnny Clifford was relieved that his side had won but felt Cork would have to improve to beat League finalists Clare in the Munster semi-final. Only time would tell!

Scorers Cork: Barry Egan 0-7; Tony O'Sullivan 0-4; Darren O'Donoghue 0-4; Alan

Browne 1-1; Kevin Murray 0-3; Kieran Morrison 0-2; Cathal Casey 0-1. **Scorers Kerry:** Pat O'Connell 0-4; Mike Hennessy 0-3; Christy Walshe 0-2; Pa O'Rourke 0-1; Brendan O'Mahony 0-1; Brendan O'Sullivan 0-1.

C O R K

	GER CUNNINGHAM	
TIMMY KELLEHER	JOHN O'DRISCOLL	JIM CASHMAN
PETER SMITH	BRIAN CORCORAN	PAT KENNEALLY
CATHAL CASEY		PAT BUCKLEY
BARRY EGAN	KEVIN MURRAY	TONY O'SULLIVAN
KIERAN MORRISON	ALAN BROWNE	DARREN RONAN

Substitutes: Darren O'Donoghue for Pat Buckley; Ger Manley for Darren Ronan; Fergal McCormack for Kevin Murray

K E R R Y

	JOHN HEALY	
JOHN FOLEY	MIKE CASEY	SEAMUS MCINTYRE
CHRISTY ROSS	MIKE HENNESSY	TONY MAUNSELL
PA O'ROURKE		DINNY MCCARTHY
BRENDAN O'MAHONY	PAT O'CONNELL	CHRISTY WALSHE
GERRY O'SULLIVAN	LIAM O'CONNOR	BRENDAN O'SULLIVAN

Substitutes: Kenneth Boyle for Liam O'Connor; Tony McCarthy for Dinny McCarthy; Joe Walsh for Jerry O'Sullivan

Cork Back row l to r: Pat Buckley, Brian Corcoran, Jim Cashman, Alan Browne, Kieran Morrison, Cathal Casey, Ger Cunningham. **Front row l to r:** Tony O'Sullivan, John O'Driscoll, Peter Smith, Pat Kenneally, Darren Ronan, Barry Egan, Timmy Kelleher. (see Cork vs Clare team picture for Kevin Murray).

Kerry Back row l to r: Mike Casey, Christy Ross, Seamus Mc Intyre, Dinny Mc Carthy, Pa O'Rourke, John Healy, Liam O'Connor, Gerry O'Sullivan. **Front row l to r:** Pat O'Connell, Christy Walsh, Brendan O'Sullivan, Mike Hennessy, John Foley, Tony Maunsell, Brendan O'Mahony.

SUNDAY MAY 21
MUNSTER SENIOR HURLING
CHAMPIONSHIP FIRST ROUND

TIPPERARY & WATERFORD

PAIRC UI CHAOIMH, CORK
REFEREE: TERENCE MURRAY LIMERICK
RESULT: TIPPERARY 4-23 WATERFORD 1-11

Tipperary sent out a warning to all-comers with their most devastating championship performance for a number of years. As League champions, Tipp went down tamely to Clare in the '94 championship; this year their league showing was indifferent, but their display against Waterford in the Munster championship opener was nothing short of vintage. Waterford, lacking in big-match experience, were unable to produce the kind of form that saw them reach the semi-final stages of the League four weeks earlier. In truth, the Decies man were over-run by a Tipp side determined to silence those who doubted their pedigree.

It was the first championship meeting of the counties since the 1989 Munster final, won impressively by Tipperary. Manager Fr. Tom Fogarty certainly opted for experience: Aidan Ryan made a welcome return to partner Colm Bonnar at midfield, while dual player Brendan Cummins took over between the posts in place of the injured Jody Grace. Damien Byrne was recalled to the Waterford team at full back while Sean Daly was drafted in at full forward.

The amicable Fr. Tom told me a few days before the game that his team had prepared diligently and were ready for the challenge. He dismissed the general view that Tipperary was a team of old stagers. It was obvious the Waterford team was a little shook up after their League semi-final collapse against Clare, nevertheless, they were reasonably confident.

If it was difficult to evaluate Tipperary's strength before the game, there was no such problem once referee Terence Murray got proceedings underway. It soon became apparent that Tipp meant business as they began to dismantle the Waterford challenge with clinical precision. Tipperary had many stars, but none more than Aidan Ryan, who turned in a superlative display and ended the day with a tally of 1-2. Waterford's midfield partnership of Johnny Brenner and Tom Fives never got to grips with Ryan and Colm Bonnar. Tourin club man, Fives was replaced at half-time by Peter Queally. Johnny Brenner was called ashore fifteen minutes from time, his place taken by Paul Connors. But try as they might, Waterford could not break the Tipp stranglehold.

At half-time, it was 0-12 to 0-5, in Tipperary's favour and Waterford's hopes looked forlorn. Centre half forward Ger Harris scored a Waterford goal after 47 minutes but it was then we saw the best of Tipperary. Pat Fox, a second half substitute for Anthony Crosse, started the scoring spree with a well-taken goal. Michael Cleary added another soon after and before the game had run its inevitable

Tipperary Back row l to r: Raymie Ryan, Noel Sheehy, Brendan Cummins, Declan Ryan, Anthony Crosse, John Leahy, Conal Bonner. **Front row l to r:** Nicky English, Michael Cleary, Colm Bonner, Michael Ryan, Tommy Dunne, Aidan Ryan, George Frend, Paul Delaney.

Waterford Back row l to r: Gary Gater, Damien Byrne, Stephen Frampton, Sean Cullinane, Sean Daly, Johnny Brenner, Paul Flynn, Tom Fives. **Front row l to r:** Billy O'Sullivan, Brian Greene, Tom Feeney, Ray Barry, Ger Harris, Tony Browne, Fergal Hartley.

course there were further goals from Aidan Ryan and Fox again. And what an impact the Eire Óg Annacarty player had on the game! He was only on the field for 26 minutes, yet ended up as Tipperary's top scorer with 2 goals and 4 points.

There was an unseemly incident late in the second half when several players from both sides became involved in a fracas. Tipperary's Paul Delaney and Michael Ryan were booked. Others were fortunate to escape punishment.

Scorers Tipperary: Pat Fox 2-4; Michael Cleary 1-4; Aidan Ryan 1-2; Declan Ryan 0-4; Nicky English 0-4; Tommy Dunne 0-3; John Leahy 0-2. **Scorers Waterford:** Ger Harris 1-1; Gary Gater 0-3; Paul Flynn 0-3; Tony Browne 0-1; Tom Fives 0-1; Billy O'Sullivan 0-1; Peter Queally 0-1.

TIPPERARY

BRENDAN CUMMINS

| GEORGE FREND | NOEL SHEEHY | MICHAEL RYAN |
| RAYMIE RYAN | CONAL BONNAR | PAUL DELANEY |

AIDAN RYAN   COLM BONNAR

| TOMMY DUNNE | DECLAN RYAN | JOHN LEAHY |
| MICHAEL CLEARY | ANTHONY CROSSE | NICKY ENGLISH |

Substitute: Pat Fox for Anthony Crosse; Conor Gleeson for Conal Bonnar

WATERFORD

RAY BARRY

| SEAN CULLINANE | DAMIEN BYRNE | TOM FEENEY |
| TONY BROWNE | STEPHEN FRAMPTON | FERGAL HARTLEY |

JOHNNY BRENNER   TOM FIVES

| GARY GATER | GER HARRIS | BRIAN GREENE |
| BILLY O'SULLIVAN | SEAN DALY | PAUL FLYNN |

Substitutes: Peter Queally for Tom Fives; Paul Connors for Johnny Brenner; John Meaney for Sean Daly

SUNDAY JUNE 4
MUNSTER SENIOR HURLING
CHAMPIONSHIP SEMI-FINAL

CLARE & CORK

GAELIC GROUNDS, LIMERICK
REFEREE: PAT O'CONNOR LIMERICK
RESULT: CLARE 2-13 CORK 3-9

It was the day Clare hurling came of age. Ger Loughnane's heroes stared defeat in the face but stubbornly refused to lose heart. Instead, they showed tremendous character and in the end clinched a third successive Munster Final appearance. Picture the scene. Cork appeared to have booked their place in the provincial decider when Kevin Murray struck the ball to the net to edge his side 2 points ahead with one minute left to play. Somehow Clare, from deep within, found the courage to strike back in dramatic style. No one epitomised their new-found spirit more than centre half back Sean McMahon, who was moved upfield to corner forward after injuring his collarbone with 15 minutes left to play.

McMahon could not be replaced as Clare had already used up their requisite number of subs, but playing through the pain barrier, the Doora/Barefield man, using just one hand, forced a line ball which eventually led to the winning goal. Fergus

Tuohy's sideline cut was finished to the net by substitute Ollie Baker much to the delight of the Clare supporters.

Victory disguised shortcomings in Clare's play and they could hardly be pleased with a total of 20 wides throughout the 70 minutes. It would be unfair to be critical on such a glorious day for the Banner County.

Although aided by the breeze in the first half, Clare, despite abundant possession, trailed by 3 points at the interval. Alan Browne scored the opening goal and then set up Ger Manley for Cork's second goal on 32 minutes to put them in front for the first time. Then Barry Egan stretched Cork's lead with the last point of the first half. Within four minutes of the restart, Cork had opened up a 5 point lead through points from Alan Browne and Kevin Murray. Clare refused to lie down. The introduction of Frank Lohan at half-time allowed Liam Doyle move to his more familiar half back position where he became much more involved and turned in an outstanding display.

Slowly Clare began to exert their dominance, and 2 points from Jamesie O'Connor followed by a point each from PJ O'Connell, Ger 'Sparrow' O'Loughlin and Ollie Baker levelled the game with 15 minutes still to play. Once again, Cork hit back with 2 points from Mark Mullins and another from Kevin Murray. The drama was only beginning! The 'Sparrow' shot to the net; O'Connell edged Clare in front with a point; four minutes later, Kevin Murray scored what appeared to be a winning goal for Cork. We reckoned without super-sub Ollie Baker, who surely guaranteed himself a special niche in Clare folklore with a 'golden' goal to win the game. After the game, Johnny Clifford announced he was stepping down as Cork manager, now that his two-year term had come to an end. After the disappointment of the League Final defeat, Clare manager Ger Loughnane expressed his delight at the way Clare had battled back and won in a tight finish. His prophecy in the dressing-room after

Clare Back row l to r: Brian Lohan, Michael O'Halloran, Jim Mc Inerney, David Fitzgerald, Stephen Sheedy, Sean Mc Mahon, Ger 'Sparrow' O'Loughlin. **Front row l to r:** P.J. O'Connell, John Chaplin, Conor Clancy, Anthony Daly, Fergal Hegarty, Jamesie O'Connor, Liam Doyle, Fergus Tuohy.

losing the League Final to Kilkenny that Clare would win the Munster title in '95 was still on course. If only just!

Scorers Clare: Ger 'Sparrow' O'Loughlin 1-3; Jamesie O'Connor 0-4; Ollie Baker 1-1; PJ O'Connell 0-2; Sean McMahon 0-1; Fergal Hegarty 0-1; Conor Clancy 0-1. **Scorers Cork:** Alan Browne 1-2; Kevin Murray 1-2; Ger Manley 1-0; Mark Mullins 0-2; Barry Egan 0-1; Kieran Morrisson 0-1; Darren O'Donoghue 0-1.

CLARE

DAVID FITZGERALD

| MICHAEL O'HALLORAN | BRIAN LOHAN | LIAM DOYLE |
| ANTHONY DALY | SEAN MCMAHON | JOHN CHAPLIN |

STEPHEN SHEEDY   FERGAL HEGARTY

| FERGUS TUOHY | PJ O'CONNELL | JAMESIE O'CONNOR |
| JIM MCINERNEY | CONOR CLANCY | GER 'SPARROW' O'LOUGHLIN |

Substitutes: Ollie Baker for Stephen Sheedy; Frank Lohan for John Chaplin; Stephen McNamara for Jim McInerney

CORK

GER CUNNINGHAM

| JIM CASHMAN | JOHN O'DRISCOLL | PAT KENNEALLY |
| PETER SMITH | BRIAN CORCORAN | TIMMY KELLEHER |

CATHAL CASEY   BARRY EGAN

| DARREN O'DONOGHUE | GER MANLEY | MARK MULLINS |
| KEVIN MURRAY | ALAN BROWNE | K IERAN MORRISSON |

Substitutes: F ergal Ryan for Cathal Casey; Sean McCarthy for Kieran Morrisson; Darren Ronan for Darren O'Donoghue

Cork Back row l to r: Ger Cunningham, Brian Corcoran, Ger Manley, Jim Cashman, Alan Browne, Kieran Morrison, Kevin Murray. **Front row l to r:** Mark Mullins, Cathal Casey, Timmy Kelleher, Peter Smith, Pat Kenneally, John O'Driscoll, Darren O'Donoghue, Barry Egan.

SUNDAY JUNE 18

MUNSTER SENIOR HURLING
CHAMPIONSHIP SEMI-FINAL

LIMERICK & TIPPERARY

PAIRC UI CHAOIMH, CORK
REFEREE: DICKIE MURPHY WEXFORD
RESULT: LIMERICK 0-16 TIPPERARY 0-15

Limerick hurlers went a long way towards exorcising the ghost of their 1994 All-Ireland Final defeat by Offaly with a one point win over old rivals and favourites Tipperary. Nothing had gone right for Limerick since Offaly produced the most astonishing turnaround in the annals of the All-Ireland Hurling Final. Limerick were leading by 5 points and cruising to victory entering the final five minutes when Johnny Dooley scored a goal from a free and inexplicably the Limerick side crumbled. The final score of Offaly 3-16 Limerick 2-13, represented a comeback of gigantic proportions.

The traumatised Shannonsiders had a best-forgotten League campaign resulting in demotion to Division Two and not too many expected them to take the honours against a Tipperary side who served notice of their championship ambitions with a 21 point drubbing of Waterford.

At the end of the day, thanks to an outstanding scoring display by Gary Kirby, Limerick, minus the injured Ger Hegarty, proved their pedigree and silenced the critics who doubted their abililty to advance to a Munster Final meeting with Clare. While Limerick sang 'Sean South From Garryowen' the talk among Tipperary folk centred on the lengthy Munster Council suspensions handed down to defenders Paul

Limerick Back row l to r: TJ Ryan, Mike Nash, Gary Kirby, Sean O'Neill, Pat Heffernan, Frankie Carroll, Dave Clarke. **Front row l to r:** Damien Quigley, Declan Nash, Joe Quaid, Mike Galligan, Mike Houlihan, Stephen Mc Donagh, Ciaran Carey, Turlough Herbert.

Delaney and Michael Ryan, following incidents in the Waterford game. Many felt it cost Tipperary a place in the provincial decider. Tipp manager, Fr Tom Fogarty conceded that Limerick deserved to win. In truth, the Tipp defence could not be faulted for this defeat; midfielder Aidan Ryan also played his part but far too many off their forwards failed to shake off the shackles of a tight-marking Limerick defence. Centre half back Ciaran Carey proved he had fully recovered from a troublesome groin injury with a *tour-de-force* performance.

Tipperary missed far too many scoring opportunities- 15 wides is not acceptable at this level- but could still have won were it not for the brilliance of Limerick centre half forward, Gary Kirby. The Patrickswell marksman scored 12 points and once again underlined his class. Tipperary, aided by the breeze, were just 2 points in front, 0-9 to 0-7, at half-time. Damien Quigley had a goal disallowed much to the displeasure of some Limerick supporters, who felt the advantage should have been played. Gary Kirby struck the resultant penalty over the bar.

Fielding 13 of the players that lost to Offaly in the All-Ireland Final, Limerick had moved one point clear fifteen minutes into the second half and the game was still evenly balanced, but points from Michael Cleary and Nicky English edged Tipp one point clear. At this stage full forward Anthony Crosse received a blow to the head and had to go off injured. Limerick continued to press forward and reeled off points from TJ Ryan, Gary Kirby and Sean O'Neill. Again Tipp rallied and when Michael Cleary pointed a free near the very end, just one point separated the sides and a draw appeared the likely outcome. But the defending Munster champions held their nerve and secured a narrow victory.

Scorers Limerick: Gary Kirby 0-12; Mike Galligan 0-1; TJ Ryan 0-1; Damien Quigley 0-1; Sean O'Neill 0-1. **Scorers Tipperary:** Michael Cleary 0-4; Nicky English 0-2; Raymie Ryan 0-2; Aidan Ryan 0-2; John Leahy 0-2; Declan Ryan 0-1; Pat Fox 0-1; Anthony Crosse 0-1.

Tipperary Back row l to r: Raymie Ryan, Noel Sheehy, Brendan Cummins, Declan Ryan, Anthony Crosse, John Leahy, Conal Bonner, Pat Fox. **Front row l to r:** Nicky English, Michael Cleary, Brendan Carroll, Tommy Dunne, George Frend, Colm Bonnar, Aidan Ryan.

L I M E R I C K

JOE QUAID

STEPHEN MCDONAGH	MIKE NASH	DECLAN NASH
DAVE CLARKE	CIARAN CAREY	TURLOUGH HERBERT
MIKE HOULIHAN		SEAN O'NEILL
FRANKIE CARROLL	GARY KIRBY	MIKE GALLIGAN
TJ RYAN	PAT HEFFERNAN	DAMIEN QUIGLEY

Substitutes: Mark Foley for Frankie Carroll; Shane O'Neill for Pat Heffernan; Mike Reale for Mike Houlihan

T I P P E R A R Y

BRENDAN CUMMINS

GEORGE FREND	NOEL SHEEHY	COLM BONNAR
RAYMIE RYAN	CONAL BONNAR	BRENDAN CARROLL
AIDAN RYAN		JOHN LEAHY
THOMAS DUNNE	DECLAN RYAN	MICHAEL CLEARY
PAT FOX	ANTHONY CROSSE	NICKY ENGLISH

Substitute: Andy Moloney for Anthony Crosse

SUNDAY JULY 9

MUNSTER SENIOR HURLING
CHAMPIONSHIP FINAL

CLARE & LIMERICK

SEMPLE STADIUM, THURLES
REFEREE: JOHNNY MCDONNELL TIPPERARY
RESULT: CLARE 1-17 LIMERICK 0-11

Sixty-three years! And nothing to talk about only hard-luck stories. Words like heartbreak were permanently linked with Clare hurling. Demoralising defeats by Cork, Tipperary, Limerick, and Waterford for good measure in 1938, had taken their toll. It all amounted to a lifetime of misery for Clare hurlers arounds the green fields of Munster.

And then it changed. From somewhere deep within, the players in saffron and blue found the courage to win a first Munster title since 1932. The famine had ended and the Banner county went wild with excitement. Inspirational captain, Anthony Daly held the Munster Cup in a vice-like grip. And then he spoke: "It's been sixty-three years of the long road back from Thurles and Limerick, but this baby's coming home tonight."

Manager Ger Loughane could harldy contain himself. He was in direct competition with his captain for the top prize in the 'biggest smile' category. Loughnane himself had endured the bad times as a player. Now those were forgotten. It was not a day to dwell on the lows. Selector Tony Considine joined in the spirit of the occasion with a rousing rendition of the Banner anthem, 'My Lovely Rose Of Clare'. The sixty-three year famine had ended!

The game itself may not have been a classic, but any shortcomings were well and truly disguised by the sheer magnitude of Clare's win. All past failures were forgotten. And forgiven! Clare had produced some outstanding teams over the years, but most promised more than they ever delivered, particularly in the championship.

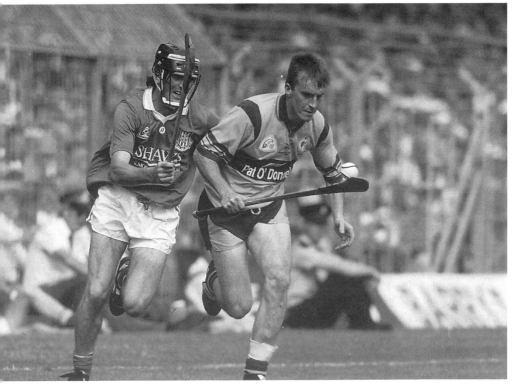

1995 Munster Final between Clare and Limerick. Fergus Tuohy of Clare with the ball followed by Tadhg Hayes, Limerick.

For some inexplicable reason, one Clare team after another failed to produce a match-winning performance in the provincial decider. Even the current crop of Clare players that eventually conquered Everest fell twice on Munster Final days, against Tipperary in '93 and Limerick in '94. But it turned out to be third time lucky on a sunny July Sunday in '95!

Ger Loughnane's prophecy in the dressing-room in the aftermath of the League final loss to Kilkenny in early May, that Clare would win the Munster title, had come true. His bold statement had a profound impact on all the players.

But spare a thought, too, for Limerick. Anthony Daly was watching last year's All-Ireland decider on television in Clare in the company of some of his friends, and as the game approached the final ten minutes he was convinced Limerick were going to beat Offaly by the proverbial cricket score, such was the Shannonsiders' dominance. Then came the most dramatic turnaround in the annals of the final. Johnny Dooley struck the ball to the net from a free. Almost immediately, Pat O'Connor scored another goal and Billy Dooley struck over some wonderful points. It was almost impossible to comprehend the drama unfolding before our eyes. Offaly scored 2-5 in the closing five minutes and won in the end by 6 points. It was a comeback of gigantic proportions. Limerick recovered very well from the trauma of losing to Offaly and showed excellent form in their gutsy defeat of Tippeary in the Munster semi-final.

Jamesie O'Connor was chosen at left half forward on the Clare team but he moved to midfield at the start in a direct switch with Fergal Hegarty.

Limerick were clear favourites to record a second successive Munster Final victory over Clare and sure enough the reigning champions, aided by the breeze, began in sprightly fashion with a point from play by Mike Galligan. But within a minute, PJ O'Connell kick-started Clare's challenge with a point from play and that was followed by a point from Ger 'Sparrow' O'Loughlin after seven minutes. But Limerick had moved 2 points clear and were playing with a good degree of confidence when Clare were awarded a penalty after 26 minutes. Goalkeeper David Fitzgerald raced up field and slotted the ball past Joe Quaid. Fitzgerald, from Sixmilebridge, was one of the many Clare heroes on the day and made some excellent saves at crucial stages.

Still, the men from the Banner County were somewhat fortunate to lead at half-time by one point, 1-5 to 0-7, as Limerick corner forward Damien Quigley struck a cracking shot off the crossbar late in the half.

The expected second half onslaught from Limerick never materialised. PJ O'Connell scored the opening point of the second half to signal Clare's intentions. Limerick centre half forward and top scorer, Gary Kirby replied with 2 points from play to level scores after 40 minutes for the fifth and last time. Jamesie O'Connor, O'Connell and Seanie McMahon added a point each to edge Clare in front. McMahon's, particularly, was an inspirational score and somehow one felt this was going to be Clare's day! Soon afterwards, corner forward, Damien Quigley missed a glorious goal-scoring opportunity for Limerick when he kicked the sliothar narrowly wide. And that was that!

An out of sorts, Limerick team scored just 2 points in the final thirty minutes while Clare tacked on 8 with a display of exhibition hurling. The final whistle signalled the end of one of the longest famines in hurling and the beginning of a mighty celebration. Semple Stadium was transfromed into a sea of saffron and blue. It was a wonderful sight. Brave Anthony Daly had a smile as wide as the Shannon as he clutched the shining Cup. His speech matched anything seen on the pitch moments earlier.

The historic win sparked off tumultous celebrations right around the county. John Joe 'Goggles' Doyle, the last Clareman to lift the Munster Cup, was not well enough to attend the final, but he was in Tulla on the Monday night to join in the celebrations. The following day, Anthony Daly visited John Joe's home with the Cup. A shared moment between two men whose names will forever be indelibly linked with two of Clare's most momentous days in hurling.

Scorers Clare: Jamesie O'Connor 0-6; PJ O'Connell 0-4; David Fitzgerald 1-0; Conor Clancy 0-2; Sean McMahon 0-1; Stephen McNamara 0-1; Fergal Hegarty 0-1; Ger 'Sparrow' O'Loughlin 0-1; Fergus Tuohy 0-1. **Scorers Limerick:** Gary Kirby 0-6; Mike Galligan 0-3; Pat Heffernan 0-1; Frankie Carroll 0-1.

C L A R E

DAVID FITZGERALD

MICHAEL O'HALLORAN	BRIAN LOHAN	FRANK LOHAN
LIAM DOYLE	SEAN MCMAHON	ANTHONY DALY
FERGAL HEGARTY		OLLIE BAKER
FERGUS TUOHY	PJ O'CONNELL	JAMESIE O'CONNOR
STEPHEN MCNAMARA	CONOR CLANCY	GER 'SPARROW' O'LOUGHLIN

Substitutes: Jim McInerney for Fergus Tuohy; Cyril Lyons for Conor Clancy

L I M E R I C K

JOE QUAID

STEPHEN MCDONAGH	MIKE NASH	DECLAN NASH
DAVID CLARKE	CIARAN CAREY	TURLOUGH HERBERT
MIKE HOULIHAN		SEAN O'NEILL
FRANKIE CARROLL	GARY KIRBY	MIKE GALLIGAN
T.J. RYAN	PAT HEFFERNAN	DAMIEN QUIGLEY

Substitutes: Tadhg Hayes for Turlough Herbert; Brian Tobin for Frankie Carroll; Donal Barry for Tadhg Hayes

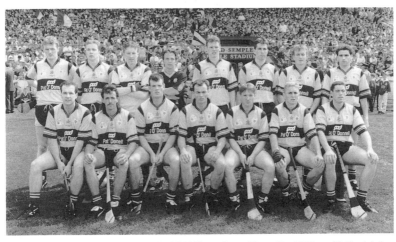

Clare Back row l to r: Brian Lohan, Michael O'Halloran, Conor Clancy, David Fitzgerald, Frank Lohan, Sean Mc Mahon, Fergus Tuohy, Ger 'Sparrow' O'Loughlin. **Front row l to r:** Liam Doyle, P.J. O'Connell, Ollie Baker, Anthony Daly, Jamesie O'Connor, Stephen Mc Namara, Fergal Hegarty.

Limerick Back row l to r: Pat Heffernan, TJ Ryan, Mike Nash, Gary Kirby, Mike Houlihan, Sean O'Neill, Frankie Carroll, Dave Clarke. **Front row l to r:** Damien Quigley, Declan Nash, Mike Galligan, Joe Quaid, Stephen Mc Donagh, Turlough Herbert, Ciaran Carey.

LEINSTER SENIOR HURLING
CHAMPIONSHIP PRELIMINARY ROUND
CARLOW & MEATH
ATHBOY
REFEREE: PADRAIG HORAN OFFALY
RESULT: CARLOW 2-11 MEATH 1-13

The main focus of attention in Gaelic games this Sunday was the National Football League Semi-Finals double-header at Croke Park where Derry defeated Tyrone and Donegal accounted for Laois to set up an all Ulster League Final. That same afternoon in Athboy far from the madding crowd, rank outsiders Carlow pulled off a shock victory over favourites Meath in the preliminary round of the Leinster Senior Hurling Championship.

Carlow's victory was all the more surprising given Meath's superb form in the League when they fashioned deserved victories over Wexford and the All-Ireland Champions Offaly. Carlow had a best-forgotten League campaign and were eventually relegated to Division Three. Talk from those close to the Carlow team the week before the game indicated Meath would be unwise to take anything for granted. A determined Carlow team showed scant regard for their opponents' new-found reputation and settled to their task with relish.

Carlow suffered a setback 21 minutes in to the first half when left half forward, Johnny Kavanagh was sent to the line by referee Padraig Horan for a foul on John Gorry. The sending off seemed to strengthen Carlow's resolve. With Johnny Nevin outstanding at centre half back, they made light of the handicap with a goal from replacement full forward, John Byrne and another, from a penalty, by top scorer, Mick Slye. Meath responded with 2 pointed frees from Pat Potterton and one apiece from Dave Martin and John Andrews to leave Carlow just 4 points in front, 2-6 to 0-8, at the half-time break.

Carlow appeared safe when they moved 6 points clear mid-way through the second half. Then a Meath goal from centre half forward David Martin after 56 minutes left just 3 points between the sides and with Leinster interprovincial player, Pat Potterton finding the range the men from the Royal county gradually reduced the deficit to the minimum. Meath missed a number of opportunities in the closing minutes as they frantically sought the levelling score, but it was not to be their day. Carlow defended bravely and held out for a slender victory to set up an unexpected meeting with Westmeath. Interestingly, Carlow used no substitutes, a rare occurence nowadays in Gaelic games.

Scorers Carlow: Mick Slye 1-4; John Byrne 1-0; Martin Farrell 0-3; David Doyle 0-2; Brendan Hayden 0-1; Niall English 0-1. **Scorers Meath:** Pat Potterton 0-7; Dave Martin 1-3; John Andrews 0-1, Mick Cole 0-1, Benny Murray 0-1.

C A R L O W

STEPHEN BAMBRICK

SEAMUS O'SHEA	EMMETT COBURN		KEVIN NOLAN
JIM ENGLISH	JOHNNY NEVIN		BRIAN LAWLOR
	BRENDAN HAYDEN	JOHN CAREY	
MICK SLYE	MARTIN FARRELL		JOHNNY KAVANAGH
DAVID DOYLE	JOHN BYRNE		NIALL ENGLISH

Substutites: None

M E A T H

MARK GANNON

ANTON O'NEILL	MARTIN SMITH		JOEY HORAN
JOHN GORRY	DECLAN MURRAY		NICKY HORAN
	PAUL DONNELLY	MICKEY MC DONNELL	
MICK COLE	DAVID MARTIN		RAY DORRAN
PAT POTTERTON	JOHN ANDREWS		BENNY MURRAY

Substitutes: Paddy Kelly for Mickey McDonnell; Martin Ennis for Ray Dorran

Carlow Back row l to r: Jim English, Martin Farrell, Emmett Coburn, Brendan Hayden, John Carey, John Byrne, Seamus O'Shea, Kevin Nolan. **Front row l to r:** Brian Lawlor, Johnny Nevin, Stephen Bambrick, Johnny Kavanagh, David Doyle, Mick Slye, Niall English.

Meath Back row l to r: Mick Cole, Nicky Horan, David Martin, Mark Gannon, John Andrews, Martin Smith, Paul Donnelly, Mickey McDonnell. **Front row l to r:** Benny Murray, Joey Horan, Declan Murray, John Gorry, Pat Potterton, Anton O'Neill, Ray Dorran.

SUNDAY MAY 14
LEINSTER SENIOR HURLING
CHAMPIONSHIP PRELIMINARY
ROUND

WESTMEATH & CARLOW

DR. CULLEN PARK, CARLOW
REFEREE: JOHN GUINAN KILKENNY
RESULT: WESTMEATH 6-6 CARLOW 3-14

This was a game that was largely ignored by hurling followers, except those closely associated with both teams. After all, a championship meeting between Westmeath and Carlow hurlers has never grabbed national headlines in the way an Offaly/Kilkenny clash invariably has. On the day Derry made front page news winning their third National Football League title, the minnows of Carlow and Westmeath produced a rip-roaring game that hung in the balance to the very end.

The final score: Westmeath 6-6 Carlow 3-14, represented the third highest aggregate score in the '95 Hurling championship. It was also the only game in which nine goals were scored.

This was an evenly balanced game throughout: Carlow, surprise winners over Meath in the first round, had the better of the exchanges in the first half and led by two points, 1-8 to 2-2, at the interval. Shortly after the restart, captain Des Murphy kicked the ball past Westmeath goalkeeper Seamus Lynch to stretch Carlow's lead to 6 points. Westmeath responded with a goal from Castlepollard club man, Barry Kennedy, and Sean McLouglin scored the first of his 3 goals after 47 minutes to level the game, Westmeath 4-3 Carlow 2-9.

Carlow substitute Barry Murphy edged his side in front with a goal three minutes

Westmeath Back row l to r: Seamus Qualter, Martin Craig, Peter Dalton, Pat Connaughton, Brian Murray, David Kilcoyne, Christo Murtagh. **Front row l to r:** Brendan Murphy, Robbie Galvin, Robert Mc Loughlin, Pat Clancy, Barry Kennedy, Peter Mullen, Seamus Lynch, Sean Mc Loughlin.

from time but almost immediately, McLoughlin struck for his third goal to clinch victory. David Doyle did score a goal for Carlow in injury time but it was not enough to deprive Westmeath of a Leinster Quarter Final meeting with Wexford.

Scorers Westmeath: Sean McLoughlin 3-1; Barry Kennedy 1-2; Robert Galvin 1-1; David Kilcoyne 1-1; Philip Galvin 0-1. **Scorers Carlow:** Des Murphy 1-4; Mick Slye 0-4; David Doyle 1-1; John Byrne 1-1; Jim English 0-1; Brendan Hayden 0-1; Martin Farrell 0-1; Tommy Murphy 0-1.

W E S T M E A T H

SEAMUS LYNCH

PETER MULLAN	BRIAN MURRAY	BRENDAN MURPHY
ROBERT MCLOUGLIN	PETER DALTON	CHRISTO MURTAGH

PAT CONNAUGHTON   MARTIN CRAIG

ROBBIE GALVIN	SEAN MCLOUGHLIN	SEAMUS QUALTER
BARRY KENNEDY	DAVID KILCOYNE	PAT CLANCY

Substitutes: Philip Galvin for Seamus Qualter; Ollie Devine for Robert McLoughlin

C A R L O W

STEPHEN BAMBRICK

SEAMUS O'SHEA	EMMETT COBURN	KEVIN NOLAN
JIM ENGLISH	JOHNNY NEVIN	BRIAN LAWLOR

BRENDAN HAYDEN   JOHN CAREY

MICK SLYE	MARTIN FARRELL	NIALL ENGLISH
DAVID DOYLE	DES MURPHY	JOHN BYRNE

Substitute: Tommy Murphy for Brian Lawlor

Carlow Back row l to r: Ritchie Kielty, Killian Griffith, Jim English, Seamus O'Shea, Emmett Coburn, Kevin Nolan, Brendan Hayden, Des Murphy, John Byrne, Mick Slye, Sean Spruhan, Brendan Doyle. **Front row l to r:** Peadar Jordan, Tommy Murphy, Niall English, Brian Lawlor, John Carey, Stephen Bambrick, David Doyle, Martin Farrell, Johnny Nevin, John Agar.

SUNDAY JUNE 4
LEINSTER SENIOR HURLING
CHAMPIONSHIP FIRST ROUND

WEXFORD & WESTMEATH

DR. CULLEN PARK, CARLOW
REFEREE: PAT AHERNE CARLOW
RESULT: WEXFORD 6-23 WESTMEATH 1-7

Westmeath were no match for a rampant Wexford team in one of the most lopsided games of the hurling championship. Nothing went right for Westmeath on the day and their 31 point anihilation represented a big setback to hurling in the county. There was a yawning gulf in class between the sides and the game served little purpose for either team. It was a totally demoralising afternoon for Westmeath while Wexford could hardly have benefited much from such a one-sided encounter.

The Westmeath team showed just one change from the side that beat Carlow; Ollie Devine, who came on as sub in that game, replaced Peter Mullan. Wexford decided to opt for a blend of youth and experience with no fewer than five players tasting senior championship action for the first time.

The newcomers were Colin Kehoe and Robert Hassey in defence; Michael Jordan at midfield and forwards Rory McCarthy and Paul Codd. Manager Liam Griffin also relied on some of the older brigade for Wexford's first hurdle in the championship. Indeed, stars of past campaigns like John and George O'Connor, Liam Dunne, Martin Storey and Tom Dempsey provided a core of experience and craft.

Wexford were forced to line out without two of their original selection; injured

Wexford Back row l to r: Dave Guiney, Billy Byrne, John O'Connor, Damien Fitzhenry, Padraig Dunbar, George O'Connor, Robert Hassey. **Front row l to r:** Rory Mc Carthy, Tom Dempsey, Paul Codd, Larry Murphy, Martin Storey, Michael Jordan, Liam Dunne, Colin Kehoe.

defenders Thomas Dunne and Larry O'Gorman were replaced by Padraig Dunbar and David Guiney. But those late changes failed to upset the rhythm of the Slaneysiders and they led comfortably, 2-8 to 0-4, at half-time.

Corner forward Larry Murphy was the chief tormentor of the Westmeath back line in the opening thirty-five minutes, scoring 2-1.

If the Clougbawn club man was the goal scoring hero of the first half, full forward Billy Byrne took the honours after the break. Byrne cracked in 3 goals in a nine minute spell early in the second half to leave Wexford, 5-10 to 0-4, in front. Indeed, so dominant was Wexford that Liam Griffin could afford the luxury of calling both Byrne and Murphy ashore. It was a purely precautionary measure by Griffin, no doubt with an eye to the upcoming semi-final meeting with Offaly. Byrne was replaced by Eamon Scallan while Murphy made way for Paul Finn.

Seamus Qualter scored Westmeath's only goal in the closing stages of the game, but as it was, Wexford outscored the midlanders in the second period by 4-15 to 1-3.

There were mixed feelings among Wexford supporters after the game. They had seen their team flatter against weaker opposition in the past and fail to land a provincial crown. Would it be different this year? The real test lay ahead in the Leinster semi-final against the All-Ireland champions Offaly.

Scorers Wexford: Billy Byrne 3-0; Larry Murphy 2-2; Tom Dempsey 1-3; Rory McCarthy 0-5; Robert Hassey 0-2; Michael Jordan 0-2; Martin Storey 0-2; Paul Codd 0-2; Eamon Scallan 0-2; Liam Dunne 0-2; George O'Connor 0-1. **Scorers Westmeath:** Robert Galvin 0-3; Sean McLouglin 0-3; Seamus Qualter 1-0; Barry Kennedy 0-1.

Westmeath Back row l to r: Sean Mc Loughlin, David Kilcoyne, Martin Craig, Pat Connaughton, Brian Murray, Oliver Devine, Peter Dalton, Brendan Murphy. **Front row l to r:** Seamus Qualter, Robbie Galvin, Seamus Lynch, Barry Kennedy, Christo Murtagh, Pat Clancy, Robert Mc Loughlin.

WEXFORD

DAMIEN FITZHENRY

COLIN KEHOE	JOHN O'CONNOR	PADRAIG DUNBAR
DAVID GUINEY	GEORGE O'CONNOR	ROBERT HASSEY
LIAM DUNNE		MICHAEL JORDAN
MARTIN STOREY	TOM DEMPSEY	RORY MCCARTHY
PAUL CODD	BILLY BYRNE	LARRY MURPHY

Substitutes: Eamon Scallan for Billy Byrne; Paul Finn for Larry Murphy; Ger Cush for Padraig Dunbar

WESTMEATH

SEAMUS LYNCH

PETER DALTON	BRIAN MURRAY	ROBERT MCLOUGHLIN
CHRISTO MURTAGH	BRENDAN MURPHY	MARTIN CRAIG
PAT CONNAUGHTON		OLLIE DEVINE
ROBBIE GALVIN	DAVID KILCOYNE	PAT CLANCY
BARRY KENNEDY	SEAN MCLOUGHLIN	SEAMUS QUALTER

Substitutes: Philip Galvin for Robert McLoughlin; Peter Mullan for Martin Craig

SUNDAY JUNE 4

LEINSTER SENIOR HURLING
CHAMPIONSHIP FIRST ROUND

KILKENNY & LAOIS

DR CULLEN PARK, CARLOW

REFEREE: WILLIE BARRETT TIPPERARY

RESULT: KILKENNY 2-14 LAOIS 2-12

Even the most supremely optimistic Laois supporter would have been hard pressed to have given their county hurlers even a remote chance of beating League champions and All-Ireland favourites, Kilkenny. A year previously, Laois, newly promoted to Division One, approached their Leinster semi-final meeting with Wexford in an extremely confident mood. Inexplicably, the Laois challenge crumbled and Wexford won with consummate ease. It was a shattering blow to morale among the Laois hurling fraternity. The 1994/95 League campaign brought little joy and ultimately resulted in demotion to Division Two. Laois hurling appeared in disarray.

Captain Joe Dollard, told me a few days before the game against Kilkenny that he still had no explanation for the way his side collapsed against Wexford. He expressed the view that the Laois hurlers were determined to make amends and put the '94 championship nightmare fully behind them. The future of Laois hurling was on the line.

At the end of an absorbing game, no-hopers Laois were extremely unlucky to lose by two points and were it not for a superb last-minute save by substitute goalkeeper Joe Dermody, from a Fint Lalor goal-bound shot, Kilkenny would have been the first major casualties of the hurling championship. DJ Carey told me immediately after the game that Kilkenny was mightily relieved to have come away with a victory. He was acutely aware how perilously close his side came to bowing out. He paid wholesome tribute to Laois. And rightly so!

Laois suffered a setback on the Friday before the game when right half forward, David Cuddy underwent an appendicitis operation. It was cruel luck on the skilful Castletown player who was replaced by PJ Peacock from the Abbeyleix club.

Kilkenny got into their stride quickly with points from DJ Carey, championship debutant Canice Brennan, and Adrian Ronan. But the expected avalanche of scores never materialised. After eight minutes, Laois midfielder Declan Conroy beat Kilkenny goalkeeper Michael Walsh for the game's opening goal. Adrian Ronan edged Kilkenny 2 points in front, but from there until the half-time whistle, it was Laois who dictated the pace and they outscored their more illustrious opponents by 5 points to 1. Laois were full value for their, 1-5 to 0-6, half-time lead.

Almost immediately after the restart, Kilkenny went ahead with a goal from corner forward, Denis Byrne. Laois were in no mood to capitulate and moved one point clear when Fint Lalor whipped the ball to the Kilkenny net 15 minutes from time. Laois sensed victory. Just when the 12,000 in attendance were bracing themselves for a shock, hurling wizard DJ Carey broke free of his marker to set up Denis Byrne for his second goal of the game. Substitute Charlie Carter added a point for Kilkenny soon after, but Laois replied with a point apiece from Fionain O'Sullivan and Fint Lalor to produce a grandstand finish.

Laois were deprived of a winning goal when Joe Dermody, a late second half substitute for Michael Walsh, came to Kilkenny's rescue with an excellent save. It was hard luck on a determined and committed Laois side who certainly restored pride to the county hurlers. Incidentally, the game marked the championship debut of two brothers, John and Fionain O'Sullivan from the Castletown club in Laois. A rare occurrence!

Kilkenny Back row l to r: Eamonn Morrissey, John Power, Canice Brennan, Pat Dwyer, Liam Simpson, Denis Byrne, Liam Keoghan, Pat O'Neill. **Front row l to r:** Eddie O'Connor, Willie O'Connor, Michael Walsh, Bill Hennessy, Adrian Ronan, P.J. Delaney, DJ Carey.

Scorers Kilkenny: Denis Byrne 2-2; Adrian Ronan 0-4; DJ Carey 0-3; Canice Brennan 0-2; Eamon Morrissey 0-1; Charlie Carter 0-1; Pat O'Neill 0-1. **Scorers Laois:** Fint Lalor 1-6; Declan Conroy 1-1; Fionain O'Sullivan 0-2; Niall Rigney 0-1; Ollie Dowling 0-1; Joe Dollard 0-1.

KILKENNY

MICHAEL WALSH

| EDDIE O'CONNOR | PAT DWYER | LIAM SIMPSON |
| LIAM KEOGHAN | PAT O'NEILL | WILLIE O'CONNOR |

CANICE BRENNAN   BILL HENNESSY

| ADRIAN RONAN | JOHN POWER | PJ DELANEY |
| EAMON MORRISSEY | DJ CAREY | DENIS BYRNE |

Substitutes: Derek Gaffney for John Power; Joe Dermody for Michael Walsh; Charlie Carter for PJ Delaney

LAOIS

RICKY CASHIN

| TOMMY DELANEY | BILL MAHER | CYRIL DUGGAN |
| NIALL RIGNEY | JOE DOLLARD | JOHN O'SULLIVAN |

OWEN COSS   DECLAN CONROY

| TOMAS KENNA | NOEL DELANEY | FINT LALOR |
| PJ PEACOCK | OLLIE DOWLING | FIONAIN O'SULLIVAN |

Substitute: PJ Cuddy for Tomas Kenna

Laois Back row l to r: Cyril Duggan, Bill Maher, Owen Coss, Ollie Dowling, Declan Conroy, Tomas Kenna, Niall Rigney. **Front row l to r:** Tommy Delaney, Fint Lalor, Joe Dollard, Ricky Cashin, Fionain O'Sullivan, P.J. Peacock, Noel Delaney, John O'Sullivan.

SUNDAY JUNE 25
LEINSTER SENIOR HURLING
CHAMPIONSHIP SEMI-FINAL

KILKENNY & DUBLIN

CROKE PARK
REFEREE: PAT DELANEY LAOIS
RESULT: KILKENNY 4-13 DUBLIN 2-10

A last minute save by substitute Kilkenny goalkeeper, Joe Dermody at Dr. Cullen Park three weeks before prevented what would have been the biggest shock of the year in hurling. The genial hurling wizard, DJ Carey, was adamant Kilkenny had not underestimated the Laois challenge and admitted 'it was just one of those days, Laois were unlucky to lose'. One fright a year, it seems, is one too many as far as the Kilkenny team is concerned and judging by the few well chosen words being uttered from their base leading up to the semi-final there was never any danger of Ollie Walsh's men treating the Dublin challenge lightly.

Regular goalkeeper Michael Walsh was declared fit to play after recovering from the hamstring injury which forced him to retire in the game against Laois, while Derek Gaffney was named at midfield in place of Canice Brennan. It was disappointing for the talented Conahy Shamrocks player to lose his place, but there was an unexpected reprieve when 'mighty' John Power was forced to pull out with injury and Brennan was drafted into the side at centre half forward.

One of the most interesting selections on the Dublin team was that of dual-star, Vinny Murphy, who was entrusted with the task of leading the Dublin attack. The Dubs introduced nine players new to championship hurling and that was a telling factor as Kilkenny dominated from early on and effortlessly pulled clear to lead by, 2-9 to 0-5, at half-time. Dublin opened the scoring with a point from John Twomey but once Eamon Morrisey slammed the ball past Dublin goalkeeper Brendan McLoughlin there was a sense of inevitability about the outcome. Vinny Murphy and Twomey kept Dublin in touch with a point apiece early on but the metropolitans' challenge crumbled beyond redemption when Denis Byrne scored Kilkenny's second goal.

Kilkenny possessed for too much craft and artistry and try as they might it was an uphill struggle for Dublin to keep within a respectable distance of the '92 and '93 All-Ireland champions.

Eamon Morrissey, before he retired injured, was the Kilkenny hero in the second half scoring, 2-3 in an 18 minute spell, which utterly demolished the Dublin challenge and left the League champions in front by 18 points, 4-12 to 0-6, with a little less than fifteen minutes still to play.

Dublin to their credit struggled against the odds and late goals from Shane Cooke and John Twomey, from a penalty, served to put a more respectable look on the scoreboard. Dublin scored 2-4, in the closing stages of the game, but by then Kilkenny had done more than enough.

Kilkenny Back row l to r: Eamonn Morrissey, Canice Brennan, Pat Dwyer, Liam Simpson, Derek Gaffney, Denis Byrne, Pat O'Neill. **Front row l to r:** Willie O'Connor, Eddie O'Connor, P.J. Delaney, Michael Walsh, Bill Hennessy, DJ Carey, Liam Keoghan, Adrian Ronan.

Dublin Back row l to r: Paddy Brady, Rory Boland, Conor Mc Cann, John Twomey, Mick Morrissey, Liam Walsh, Sean Deignan, Andy O'Callaghan. **Front row l to r:** Sean McDermott, Shane Cooke, Brendan Mc Loughlin, John Power, John Morris, Vinny Murphy, John Small.

Scorers Kilkenny: Eamon Morrissey 3-3; Denis Byrne 1-1; Adrian Ronan 0-3; Canice Brennan 0-2; DJ Carey 0-2; Bill Hennessy 0-2. **Scorers Dublin:** John Twomey 1-3; Shane Cooke 1-0; Vinny Murphy 0-3; John Small 0-1; Sean McDermott 0-1; Brian McMahon 0-1; Dermot Harrington 0-1.

KILKENNY

MICHAEL WALSH

EDDIE O'CONNOR	PAT DWYER	LIAM SIMPSON
LIAM KEOGHAN	PAT O'NEILL	WILLE O'CONNOR
BILL HENNESSY		DEREK GAFFNEY
ADRIAN RONAN	CANICE BRENNAN	PJ DELANEY
EAMONN MORRISSEY	DJ CAREY	DENIS BYRNE

Substitutes: Mark Dowling for Derek Gaffney; Charlie Carter for PJ Delaney; Liam McCarthy for Eamon Morrissey

DUBLIN

BRENDAN MCLOUGHLIN

SEAN DEIGNAN	JOHN POWER	PADDY BRADY
LIAM WALSH	MICK MORRISSEY	RORY BOLAND
ANDY O'CALLAGHAN		CONOR MCCANN
JOHN SMALL	VINNY MURPHY	SHANE COOKE
SEAN MCDERMOTT	JOHN TWOMEY	JOHN MORRIS

Substitutes: Brian McMahon for John Morris; Joe Dalton for John Small; Dermot Harrington for Conor McCann

Offaly Back row l to r: Shane McGuckin, Daithi Regan, Kevin Martin, David Hughes, PJ Martin, Kevin Kinahan, Brian Whelehan. **Front row l to r:** Michael Duignan, John Troy, Martin Hanamy, Johnny Pilkington, Brendan Kelly, Declan Pilkington, Joe Dooley, Johnny Dooley.

SUNDAY JUNE 25
LEINSTER SENIOR HURLING CHAMPIONSHIP SEMI-FINAL
OFFALY & WEXFORD
CROKE PARK
REFEREE: AODÁN MAC SUIBHNE DUBLIN
RESULT: OFFALY 2-14 WEXFORD 1-10

It was felt by many observers that 1995 would be the year when Wexford would exorcise the ghost of past failures and maybe, just maybe, claim a first Leinster title since 1968. The Slaneysiders trounced Westmeath in their opening game and manager Liam Griffin and his selectors had reason to approach the game against All-Ireland champions, Offaly with a reasonable confidence. When the team was announced on the Tuesday night, it showed three changes from the Westmeath game; with Sean Flood and Tomas Dunne taking over from Dave Guiney and Padraig Dunbar in defence and Paul Finn replacing Michael Jordan in midfield. Just when it appeared the Wexford players were in exactly the right frame of mind to tackle the champions, Liam Dunne was sensationally stripped of the captaincy for assisting his club, Oulart-the-Ballagh, against management instructions, in a midweek club game.

The captaincy was given to veteran St Martins' club man George O'Connor and not Dunne's Oulart teammate, Martin Storey, who didn't play in the club match. The controversy generated much debate and may have unsettled the Wexford players. In a frank interview for RTE Radio Sport, Liam Griffin told me that the captaincy was being taken from the Oulart club only, and that Liam Dunne understood the situation. He was adamant that the decision would not affect morale among the players. Fears that Dunne and the other members of Oulart would withdraw their services to the county proved unfounded. Offaly were forced to line out without injured Hubert Rigney and Billy Dooley, whose corner forward position was filled by Michael Duignan. Rigney's place at centre half back was taken by '1995 Hurler Of The Year', Brian Whelehan, with Kevin Martin moved out to fill Whelehan's customary right half back position, and Kevin's brother's PJ chosen at left half back.

Whether the 'storm in a teacup', as some people in Wexford termed it, was to blame or not is a matter of conjecture, but whatever the reason, Wexford, despite a spirited rally in the second half, turned in a disjointed performance against a less than sure-footed Offaly team. Brothers Johnny and Joe Dooley scored 1-7 between them and John Troy accounted for 1-2. His goal came at a crucial juncture very near the end and by which time Wexford had cut the deficit to just 4 points.

Offaly took command early on and were comfortably in control, 0-12 to 0-5, at half-time but had Wexford taken even half of the opportunities that presented themselves the scoreboard would have had a signficantly kinder look about it.

To make matter worse for Wexford, Joe Dooley whipped the ball to the net past

Damien Fitzhenry some seven minutes after the restart and the energetic Michael Duignan struck the ball over the bar a minute later to increase Offaly's lead to 10 points, 1-13 to 0-6. Wexford's Leinster aspirations were in tatters. Billy Byrne pulled a goal back for Wexford and when Liam Dunne fired over a point from a free after 58 minutes just 4 points separated the sides. Then the elusive John Troy scored the insurance goal to set up a Leinster Final meeting with Kilkenny.

Scorers Offaly: Johnny Dooley 0-6; John Troy 1-2; Joe Dooley 1-1; Michael Duignan 0-3; Pat O'Connor 0-1; Johnny Pilkington 0-1. **Scorers Wexford:** Billy Byrne 1-2; Liam Dunne 0-4; Tom Dempsey 0-3; Martin Storey 0-1.

O F F A L Y

DAVID HUGHES

| SHANE McGUCKIN | KEVIN KINAHAN | MARTIN HANAMY |
| KEVIN MARTIN | BRIAN WHELEHAN | PJ MARTIN |

JOHNNY PILKINGTON   DAITHI REGAN

| JOHNNY DOOLEY | JOHN TROY | JOE DOOLEY |
| MICHAEL DUIGNAN | BRENDAN KELLY | DECLAN PILKINGTON |

Substitutes: Gary Cahill for PJ Martin; Pat O'Connor for Declan Pilkington; Declan Pilkington for Brendan Kelly

W E X F O R D

DAMIEN FITZHENRY

| COLIN KEHOE | JOHN O'CONNOR | TOMAS DUNNE |
| SEAN FLOOD | GEORGE O'CONNOR | ROBERT HASSEY |

LIAM DUNNE   PAUL FINN

| MARTIN STOREY | TOM DEMPSEY | RORY MCCARTHY |
| PAUL CODD | BILLY BYRNE | LARRY MURPHY |

Substitutes: Aidran Fenlon for Rory McCarthy; Larry O'Gorman for Robert Hassey; Eamon Scallan for Paul Codd

Wexford Back row l to r: Ciaran Roche, Dave Guiney, Rory McCarthy, Damien Fitzhenry, George O'Connor, Paul Finn, Tomas Dunne, John O'Connor, Robert Hassey, Seamus Kavanagh, Eamon Scallan. **Front row l to r:** Tom Dempsey, Paul Codd, Liam Dunne, Martin Storey, Sean Flood, Larry Murphy, Colin Kehoe, Billy Byrne, Adrian Fenlon, Michael Jordan.

SUNDAY JULY 16
LEINSTER SENIOR HURLING CHAMPIONSHIP FINAL
OFFALY & KILKENNY
CROKE PARK
REFEREE: DICKIE MURPHY WEXFORD
RESULT: OFFALY 2-16 KILKENNY 2-5

It is extremely unlikely that any team in the country would have lived with Offaly on that wet July Sunday, such was the awesome power of their performance against a Kilkenny side that completely capitulated in the second half. This was one of the most absorbing games of the Hurling championship. Afterwards, a number of the euphoric Offaly players stated how they got perhaps more pleasure from the manner of victory over their old rivals than from last year's dramatic All-Ireland Final win over Limerick. Perhaps no one should have been too surprised at such utterances, given the intensity of the rivalry between the two counties on the hurling fields of Leinster.

The traditional counties are finding it difficult to absorb all the implications, but judging by their performance in trouncing Kilkenny by 11 points in this year's provincial decider, Offaly appear to be in no hurry whatsoever to move aside.

Kilkenny were clear favourites to regain the Leinster crown, particularly after their win over Offaly in the League semi-final, a game in which DJ Carey scored 3 goals. But Kilkenny's form on the way to the final had been somewhat erratic and Laois came within a whisker of causing a major shock at Dr. Cullen Park in the first round when it took a superb last-minute save from sub goalkeeper, Joe Dermody to keep their hopes alive.

Underdogs Offaly, angry at being written off, were out to prove that the previous year's Leinster Final success was no one-match wonder. Kilkenny made two changes from the game against Dublin and appeared to have selected their strongest possible line-out. Michael Phelan returned from injury to play at midfield for the 'Cats' in place of Derek Gaffney while John Power, who missed the semi-final because of a hamstring injury, was chosen ahead of Canice Brennan at centre half forward.

Hubert Rigney, Billy Dooley and Pat O'Connor were in the Offaly starting line-up in place of PJ Martin, Declan Pilkington and Brendan Kelly, all of whom played against Wexford in the semi-final.

Thunder and lightning delayed the start of the game by seven minutes, but the treacherous conditions failed to dampen the enthusiasm of both sets of players. The first half represented everything positive and enriching in the ancient game. Both defences were outstanding and Kilkenny only trailed by 2 points at the break. The second half turned into a nightmare for the League Champions as Offaly ruthlessly brushed aside their challenge. This was Offaly hurling at its brilliant best. Few could

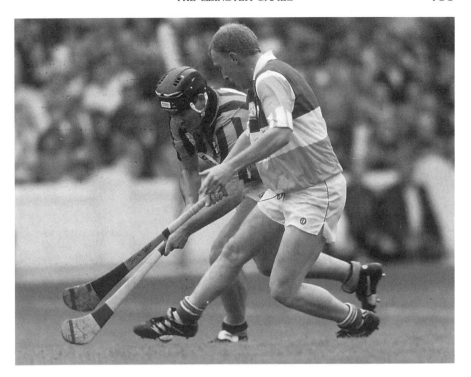

Liam Simpson of Kilkenny and John Troy of Offaly.

have predicted what was about to unfold seven minutes after the restart when Daithi Regan struck a high ball towards the Kilkenny goal which came off the chest of goalkeeper, Michael Walsh and crossed the line. That controversial score changed everything. Inexplicably, the Kilkenny challenge fell asunder and the game was finished as a contest long before Pat O'Connor swept the ball to the net for Offaly's second goal nine minutes from time. It was difficult to comprehend the scoreline at that stage: Offaly 2-14 Kilkenny 0-5.

DJ Carey scored 2 late goals for Kilkenny but by then Offaly had wreaked enough havoc to establish themselves as firm favourites to win the All-Ireland crown. Incredibly, Kilkenny scored just twice from play in a game that will be talked about for a long time to come.

Scorers Offaly: Michael Duignan 0-3; Billy Dooley 0-5; Pat O'Connor 1-1; Johnny Dooley 0-3; Daithi Regan 1-0; John Troy 0-2; Brian Whelehan 0-1; Johnny Pilkington 0-1.
Scorers Kilkenny: DJ Carey 2-0; Adrian Ronan 0-3; Pat O'Neill 0-1; P.J. Delaney 0-1.

OFFALY

DAVID HUGHES

SHANE MCGUCKIN	KEVIN KINAHAN	MARTIN HANAMY
BRIAN WHELEHAN	HUBERT RIGNEY	KEVIN MARTIN

JOHNNY PILKINGTON   DAITHI REGAN

JOHNNY DOOLEY	JOHN TROY	JOE DOOLEY
MICHAEL DUIGNAN	PAT O'CONNOR	BILLY DOOLEY

Substitutes: Brendan Kelly for Joe Dooley; Declan Pilkington for Johny Pilkington

KILKENNY

MICHAEL WALSH

EDDIE O'CONNOR	PAT DWYER	LIAM SIMPSON
LIAM KEOGHAN	PAT O'NEILL	WILLIE O'CONNOR

MICHAEL PHELAN   BILL HENNESSY

ADRIAN RONAN	JOHN POWER	PJ DELANEY
EAMONN MORRISSEY	DJ CAREY	DENIS BYRNE

Substitutes: Derek Gaffney for Denis Byrne; Canice Brennan for Michael Phelan; Charlie Carter for Adrian Ronan

Offaly Back row l to r: Daithi Regan, Shane Mc Guckin, Kevin Martin, Johnny Pilkington, Kevin Kinahan, David Hughes, Hubert Rigney, Brian Whelehan. **Front row l to r:** Billy Dooley, John Troy, Pat O'Connor, Michael Duignan, Martin Hanamy, Joe Dooley, Johnny Dooley.

Kilkenny Back row l to r: Eamonn Morrissey, Michael Phelan, Pat Dwyer, Liam Simpson, John Power, Denis Byrne, Pat O'Neill. **Front row l to r:** Adrian Ronan, DJ Carey, Michael Walsh, P.J. Delaney, Bill Hennessy, Liam Keoghan, Eddie O'Connor, Willie O'Connor.

ULSTER SENIOR HURLING
CHAMPIONSHIP FINAL

DOWN & ANTRIM

CASEMENT PARK, BELFAST
REFEREE: AODÁN MAC SUIBHNE DUBLIN
RESULT: DOWN 3-7 ANTRIM 1-13

On the day Clare hurlers grabbed all the headlines as emerging kingpins of Munster for the first time since 1932, Antrim came perilously close to losing their Ulster crown in front of their home supporters in sun-scorched Casement Park. It took a point in injury time from Antrim's top scorer Gregory O'Kane to force a dramatic draw with outsiders Down in what was a largely disappointing provincial decider.

Antrim needed to win this game with something to spare if only to convince themselves of their well-being after suffering a shattering defeat by Limerick in last year's All-Ireland semi-final, but in the end they were extremely fortunate to escape with a draw after surviving a grandstand finish by the Mournemen.

Antrim appeared safe when they led by 1-12 to 1-7, with less than three minutes left to play, but then Down hit back in style with a goal from a free by Kevin Coulter. When the same player struck the ball to the net from a 65, two minutes later, Down had edged 1 point ahead. But Antrim showed great character and O'Kane rescued the game with the levelling point in injury time. It was a scare Antrim supporters could have done without particularly after witnessing their team hit up to 25 wides and lose a 5 point lead in the closing minutes.

The dramatic finish disguised an otherwise mediocre game and afterwards Down manager Sean McGuinness and his Antrim counterpart, Dominic McKinley both admitted their teams were capable of much better. Both defences were on top throughout most of the game but Down were unlucky on occasions: Conor Arthurs hit the upright and two-goal hero Kevin Coulter had a penalty saved early in the second half.

Antrim had raced into a 4 point lead before Down registered their opening score, a point from play by Hugh Gilmore. The defending champions led by 0-6 to 0-4, at half-time and Paul Donnelly extended their lead with a point just after the restart. Then 2 points from Gilmore and a goal from captain, Dermot O'Prey, twelve minutes into the second half, edged Down 2 points in front, 1-6 to 0-7.

Antrim awoke from their slumber and produced some of their best hurling for the next 20 minutes during which time they registered 1-5, and restricted Down to a solitary point. The goal from substitute Joe Boyle seven minutes from the end looked to have sealed victory for the Antrim men. But 2 goals from Kevin Coulter left Antrim in a desperate fight for survival until Gregory O'Kane rescued the situation with a last gasp equalising point.

Down Back row l to r:. Ger Coulter, Hugh Gilmore, Danny Hughes, Gary Savage, Noel Keith, Kevin Coulter, Michael Blaney, Conor Arhurs. **Front row l to r:** Martin Mallon, Dermot Woods, Dermot O'Prey, Paul Coulter, Paddy Braniff, Paul McMullan, Noel Sands.

Antrim: for team photo see below page 160. The team line-out for both games was the same.

Scorers Down: Kevin Coulter 2-1; Hugh Gilmore 0-4; Dermot O'Prey 1-0; Paul Coulter 0-1; Michael Blaney 0-1.**Scorers Antrim:** Gregory O'Kane 0-5; Joe Boyle 1-0; John Carson 0-2; Paul Donnelly 0-2; Terence McNaughton 0-2; Sean Paul McKillop 0-1; Gary O'Kane 0-1.

D O W N

	NOEL KEITH	
KEVIN COULTER	GER COULTER	PADDY BRANNIFF
MARTIN MALLON	GARY SAVAGE	DERMOT WOODS
DANNY HUGHES		PAUL COULTER
MICHAEL BLANEY	PAUL McMULLAN	DERMOT O'PREY
CONOR ARTHURS	HUGH GILMORE	NOEL SANDS

Substitutes: Sean Mallon for Michael Blaney; Michael Branniff for Paul McMullan; Gerard McGrattan for Conor Arthurs

A N T R I M

	SHANE ELLIOT	
EOIN COLGAN	EOIN McCLUSKEY	SEAN McILHATTON
SEAMUS McMULLAN	GARY O'KANE	RONAN DONNELLY
SEAN PAUL McKILLOP		NIGEL ELLIOT
CONOR McCAMBRIDGE	JOHN CARSON	PAUL DONNELLY
GREGORY O'KANE	TERENCE McNAUGHTON	ALASTAIR ELLIOT

Substitutes: Joe Boyle for John Carson; Jimmy Wilson for Conor McCambridge; Paul McKillen for Paul Donnelly

From the Ulster Hurling Final 1995. Kevin Coulter, Down, challenging Antrim's Paul Donnelly.

SUNDAY JULY 16
ULSTER SENIOR HURLING
CHAMPIONSHIP FINAL (REPLAY)

DOWN & ANTRIM

CASEMENT PARK, BELFAST
REFEREE: AODÁN MAC SUIBHNE DUBLIN
RESULT: DOWN 1-19 ANTRIM 2-10

It was one of the best ever displays by the hurlers of Down. Perhaps, the best ever! The drawn game had fallen some way short of expectations but finished in a welter of excitement. There was to be no late reprieve second time round for Antrim and the men from the Ards Peninsula deservedly earned an All-Ireland quarter final place against 'B' Champions, London at Ruislip.

Although his team's lack of experience was a factor in the closing stages of the drawn game, Antrim manager and former star player, Dominic McKinley gave a vote of confidence to the same fifteen that started the first day. Down suffered a setback when captain Dermot O'Prey failed a late fitness test. His place at left half forward was filled by Michael Blaney.

The dramatic finish to the drawn game went some way towards compensating for the largely disappointing fare served up by both teams throughout the seventy minutes. The replay was entirely different and infinitely better. It represented everything positive about the game. Down's experience was vital at crucial stages but it still took them some time to settle down and Antrim led by 1-2 to 0-1, after seven minutes. The goal came about when full forward Terence 'Sambo' McNaughton, hero of many battles in the saffron and white, handpassed the ball to Gregory O'Kane and he struck it past Down goalkeeper Noel Keith (captain for the day in place of his Ballycran club mate, Dermot O'Prey).

Antrim had moved, 1-5 to 0-3 ahead, after 15 minutes but it was then we saw the best of Down. They restricted the favourites to just 2 points for the remainder of the half while they themselves proceeded to score 1-8. The goal near the end of the half from corner forward Noel Sands left Down ahead, 1-11 to 1-7, at half-time. Danny Hughes and John McCarthy were outstanding at midfield for Down and the Antrim half backs were never allowed the scope to move upfield in search of scores.

Antrim seemed obsessed with going all out for goals in the second half when points appeared the obvious option. The tactic also mis-fired badly from the point of view that Noel Keith was outstanding between the Down posts. Keith has been a member of the Down team since 1978 and has rarely played better.

Down scored the first 3 points after the restart, but midway through the second half Antrim were handed a lifeline when the referee Aodán Mac Suibhne awarded a penalty. Unfortunately for Antrim, Seamus McMullan's shot was deflected over the bar for a point. The chance was lost and Antrim never looked likely to win from there on, though adding a John Carson goal from a free near the end.

Down Back row l to r:. Hugh Gilmore, John Mc Carthy, Gerard Coulter, Gary Savage, Noel Keith, Dermot Woods, Danny Hughes, Kevin Coulter. **Front row l to r:** Martin Mallon, Noel Sands, Paul McMullan, Paul Coulter, Paddy Braniff, Conor Arthurs, Michael Blaney.

There were jubilant scenes around Casement Park when Noel Keith lifted the Liam Harvey Cup. A quite astonishing achievement for a county with just three senior clubs; Ballycran, Ballygalget and Portaferry.

The memory of Ned Purcell, the Tipperary man who first introduced hurling to the Ards Peninsula, still lives on. The hurling men of the Ards were crowned Ulster Champions for the second time in the Nineties! Antrim man Sean McGuinness, Down manager for six years, was rightly hailed as a hero. A remarkable man and a remarkable team. Next stop Ruislip in London!

Scorers Down: Noel Sands 1-2; John McCarthy 0-4; Hugh Gilmore 0-4; Kevin Coulter 0-3; Danny Hughes 0-2; Paul Coulter 0-1; Marty Mallon 0-1; Dermot Woods 0-1; Conor Arthurs 0-1. **Scorers Antrim:** Gregory O'Kane 1-5; John Carson 1-0; Terence McNaughton 0-1; Alastair Elliot 0-1; Seamus McMullan 0-1; Conor McCambridge 0-1; Sean Paul McKillop 0-1.

<table>
<tr><td colspan="3" align="center">D O W N</td></tr>
<tr><td></td><td align="center">NOEL KEITH</td><td></td></tr>
<tr><td>KEVIN COULTER</td><td align="center">GERARD COULTER</td><td align="right">PADDY BRANNIFF</td></tr>
<tr><td>MARTIN MALLON</td><td align="center">GARY SAVAGE</td><td align="right">DERMOT WOODS</td></tr>
<tr><td align="center" colspan="2">DANNY HUGHES</td><td align="center">JOHN MCCARTHY</td></tr>
<tr><td>PAUL COULTER</td><td align="center">PAUL MCMULLAN</td><td align="right">MICHAEL BLANEY</td></tr>
<tr><td>CONOR ARTHURS</td><td align="center">HUGH GILMORE</td><td align="right">NOEL SANDS</td></tr>
</table>

Substitutes: Barry Coulter for Dermot Woods; Michael Branniff for Paul McMullan; Sean Mallon for Hugh Gilmore

<table>
<tr><td colspan="3" align="center">A N T R I M</td></tr>
<tr><td></td><td align="center">SHANE ELLIOTT</td><td></td></tr>
<tr><td>EOIN COLGAN</td><td align="center">EOIN MCCLOSKEY</td><td align="right">SEAN MCILHATTON</td></tr>
<tr><td>SEAMUS MCMULLAN</td><td align="center">GARY O'KANE</td><td align="right">RONAN DONNELLY</td></tr>
<tr><td align="center" colspan="2">SEAN PAUL MCKILLOP</td><td align="center">NIGEL ELLIOTT</td></tr>
<tr><td>CONOR MCCAMBRIDGE</td><td align="center">JOHN CARSON</td><td align="right">PAUL DONNELLY</td></tr>
<tr><td>GREGORY O'KANE</td><td align="center">TERENCE MCNAUGHTON</td><td align="right">ALASTAIR ELLIOTT</td></tr>
</table>

Substitutes: Jimmy Wilson for Sean Paul McKillop; Colm McGuckian for Conor McCambridge; Frankie McMullan for Alastair Elliott

Antrim Back row l to r: Alastair Elliot, Seamus Mc Mullan, John Carson, Ronan Donnelly, Gregory O'Kane, Sean Mc Ilhatton, Sean Paul Mc Killop, Terence Mc Haughton. **Front row l to r:** Paul Donnelly, Conor Mc Cambridge, Eoin Colgan, Gary O'Kane, Shane Elliot, Nigel Elliot, Eoin Mc Cluskey.

Galway Back row l to r: Justin Campbell, Ollie Fahy, Joe Rabbitte, Tom Helebert, Richard Burke, Michael Coleman, Brendan Keogh, Cathal Moran. **Front row l to r:** Padraig Kelly, Gregory Kennedy, Nigel Shaughnessy, Pat Malone, Francis Forde, Conor O'Donovan, Joe Cooney.

CONNACHT SENIOR HURLING FINAL

GALWAY & ROSCOMMON

DR. HYDE PARK, ROSCOMMON
REFEREE: PAT DELANEY LAOIS
RESULT: GALWAY 2-21 ROSCOMMON 2-12

The meeting of Roscommon and Galway in the first Connacht Senior Hurling Championship final for 72 years was never likely to throw up a shock result. It would be unfair to say that overwhelming favourites Galway won as they pleased but conversely the Tribesmen were always in control and claimed the MJ Inky Flaherty Memorial Cup with some ease. When the Galway team was announced midweek, sports fans everywhere rejoiced at the news that captain Pat Malone was once again back in the maroon and white jersey. There were fears that the brilliant midfielder would never again play hurling after a serious eye injury threatened to end his career. But the Oranmore-Maree clubman returned to partner 'old buddy' Michael Coleman at midfield. Malone had a quiet afternoon and was substituted late in the game, but one sensed he had already crossed the biggest hurdle by just taking part.

Roscommon continue to make progress on the hurling front and enthusiastic team manager, Michael Kelly, and his supporters deserve credit for trojan work in attempting to raise the level of the game within the county. After their success in the All-Ireland B Championship, Roscommon played Galway in last year's All-Ireland quarter final and despite losing by 15 points there were many positive aspects to their game. This time Galway's winning margin was 9 points and from Roscommon's standpoint that was progress. From small acorns, big oaks grow.

Playing against the breeze, Roscommon enjoyed a good opening spell and a goal from Padraic Feeney left the home side in front, 1-2 to 0-2, after just six minutes play. Indeed Roscommon were still in touch twenty minutes later when Colm Kelly struck over a point to level the game. But soon after, Justin Campbell scored a goal and from there until the half-time whistle, Galway took complete control and led at the break by 7 points, 1-12 to 1-5.

Roscommon at times played some excellent hurling in the second half, but they were always chasing the game and Joe Cooney's goal put Galway, 2-18 to 1-8 in front, with over fifteen minutes still left to play. Galway eased up, Roscommon rallied and a Tom Killian shot, fielded just under the crossbar by Richard Burke, was adjudged to be a goal and the umpire raised the green flag.

The general consensus at Hyde Park was that Galway would need to improve before they could harbour any ambitions of lifting the Liam McCarthy Cup from the clutches of Offaly and the rest!

Scorers Galway: Joe Cooney 1-4; Francis Forde 0-4; Justin Campbell 1-1; Padraig Kelly 0-3; Joe Rabbitte 0-2; Cathal Moran 0-2; Michael McGrath 0-2; Brendan Keogh 0-1; Michael Coleman 0-1; Ollie Fahy 0-1. **Scorers Roscommon:** Padraic Feeney 1-1; Colm

Kelly 0-3; Tom Killian 1-0; Michael Cunniffe 0-2; Ronnie Dooley 0-1; Liam Murray 0-1; Brendan Boyle 0-1; Joe Mannion 0-1; Adrian Kelly 0-1; Ray Mulvey 0-1.

GALWAY

	RICHARD BURKE	
GREGORY KENNEDY	TOM HELEBERT	CONOR O'DONOVAN
PADRAIG KELLY	BRENDAN KEOGH	NIGEL SHAUGNESSY
	PAT MALONE	MICHAEL COLEMAN
JUSTIN CAMBBELL	JOE RABBITTE	JOE COONEY
CATHAL MORAN	OLLIE FAHY	FRANCIS FORDE

Substitutes: Michael McGrath for Cathal Moran; Gerry McInerney for Gregory Kennedy; Joe McGrath for Pat Malone

ROSCOMMON

	ADRIAN TULLY	
MICHAEL HUSSEY	ADRIAN KELLY	PADRAIC MANNION
TOMMY HEALY	TOM KILLIAN	NIALL CUNNINGHAM
	MIKE CUNNIFFE	RONNIE DOOLEY
LIAM MURRAY	COLM KELLY	BRENDAN BOYLE
JOE MANNION	PADRAIC FEENEY	RAY MULVEY

Substitutes: Marty Healy for Michael Hussey; Kevin McGeeney for Liam Murray; Padraic Cuddy for Brendan Boyle

Roscommon Back row l to r: Brendan Boyle, Ray Mulvey, Adrian Kelly, Adrian Tully, Mike Cunniffe, Padraic Feeney, Padraig Mannion. **Front row l to r:** Tom Healy, Joe Mannion, Ronnie Dooley, Mike Hussey, Tom Killian, Liam Murray, Niall Cunningham, Colm Kelly.

ALL-IRELAND SENIOR HURLING 'B'
CHAMPIONSHIP FIRST ROUND

WICKLOW & LOUTH

O'RAGHALLAIGH'S, DROGHEDA
REFEREE: HP MCCUSKER DOWN
RESULT: WICKLOW 6-16 LOUTH 0-8

Former Armagh player, Paddy Devlin from the Hollywood club, was the hero of the day as Wicklow recorded the second highest win of the entire hurling championship against an altogether out of sorts Louth team. Their 26 point winning margin was all the more surprising given the fact that Louth had beaten Wicklow in their Division Three League game last February. But there was never any danger of a repeat victory by the men from the Wee County. Wicklow were far more fluent on this occasion and, despite playing against the breeze, restricted Louth to just four points in the opening half. Timmy Collins scored Wicklow's first goal thirteen minutes into the opening half and soon after Devlin struck the ball to the net. The ace marksman scored his second goal before half-time to leave Wicklow in front at the break, 3-6 to 0-4.

Shortly after the resumption, Sean Byrne scored a splendid goal from a narrow angle to effectively kill off the Louth challenge. Before the game had run its inevitable course, Devlin scored 2 further goals to crown one of his best ever displays in a Wicklow jersey. He finished the game with a tally of 4-1, the highest individual score of the entire senior hurling championship. Furthermore, Devlin was the only player in both the '95 hurling and football championship campaign to score 4 goals in ine game. Quite an achievement!

Louth manager Tony Melia was naturally enough bitterly disappointed with the manner of his team's defeat.

"Wicklow got the bit between the teeth after their defeat in the League and they obviously decided they were going to reverse the result in the championship. We had a number of important players out through injury and of course in the first place we'd be working from a very small pool, so any defections would hit us hard as there are only four senior clubs in the county."

Louth PRO Micheal O'Broin, who has put in huge effort over the years to promote the ancient game in the county, admitted that Louth had trained hard for the game but that nothing went right on the day. "The success of the team in the League would be as a direct result of work done at juvenile level in the county and that was very satisfying. The absence of key players in the championship was a factor, but having said that, Wicklow thoroughly deserved their victory on the day."

Scorers Wicklow: Paddy Devlin 4-1; Sean Byrne 1-2; John Keogh 0-5; Don Hyland 0-4; Timmy Collins 1-1; Christy O'Toole 0-1; Shane O'Loughlin 0-1; Colin Byrne 0-1.**Scorers Louth**: Michael Gormley 0-3; John Murphy 0-2; David Dunne 0-2; Emmet Downey 0-1

W I C K L O W

MICHAEL NEARY

| LAR BYRNE | JOHN HENDERSON | | TOM BYRNE |
| COLIN BYRNE | CASEY O'BRIEN | | ROBERT DOYLE |

NIGEL BYRNE   CHRISTY O'TOOLE

| SHANE O'LOUGHLIN | PADDY DEVLIN | | TIMMY COLLINS |
| JOHN KEOGH | SEAN BYRNE | | DON HYLAND |

Substitutes: David Moran for Christy O'Toole; Brian Gleeson for Tom Byrne; Stephen Kennedy for Colin Byrne;

L O U T H

BRIAN BRADY

| EMMET DOWNEY | DIARMUID MCCARTHY | | SEAN MATTHEWS |
| PAUL DYAS | PAUL CALLAN | | AARON HOEY |

COLLINS CONNOLLY   DAVID DUNNE

| TONY CORCORAN | CIARAN SOMERS | | EDDIE MCARDLE |
| PAUL DUNNE | MICK GORMLEY | | JAMES COBURN |

Substitutes: John Murphy for Paul Dunne; David Black for Sean Matthews

SUNDAY MAY 7

A L L - I R E L A N D   S E N I O R   H U R L I N G   ' B '
C H A M P I O N S H I P   F I R S T   R O U N D

KILDARE & ARMAGH

KEADY

RESULT: KILDARE 2-13 ARMAGH 1-10

O n the same day as the hurlers of Kilkenny and Clare were squaring up to each other in the League Final at Thurles, the minnows of Kildare and Armagh were having their own private battle up north at Keady in the first round of the All-Ireland Senior 'B' Championship. It turned out to be quite a rewarding day for the Leinster representatives. Kilkenny easily defeated Clare by double scores, 2-12 to 0-9, while Kildare saw off the challenge of the home-side by 2-13 to 1-10.

Kildare won the game with a blistering spell midway through the first half when corner forward Damien Bowden of Leixlip scored 2 goals inside five minutes. Vincent Mone kept Armagh in touch throughout and finished with a very respectable tally of 1-6, but not enough to deprive Kildare of their victory. Midfielders, Pat Rohan and Eamonn Kelly scored 2 points apiece in the opening half, to leave Kildare in front, 2-5 to 0-6, at half-time.

Armagh came back strongly early in the second half and were rewarded by a goal by top-scorer Vincent Mone which lifted the spirits of the Orchard county supporters. Kildare replied with a point each from Eamonn Kelly and borthers John Colin and Ronan Byrne to finishe strongly and win by 6 points. Kildare were never in any dnager of losing this game after the Bowden goals.

Kildare manager, John Reidy expressed himself well satisfied that his young side had played so well against a very determined Amragh team.

"From a Kildare point of view this match was a make or break situation for our young team as we had lost to Armagh in the last round of the League at Newbridge.

Make no mistake, it was an excellent achievement for our lads to beat a strong Armagh team in their home territory. As always, Armagh gave their all, fairly, but those 2 early goals from Damien turned the tide completely in our favour. Armagh tried very hard to come back into the game, but they got no change from our half back line."

Manager of the Armagh team, Jimmy Carlisle was expecting a much more positive result based on previous encounters between the sides.

"We beat Kildare in the league in Kildare and certainly we were expecting to beat them in the championship as well, unfortunately our midfielder, Francis Fulton had to go off injured in the first six minutes. Kildare got on top for the rest of the first half, but Armagh came back strongly in the second half, although not enough to win the game. Being a football county, hurling has always come second best in Armagh and to get players to come to training has always been a serious problem. The future looks bright as we have many very good under age players."

Scorers Kildare: Damien Bowden 2-1; Eamonn Kelly 0-3; Colm Byrne 0-3; Ronan Byrne 0-2; Pat Rohan 0-2; Pat Byrne 0-1; John Byrne 0-1. **Scorers Armagh:** Vincent Mone1-6; Damien Short 0-1; Michael McKee 0-1; Mattie Lennon 0-1; Chris Shine 0-1.

KILDARE

		LEO DEERING		
ROBBIE WINDERS		JAMES O'DONNELL		ANTHONY CROSS
PAT BYRNE		PAURIC O'MALLEY		NIALL SWAN
	PAT ROHAN		EAMONN KELLY	
MICK MALONEY		JOHN BYRNE		COLM BYRNE
RONAN BYRNE		GREG DEERING		DAMIEN BOWDEN

Substitutes: Barry Kinlon for Ronan Byrne; John Brennan for Pauric O'Malley

ARMAGH

		BRENDAN DONNELLY		
GARETH BURKE		MARTIN LENNON		PC GORMLEY
FRANCIS FULTON		SYLVVESTER MC CONNELL		PADDY LAVERY
	MATTIE LENNON		EAMON MCKEE	
VINCENT MONE		DAMIEN SHORT		NED MCCANN
ARTHUR HUGHES		MICHAEL MCKEE		CHRIS SHINE

Substitutes: Paul Doyle for Francis Fulton

SUNDAY MAY 14

ALL-IRELAND SENIOR HURLING 'B' CHAMPIONSHIP FIRST ROUND

FERMANAGH & MAYO

ENNISKILLEN

REFEREE: OLIVER O'NEILL MEATH

RESULT: FERMANAGH 3-11 MAYO 3-8

Olly McShea was the star of the day as Fermanagh staged a great second half fighback to beat Mayo by three points and earn a Home Semi-Final clash with Wicklow a week later. The Lisbellaw club man scored 2-6, the third highest individual score of the hurling championship, and his first goal from a close in free just before half-time gave Fermanagh a welcome boost.

Mayo completely dominated the first half, and a goal apiece from brothers, Dom and Declan Greally, ensured the visitors held a 7 point interval advantage, 2-7 to 1-3. Fermanagh manager Seamus Donegan moved McShea from full forward to bolster the midfield sector at the start of the second half and he made an immediate impact. McShea ruled his patch with authority and added 1-4 to his first half total as the Mayo challenge fell away. McShea's club mate, Shane O'Donnell, helped himself to 1-2 and Cyril Dunne and Sean Duffy scored a point apiece as Fermanagh outscored the Connacht side by 2-8 to 1-1 in the second half.

Mayo player/selector Joe Greaney admitted afterwards that the loss of Keith Guthrie through injury early in the second half was a huge setback. "Our game plan was working very well in the first half, but the injury to Keith changed our pattern of play and Fermanagh had the experience to exploit our weaknesses in that area. There was a lot of very good hurling played throughout the seventy minutes and, as Division Four teams, both ourselves and Fermanagh took great pleasure from having played in such a fast and skilful game."

Fermanagh manager Seamus Donegan was of the opinion that his team's second half display was one of the best ever.

"I was very pleased with the players attitude after the break. To come back from 7 points down at half-time and win the game by 3 points against a very good Mayo team, who dominated the first half, certainly showed the great character that's in this team."

Scorers Fermanagh: Olly McShea 2-6; Shane O'Donnell 1-3; Sean Duffy 0-1; Cyril Dunne 0-1. **Scorers Mayo:** Declan Greally 2-1; Johnny Cunnane 0-4; Dom Greally 1-1; Sean Granahan 0-1; Vinny O'Hora 0-1

F E R M A N A G H

STEPHEN HANNA

| BRIAN JOHNSTON | DONAL MCSHEA | SEAMUS MCCUSKER |
| JOHN MCCUSKER | KEVIN MCKEOGH | SEAMUS BRESLIN |

SEAN DUFFY   PAULINUS LEONARD

| NOEL MCDONNELL | JIMMY DONOVAN | JASON MCMANUS |
| SHANE O'DONNELL | OLLY MCSHEA | CYRIL DUNNE |

Substitutes: Rory O'Donnell for Brian Johnston; Ciaran Dunne for Jimmy Donovan

M A Y O

PAT DELANEY

| KEITH GUTHRIE | JOHN KENNEDY | RORY DELANEY |
| PAUL HUNT | GER GREALLY | KENNY GOLDEN |

OWEN SHAUGHNESSY   BRIAN DELANEY

| JOHNNY CUNNANE | DOM GREALLY | SEAN GRANAHAN |
| VINNY O'HORA | DECLAN GREALLY | FERGAL DELANEY |

Substitute: Joe Greaney for Keith Guthrie

SUNDAY MAY 21
ALL-IRELAND SENIOR HURLING 'B'
HOME SEMI-FINAL
KILDARE & DERRY
DUNDALK
REFEREE: TOMMY MCINTYRE ANTRIM
RESULT: KILDARE 0-14 DERRY 1-9

Kildare survived a late Derry rally to deservedly qualify for the the All-Ireland Senior 'B' Hurling Championship Home Final against near neighbours Wicklow. Kildare mostly held the upper hand throughout the game and the Ulster side found it hard to cope with the Lilywhites superior strength and more direct style of play. Although reduced to fourteen men late in the opening half after corner back Robbie Winders was sent off, Kildare still held a 5 point advantage, 0-8 to 0-3, at half-time.

Kildare appeared to be in total control until rocked back on their heels with a goal from Derry centre half forward Oliver Collins, that brought the game to life. Man of the match, Collins handed the Oak Leaf county a lifeline when he shot to the net and Kildare had to survive some anxious moments before the final whistle sounded. The Ulster interprovincial star had an oustanding game and, against the odds, scored all but 2 points of Derry's total. But all too often, Collins was left to plough a lonely furrow and that ultimately proved Derry's downfall.

Derry manager Joe McGurk was very disappointed with the lack of penetration in the forward line where apart from Collins, only Malachy McKenna got his name on the scoresheet.

"We were confident going into the game, but Kildare certainly deserved to win on the day. They were hungrier for success and were physically stronger all round. We were in the process of team building and lacked experience, but I think there's a great future ahead for this team. Kildare played a very direct game and it would be fair to say they won most of the man-to-man exchanges."

Kildare manager John Reidy maintained afterwards that the switching of Richie Coyle to his customary full back position after Robbie Winders was sent off played a key part in curtailing the Derry forwards.

"This was one of the best displays by a Kildare side since 1990 when we won the Home Final against Meath. We showed the kind of true grit and spirit which has been sadly lacking in Kildare hurling over the past three years. I was proud to be associated with the players on such a great occasion."

Scorers Kildare: Colm Byrne 0-6; Mick Maloney 0-2; John Byrne 0-2; Eamonn Kelly 0-1; Richie Coyle 0-1; Greg Deering 0-1; Damien Bowden 0-1. **Scorers Derry:** Oliver Collins 1-7; Colm McGurk 0-1; Malachy McKenna 0-1.

KILDARE

	LEO DEERING	
ROBBIE WINDERS	JAMES O'DONNELL	ANTHONY CROSS
PAT BYRNE	PAURIC O'MALLEY	NIALL SWAN
PAT ROHAN		EAMONN KELLY
MICK MALONEY	JOHN BYRNE	COLM BYRNE
RICHIE COYLE	GREG DEERING	DAMIEN BOWDEN

DERRY

	FERGAL MCNALLY	
MICHAEL MURRAY	CONOR MURRAY	JOE YOUNG
COLM MCGURK	PATRICK MCCLOY	COLIN MCELDOWNEY
NIALL MULLAN		BRENDAN WARD
DECLAN CASSIDY	OLIVER COLLINS	ADRIAN MCCRYSTAL
PATRICK CASSIDY	MICHAEL COLLINS	MALACHY MCKENNA

Substitutes: Sean Lockhart for Michael Murray;Diarmuid Murray for Adrian McCrystal; Padraig O'Mianian for Brendan Ward

SUNDAY MAY 21

ALL-IRELAND SENIOR HURLING 'B'
CHAMPIONSHIP HOME SEMI-FINAL

WICKLOW & FERMANAGH

DUNDALK

REFEREE: MEL MC CORMACK MEATH

RESULT: WICKLOW 2-16 FERMANAGH 1-6

Wicklow advanced to the Home Final of the Senior B Hurling Championship with a comprehensive 13 point victory over a Fermanagh side that never appeared likely to cause an upset. Although always in control, Wicklow rarely struck the rich vein of form that saw them dispose of Louth in the previous round by a margin of 26 points.

Wicklow started in blistering fashion and were 1-3 to no score in front after just ten minutes of play. Don Hyland opened the scoring with a point from play and soon after corner forward Shane O'Loughlin beat Fermanagh goalkeeper Stephen Hanna to score an excellent goal. The Fermanagh defence was under constant pressure in the early stages and Hyland and Sean Byrne stretched Wicklow's lead with a point each. But the expected rout never materialised!

Wicklow forwards, in particular, missed numerous scoring opportunities and, despite an abundance of possession, the Leinster side could only muster three further points during the remainder of the opening half. Fermanagh's paltry return amounted to a solitary point.

Corner forward John Keogh struck over 2 points early in the second half to increase Wicklow's lead and Fermanagh's fate was sealed when Sean Byrne scored a goal with about twenty minutes left to play. Fermanagh's play improved considerably in the second half and they registered 1-5, the goal coming from substitute Adrian McPhilips. Wicklow finished much the stronger and scored 7 points in the closing stages to run out comfortable winners.

Fermanagh manager, Seamus Donegan accepted that Wicklow were far and away the more accomplished team on the day, but he was not too despondent.

"There's no doubt we were beaten by a better team. Wicklow have some outstanding hurlers and I was particularly impressed with their centre half back, Casey O'Brien. Unfortunately, very early on we lost some key players through injury which upset the balance of the team. It was our first time in the 'B' Championship, so it was a learning experience and hopefully we'll advance further in the competition next year."

Scorers Wicklow: Don Hyland 0-6; John Keogh 0-5; Sean Byrne 1-2; Shane O'Loughlin 1-0; Timmy Collins 0-1; Colin Byrne 0-1; Ned Cremin 0-1. **Scorers Fermanagh**: Adrian McPhillips 1-0; Ollie McShea 0-2; Shane O'Donnell 0-2; Seamus Breslin 0-1; Sean Duffy 0-1.

WICKLOW
MICHAEL NEARY

LAR BYRNE	JOHN HENDERSON		TOM BYRNE
COLIN BYRNE	CASEY O'BRIEN		ROBERT DOYLE
	CHRISTY O'TOOLE	NIGEL BYRNE	
SHANE O'LOUGHLIN	PADDY DEVLIN		TIMMY COLLINS
JOHN KEOGH	SEAN BYRNE		DON HYLAND

Substitutes: Ned Cremin For Paddy Devlin; David Moran For Nigel Byrne

FERMANAGH
STEPHEN HANNA

BRIAN JOHNSTON	DONAL MCSHEA		JOHN MC CUSKER
PAULINUS LEONARD	KEVEN MCKEOGH		SEAMUS BRESLIN
	SEAN DUFFY	OLIVER MCSHEA	
NOEL MCDONNELL	JIMMY DONOVAN		PAUL MCMANUS
SHANE O'DONNELL	JOE MCGOLDRICK		JASON MCMANUS

Substitutes: Rory O'Donnell for Brian Johnston;Adrian McPhillips for Noel McDonnell; Cyril Dunne for Joe McGoldrick

SATURDAY JUNE 3
ALL-IRELAND SENIOR HURLING 'B' HOME FINAL

Wicklow Back row l to r: Sean Byrne, Lar Byrne, Tom Byrne, Colin Byrne, Casey O'Brien, Christy O'Toole, John Keogh, John Henderson. **Front row l to r:** Timmy Collins, Nigel Byrne, Ned Cremin, Michael Neary, Robert Doyle, Shane O'Loughlin, Don Hyland.

WICKLOW & KILDARE

NOWLAN PARK
REFEREE: JOHN MCDONNELL TIPPERARY
RESULT: WICKLOW 3-12 KILDARE 1-8

Wicklow hurlers have had few enough great moments to savour in the lifetime of the ancient game in the county, but their win over Kildare in the final of the All-Ireland Senior Hurling 'B' Championship more than compensated for the heartbreak and disappointment endured. Manager Jack Murray had spoken during the year of the 'happy family atmosphere' among the Wicklow players and certainly their unity of purpose was very much in evidence against the Lilywhites.

Afterwards, Chairman of the Wicklow County Hurling Board, Jackie Napier, expressed confidence that winning the 'B' title would be a huge boost to hurling within the county.

"It was a marvellous evening in Nowlan Park and fair play to Kilkenny County Board who treated the 'B' final with the respect it deserved. The teams were paraded around the pitch and there was a wonderful atmosphere which added to the occasion. The lads going out to play for Wicklow wanted to win badly and in the end they deserved to win. I've been on the fringes of Wicklow hurling teams since the early Sixties and winning the 'B' Home Final would have meant just as much to the county as when we won the Junior All-Irelands in '67 and '71."

Despite playing against the breeze in the first half, Wicklow held a 3 point advantage at the interval, 1-8 to 1-5. Even at that early stage, twice winners, Kildare knew they had a mountain to climb. Full forward Sean Byrne gave Wicklow the perfect start with a text-book goal after just one minute to set the trend for the game. Kildare kept in touch throughout the opening half and the sides were level 1-4 apiece, after 24 minutes. Brian Coulston, operating at corner forward, was the Kildare goal-scorer.

Kildare strove might and main to turn the game around in the second half, but they came up against a fiercely determined Wicklow side that had many heroes, none more so than minor star, John Keogh, who emerged top scorer with 1-4. Wicklow outscored their near neighbours by, 2-4 to 0-3, in the second half to emerge worthy winners by 10 points.

A gracious Kildare manager, John Reidy, made no excuses after the game, but naturally expressed disappointment that his team had failed to play to its full potential.

"We came up against a very strong and determined Wicklow team who took their scores well and they deserved their victory. Naturally enough, our players were a little nervous taking part in such a big game for the first time and that certainly was a factor. But fair play to Wicklow, who played strong and direct hurling and we just couldn't match them on the day. I thought their half forward line in particular played exceptionally well."

Scorers Wicklow: John Keogh 1-4; Sean Byrne 1-1; Ned Cremin 1-0; Timmy Collins 0-4; Don Hyland 0-2; Colin Byrne 0-1. **Scorers Kildare:** Greg Deering 0-5; Brian Coulston 1-0; Colm Byrne 0-3.

WICKLOW

MICHAEL NEARY

LAR BYRNE	JOHN HENDERSON		TOM BYRNE
ROBERT DOYLE	CASEY O'BRIEN		COLIN BYRNE
	NIGEL BYRNE	CHRISTY O'TOOLE	
SHANE O'LOUGHLIN	DON HYLAND		TIMMY COLLINS
JOHN KEOGH	SEAN BYRNE		NED CREMIN

Substitutes: Vinny Mulroe for Casey O'Brien; Paddy Devlin for Ned Cremin

KILDARE

LEO DEERING

JAMES O'DONNELL	RICHIE COYLE		ANTHONY CROSS
PAT BYRNE	PAURIC O'MALLEY		NIALL SWAN
	COLM BYRNE	EAMONN KELLY	
MICK MALONEY	PAT ROHAN		JOHN BYRNE
BRIAN COULSTON	GREG DEERING		DAMIEN BOWDEN

Substitutes: John Brennan for Anthony Cross; Mark Hennessy for Pat Rohan; John Coulston for Brian Coulston

Kildare Back row l to r: James O'Donnell, Eamonn Kelly, Greg Deering, Padraig O'Malley, Pat Rohan, John Byrne, Pat Byrne, Colm Byrne. **Front row l to r:** Mick Maloney, Niall Swan, Damien Bowden, Leo Deering, Richie Coyle, Brian Coulston, Anthony Cross.

SUNDAY JUNE 25
ALL-IRELAND B HURLING CHAMPIONSHIP
LONDON & NEW YORK
CROKE PARK
REFEREE: DICKIE MURPHY WEXFORD
RESULT: LONDON 4-12 NEW YORK 5-7

London signalled their intentions very early on and were, 2-5 to 0-1 ahead, after only fifteen minutes. New York opened the scoring with a point from Ray Sampson but London replied with goals from star players Tom Galway and Michael Cunningham. Ten points down and struggling, New York looked doomed but their fight-back began in earnest with a goal from Ray Sampson. That score sparked an astonishing revival and before the half had run its course, a rejuvenated and very assured New York side had added three further goals courtesy of Ian Conroy, Nicky Potterton and Seamus Collison. The London defence was in tatters but just when it seemed New York were about to take complete control, London full forward Michael Cunningham scored his second goal to leave London ahead by just three points, 3-8 to 4-2, at half-time.

New York forwards were not allowed nearly as much scope in the second half as London tightened their defence; Andy Comerford was outstanding at centre half back and goalkeeper John O'Farrell brought off a number of good saves. It was an evenly balanced second half as both sides missed a number of scoring opportunities, with New York perhaps the most guilty in that department. Centre half forward, Tommy Corbett looked to have sealed victory when he scored London's fourth goal nine minutes from time but New York rallied again with a goal from substitute Ritchie Hogan. Then Owen Cummings fired over 2 points to leave the minimum between the sides, but London centre half forward Tommy Corbett had the last say with a well-taken point. New York deserve great credit for their astonishing recovery after a disastrous start, but to the victor the spoils, and to the great delight of their small band of supporters, London did enough to qualify to meet Wicklow in the All-Ireland B Hurling Championship Final.

Scorers London: Tom Galway 1-5; Michael Cunningham 2-1; Tommy Corbett 1-2; Willie Lohan 0-1; James O'Donoghue 0-1; Freddie Moran 0-1; Donal Murphy 0-1. **Scorers New York:** Ray Sampon 1-4; Owen Cummins 0-3; Ian Conroy 1-0; Nicky Potterton 1-0; Seamus Collison 1-0; Richie Hogan 1-0.

L O N D O N

JOHN O'FARRELL

DECLAN O'HANLON	TONY LOHAN	NOEL HANLEY
J.J SHEIL	ANDY COMERFORD	DAN MCKENNA

WILLIE LOHAN   DAMIEN POWER

JAMES O'DONOGHUE	TOMMY CORBETT	FREDDIE MORAN
DONAL MURPHY	MICHAEL CUNNINGHAM	TOM GALWAY

Substitutes: Kevin Leahy for Freddie Moran; Jimmy Kennedy for Willie Lohan

N E W   Y O R K

JOHN CAGNEY

JIM LYONS	TOM CANTY	JIM MILLER
BRIAN BARCO	OWEN CUMMINS	JOHN KENNEDY

BRIAN MCCABE   JOHN MADDEN

NICKY POTTERTON	JOHN MCDONNELL	SEAMUS COLLISON
RAY SAMPSON	IAN CONROY	DANNY GREALISh

Substitutes: Richie Hogan for Danny Grealish

SUNDAY JULY 2

ALL-IRELAND B SENIOR HURLING
CHAMPIONSHIP FINAL

LONDON & WICKLOW

O'MOORE PARK, PORTLAOISE
REFEREE: AODÁN MACSUIBHNE DUBLIN
RESULT: LONDON 2-7 WICKLOW 0-8

When it was all over and some time after the Cup had been presented by the President of the GAA, Jack Boothman, the London captain, Limerickman Dan O'Brien, spoke with me about what the win would mean to hurling in the greater London area. He was convinced that winning the All-Ireland B title would be a huge boost to hurling and would be a great incentive to the hard working players and officials who have devoted their lives to the promotion of the game. At one stage in the course of the interview, he stopped for a moment as if to convince himself it was all for real, and then said determinedly: "We made up our minds we were not going back without the Cup, it was a simple as that." London had conceded 5 goals in the game against New York but manager Tommy Harrell refused to panic and made no changes apart from one positional switch; Dan McKenna, left half back against New York, was moved into the corner back position in a direct switch with Declan O'Hanlon.

I was speaking with Mr. Boothman before the game and he was in great form as usual and reminded me in his own inimitable style that only Wicklow and Galway could now achieve the double.

It turned out to be a dissapointing afternoon for the Garden County followers! It was the first time the county had two senior teams competing at championship level on the one day, but there was to be no fairytale ending. Meath took only five minutes or so to dash the hopes of their footballers when Tommy Dowd and Brian Stafford scored 2 early goals. There was no way back and Wicklow lost out in the end by 3-14 to 0-9. It was an entirely different story for the Wicklow hurlers. Aided by the breeze, they led at half-time by 0-6 to 0-2, after failing to take full advantage of the scoring opportunities that came their way.

The game turned in London's favour ten minutes into the second half when right corner forward Donal Murphy fired home a goal and two minutes later Freddie Moran cracked the ball to the Wicklow net. Little went right for Wicklow in the second half and they only scored 2 points and hit an inordinate amount of wides. London had many heroes, none more so than corner forward, Tom Galway from Wexford, who scored 5 points on this a never-to-be-forgotten day for the 'exiles'.

Scorers London: Tom Galway 0-5; Donal Murphy 1-0; Freddie Moran 1-0; Michael Cunningham 0-2. **Scorers Wicklow:** John Keogh 0-4; Don Hyland 0-3; Ned Cremin 0-1.

LONDON

JOHN O'FARRELL

DAN MCKENNA	TONY LOHAN	NOEL HANLEY
J.J. SHEIL	ANDY COMERFORD	DECLAN O'HANLON

WILLIE LOHAN DAMIEN POWER

JAMES O'DONOGHUE	TOMMY CORBETT	FREDDIE MORAN
DONAL MURPHY	MICHAEL CUNNINGHAM	TOM GALWAY

Substitutes: Jimmy Kennedy for Declan O'Hanlon; Mick O'Meara for Tommy Corbett; Kevin Leahy for Freddie Moran

WICKLOW

MICHAEL NEARY

LAR BYRNE	JOHN HENDERSON	TOM BYRNE
ROBERT DOYLE	CASEY O'BRIEN	COLIN BYRNE

NIGEL BYRNE CHRISTY O'TOOLE

SHANE O'LOUGHLIN	DON HYLAND	TIMMY COLLINS
JOHN KEOGH	SEAN BYRNE	NED CREMIN

Substitutes: David Bury for Ned Cremin; Paddy Devlin for John Keogh

London Back row l to r: Donal Murphy, Noel Hanley, Jamesie Donoghue, Jimmy Kennedy, Martin Carroll, Freddie Moran, Damien Power, Liam Wyer, Mick O'Meara, Cormac Galvin, Kevin Leahy. **Front row l to r:** Willie Lohan, Tom Corbett, Tom Galway, J.J. Sheil, Mick Cunningham, John O'Farrell, Andy Comerford, Declan O'Hanlon, Dan Mc Kenna, Tony Lohan, PJ Horan.

Wicklow Back row l to r: Sean Byrne, Nigel Byrne, Lar Byrne, Casey O'Brien, Colin Byrne, Michael Neary, Tom Byrne, John Henderson. **Front row l to r:** Christy O'Toole, Don Hyland, Timmy Collins, John Keogh, Ned Cremin, Shane O'Loughlin, Robert Doyle.

SUNDAY JULY 23
ALL-IRELAND SENIOR HURLING QUARTER FINAL

DOWN & LONDON

RUISLIP

REFEREE: SEOSAMH O'LAOIRE CORK

RESULT: DOWN 0-16 LONDON 0-9

Ulster champions Down advanced to an All-Ireland semi-final meeting with Offaly following a decisive 7 point victory over Senior B Champions London at Ruislip. It was by no means a classic game. Down coped better with the searing temperatures and rock-hard surface, and their superior teamwork was evident from very early on. Favoured by the breeze, the men from the Ards, courtesy of 2 points apiece from Noel Sands and Hugh Gilmore, had moved 0-4 to 0-2 ahead at the end of a first quarter in which London more than held their own without ever inspiring confidence. Former Wexford under-21 player, Tom Galway got London's opening point after 12 minutes, and in the sixteenth minute Jimmy Kennedy finished off a good movement with a point from play.

Down outscored the home side by 8 points to 2 in the second quarter with 3 of those points from long-hitting corner back Kevin Coulter and one each from Conor Arthurs, John McCarthy, Barry Coulter, Martin Mallon, and the closing score of the half from Michael Blaney. London squandered far too many scoring opportunites in that period and their only tangible reward was a point each from Tom Corbett and Michael Cunningham, who was also deprived of a goal earlier in the half when his powerfully struck shot was brilliantly saved by the ever alert Down goalkeeper, Noel Keith. Down led at half-time by eight points, 0-12 to 0-4, and even at that early stage the signs were ominous.

London corner back Dan McKenna scored a wonderful long-range point shortly after the restart and a further 2 points from Tom Galway cut the deficit to just 5 points. Players from both sides were guilty of poor marksmanship, before Kevin Coulter sent over another 'long distance special' to increase the Ulster champions' lead. London needed a goal to salvage the game, but the Down defence stood firm and Conor Arthurs wrapped up the scoring with an injury-time point, his third of the afternoon. It was a richly deserved victory for Down, but a spirited London side can also take heart from their gutsy performance.

London fielded a good number of players with inter-county experience from the traditional hurling counties and manager Tommy Harrell was confident his team would have had the measure of the Ulster champions. But too many players failed to lift their game sufficiently and Down richly deserved their victory.

"Unfortunately, our forwards missed far too many chances and, as well as that, a couple of our defenders failed to show their true form. But having said that, Down deserved their victory and there's no doubt we were beaten by a better team. But we'll be back again!"

Scorers Down: Kevin Coulter 0-4; Conor Arthurs 0-3; Hugh Gilmore 0-3; Noel Sands 0-2; Michael Blaney 0-1; Barry Coulter 0-1; John McCarthy 0-1; Martin Mallon 0-1.
Scorers London: Tom Galway 0-3; Michael Cunningham 0-2; Dan McKenna 0-1; Tom Corbett 0-1; Jimmy Kennedy 0-1; Paul Sharkey 0-1.

D O W N

	NOEL KEITH	
KEVIN COULTER	GERARD COULTER	PADDY BRANNIFF
MARTIN MALLON	GARY SAVAGE	PAUL MCMULLEN
DANNY HUGHES		JOHN MCCARTHY
PAUL COULTER	BARRY COULTER	MICHAEL BLANEY
CONOR ARTHURS	HUGH GILMORE	NOEL SANDS

Substitutes: Michael Branniff for Paddy Branniff; Dermot Oprey for Noel Sands

L O N D O N

	JOHN FARRELL	
DAN MCKENN	A TONY LOHAN	NOEL HANLEY
JJ SHEIL	ANDY COMERFORD	WILLIE LOHAN
DAMIEN POWER		DECLAN O'HANLON
DONAL MURPHY	TOMMY CORBETT	JIMMY KENNEDY
JAMES O'DONOGHUE	MICHAEL CUNNINGHAM	TOM GALWAY

Substitutes: Kevin Leahy for JJ Sheil; Paul Sharkey for Tom Corbett; Brian Minogue for Jimmy Kennedy

Down Back row l to r: Gerard Coulter, Kevin Coulter, Gary Savage, Noel Keith, Barry Coulter, John Mc Carthy, Danny Hughes. **Front row l to r:** Hugh Gilmore, Martin Mallon, Conor Arthurs, Michael Blaney, Noel Sands, Paul McMullan, Paul Coulter. (see Down vs Antrim team picture for Paddy Braniff) .

CLARE & GALWAY

CROKE PARK
REFEREE: DICKIE MURPHY WEXFORD
RESULT: CLARE 3-12 GALWAY 1-13

It was a wonderful sight! Croke Park was turned into a sea of saffron and blue. Clare had reached an All-Ireland senior hurling semi-final for the first time in 63 years. Hurling is a way of life in Clare and the players had attained celebrity status after their epic Munster Final triumph. Those same players once again underlined their class by overcoming a stubborn Galway challenge to advance to an All-Ireland final clash with defending champions, Offaly.

Captain Anthony Daly told me a few days before the semi-final that as far as the traditional counties are concerned, Clare would be regarded as nobodies in the hurling world and would always be seen as a soft touch to the strong powers in Munster. He also made the point that standards have levelled out and that teams are much better prepared than ever before. He was adamant that Clare would have to concentrate totally on the game and not on a big weekend in Dublin.

"Galway are keeping nice and quiet about the whole thing but they're deadly dangerous on a given day. If we're not focussed as well as we should, Galway will wipe the floor with us" Anthony warned.

Clare manager Ger Loughnane and his selectors gave a vote of confidence to the team which beat Limerick in the Munster Final but there was one positional change; Jamesie O'Connor was chosen at midfield with Fergal Hegarty named at left half forward. O'Connor was originally selected at left half forward for the Munster Final, but he was moved to midfield from the start of the game in a direct swap with Hegarty. Nigel Shaughnessy was chosen to partner Michael Coleman at midfield for Galway instead of inspirational captain Pat Malone, struggling to regain form after an eye injury.

Ger Loughnane's bold statement in the dressing-room in the aftermath of the League Final loss to Kilkenny that Clare would win the Munster title had a profound impact on goalkeeper David Fitzgerald. "To say that, at the time, was unbelieveable. The fact that he showed so much faith in us put the lads thinking. I remember talking with P.J. Delaney in the car park after the game and I said to him: 'Hopefully, we'll be seeing you in Croke Park in September.' He probably thought I was off my head. But Ger's words had already sunk in."

The sight of Anthony Daly and the Clare team emerging from the tunnel sent the Banner supporters into ecstasy and the noise reached a crescendo when Ger 'Sparrow' O'Loughlin collected goalkeeper David Fitzgerald's long delivery to put over the opening point of the game. Galway struck back with 3 unanswered points

Clare Back row l to r: Brian Lohan, Michael O'Halloran, Frank Lohan, David Fitzgerald, Fergal Hegarty, Sean Mc Mahon, Ger 'Sparrow' O'Loughlin, Conor Clancy. Front row l to r: Stephen McNamara, Liam Doyle, Anthony Daly, Jamesie O'Connor, Ollie Baker, P.J. O'Connell, Fergus Tuohy.

from Ollie Fahy, Justin Campbell and Joe Cooney. O'Loughlin came to Clare's rescue with a goal after 16 minutes and when Stephen McNamara rounded Christy Helebert to kick to the net after 22 minutes, the Munster champions had edged 3 points clear. Those killer goals rocked Galway!

It was Clare 2-6 Galway 0-7 at the interval. The 'Sparrow' scored his second goal of the game two minutes after the restart. It was unwise even to blink at this stage.

Galway corner forward Francis Forde then turned a Joe Cooney shot into the Clare net, but almost immediately the energetic Jamesie O'Connor struck over a Clare point. Midfielder Michael Coleman was the launching pad for a Galway fightback during which they scored 4 points without reply, but with the game on a knife-edge the Connacht champions missed opportunities that were to prove extremely costly.

Galway Back row l to r: Liam Burke, Ollie Fahy, Joe Rabbitte, Christy Helebert, Richard Burke, Justin Campbell, Michael Coleman, Brendan Keogh. Front row l to r: Joe Cooney, Gerry McInerney, Sean Treacy, Nigel Shaughnessy, Francis Forde, Conor O'Donovan, Padraig Kelly.

Clare weathered the storm and finished the stronger, outscoring Galway by 4 points to one in the closing 14 minutes. The Clare shout would be heard on All-Ireland hurling final day for the first time since 1932!

Scorers Clare: Ger O'Loughlin 2-1; Jamesie O'Connor 0-7; Stephen McNamara 1-1; Fergus Tuohy 0-1; P.J. O'Connell 0-1; Liam Doyle 0-1. **Scorers Galway:** Joe Cooney 0-6; Francis Forde 1-1; Ollie Fahy 0-2; Justin Campbell 0-2; Liam Burke 0-1; Michael Coleman 0-1.

CLARE

DAVID FITZGERALD

| MICHAEL O'HALLORAN | BRIAN LOHAN | FRANK LOHAN |
| LIAM DOYLE | SEAN MCMAHON | ANTHONY DALY |

JAMESIE O'CONNOR　　　　OLLIE BAKER

| FERGUS TUOHY | P.J. O'CONNELL | FERGAL HEGARTY |
| STEPHEN MCNAMARA | CONOR CLANCY | GER O'LOUGHLIN |

Substitutes: Jim McInerney for Fergus Tuohy; Alan Neville for Fergal Hegarty

GALWAY

RICHARD BURKE

| CONOR O'DONOVAN | SEAN TREACY | CHRISTY HELEBERT |
| PADRAIG KELLY | BRENDAN KEOGH | GERRY MCINERNEY |

MICHAEL COLEMAN　　　　NIGEL SHAUGHNESSY

| JUSTIN CAMPBELL | JOE RABBITTE | OLLIE FAHY |
| FRANCIS FORDE | JOE COONEY | LIAM BURKE |

Substitutes: Tom Helebert for Christy Helebert; Michael McGrath for Joe Rabbitte; Joe McGrath for Brendan Keogh

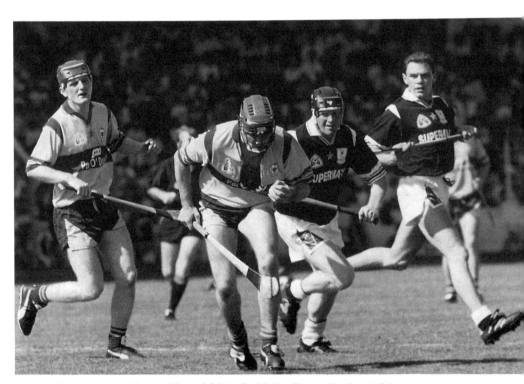

All-Ireland semi-final between Clare and Galway. Frank Lohan, Clare, and Joe Cooney, Galway.

SUNDAY AUGUST 6TH
ALL-IRELAND SENIOR HURLING
SEMI-FINAL

OFFALY & DOWN

CROKE PARK
REFEREE: WILLIE BARRETT TIPPERARY
RESULT: OFFALY 2-19 DOWN 2-8

Ulster champions, Down, had to play one game more than Leinster kingpins, Offaly to reach the All-Ireland semi-final stage. The men from the Ards Peninsula defeated Antrim after a replay in Ulster and then accounted for London in the All-Ireland quarter final while Offaly had two outings and both ended in comfortable victories. They beat Wexford by, 2-14 to 1-10, and then had an impressive, 2-16 to 2-5 victory over favourites, Kilkenny in the Leinster decider. It is a very rare occurrence for the 'Cats' to be beaten by double scores! All the more reason then why Offaly started as overwhelming favourites against a Down team making only their second appearance at an All-Ireland semi-final. They had lost by 9 points to Cork in their first ever senior semi-final outing in 1992.

Offaly manager, Eamon Cregan made it abundantly clear before the game that his side would not be lulled into a false sense of well-being. Offaly had learned a hard lesson in the 1989 semi-final when Antrim dumped them out of the championship.

Down suffered a setback before the start when corner forward, Conor Arthurs, had to withdraw with a hand injury, but were fortunate to be able to call on Gerard McGrattan, the first hurler from the county to win an All-Star Award.

The game was no more than a minute old with long-hitting corner back Kevin Coulter opened the scoring with point from a free. It was the first and only time during the game when Down led Offaly. In fairness, they fought for everything but their first touch seemed to desert them at crucial stages. Offaly were always more fluent and economical without ever reaching the level of performance that destroyed Kilkenny in the Leinster final.

John Troy cancelled out Coulter's opening point and from there on Offaly were the masters. Michael Duignan scored an Offaly goal after six minutes and by the midway point of the half, the champions had moved, 1-8 to 0-1, ahead. But a goal from Noel Sands handed Down a lifeline and kept the interval score to a respectable margin of 6 points. In fact, Down scored 1-3 to Offaly's 0-2 during the second quarter.

Offaly added 2 quick points early in the second half and then Billy Dooley showed his class with a superb individual goal. There was to be no way back for Down. Paul Coulter did score a goal in the fifteenth minute of the half, but Offaly were much too strong. The three Dooley brothers between them scored 1-14; top marksman, Johnny, the hero of the 1994 All-Ireland final, emerged top scorer with 11 points; Billy scored 1-2 while Joe, the oldest member of the famous trio, landed one point.

Scorers Offaly: Johnny Dooley 0-11; Billy Dooley 1-2; Michael Duignan 1-1;Brian Whelehan 0-1; Johnny Pilkington 0-1; John Troy 0-1; Joe Dooley 0-1; Pat O'Connor 0-1.
Scorers Down: Noel Sands 1-2; Paul Coulter 1-0; Hugh Gilmore 0-3; Danny Hughes 0-1; John McCarthy -0-1; Kevin Coulter 0-1.

O F F A L Y

DAVID HUGHES

| SHANE MCGUCKIN | KEVIN KINAHAN | MARTIN HANAMY |
| BRIAN WHELEHAN | HUBERT RIGNEY | KEVIN MARTIN |

DAITHI REGAN   JOHNNY PILKINGTON

| JOHNNY DOOLEY | JOHN TROY | JOE DOOLEY |
| BILLY DOOLEY | PAT O'CONNOR | MICHAEL DUIGNAN |

Substitute: Joe Errity for Hubert Rigney; Declan Pilkington for Daithi Regan; Brendan Kelly for John Troy

D O W N

NOEL KEITH

| KEVIN COULTER | GERARD COULTER | DERMOT WOODS |
| MARTIN MALLON | GARY SAVAGE | PAUL MCMULLAN |

DANNY HUGHES   JOHN MCCARTHY

| PAUL COULTER | BARRY COULTER | DERMOT O'PREY |
| GERARD MCGRATTAN | HUGH GILMORE | NOEL SANDS |

Substitute: Michael Braniff for Hugh Gilmore

Gathering the ball in the All-Ireland semi-final, Offaly and Down. Pat O'Connor, Offaly being challenged by Down's Gerard Coulter.

Offaly Back row l to r: Shane McGuckin, Daithi Regan, Kevin Kinahan, Kevin Martin, Hubert Rigney, Michael Duignan, David Hughes, Brian Whelehan. **Front row l to r:** Billy Dooley, John Troy, Martin Hanamy, Johnny Pilkington, Pat O'Connor, Joe Dooley, Johnny Dooley.

Down Back row l to r:. Hugh Gilmore, Barry Coulter, Gerard Coulter, Gary Savage, Gerard Mc Grattan, John Mc Carthy, Danny Hughes, Kevin Coulter. **Front row l to r:** Noel Sands, Martin Mallon, Paul Coulter, Noel Keith, Dermot O'Prey, Paul McMullan, Dermot Woods.

CLARE v OFFALY- BEFORE THE FINAL

OFFALY & THE DOOLEY BROTHERS

Joe, Billy and Johnny! No need for a surname. Everyone in hurling knows the famous Dooley brothers from the tiny parish of Clareen in Offaly. It is the parish with no pub, and the place where hurling has always been an integral part of community life. The ancient game comes as natural as breathing to the Dooleys. Huring has long been the centre of their world and the game in turn has been kind to them.

There's a proud tradition of hurling on both sides of the family. Their grandfather, Jim Carroll from Coolderry, and his brohter Joe both won All-Ireland medals when Offaly claimed the Junior hurling crown for the first time in 1923. Another grand-uncle, Tom Dooley won and All-Ireland junior medal with Offaly in 1929.

Coming from such a family, it was only natural that the young lads would eventually take up the game. Their father Sean and mother Betty encouraged their offspring at every opportunity.

Joe, the eldest in a family of nine, knew he had found a kindred spirit the first time he picked up a hurley. Neighbours still recall the fairhaired youngster who never seemed to go anywhere without the hurley in his hand. "If we spent as much time praying as we did talking about hurling, we'd all be canonised by now,"Joe says. "We're all very thankful to our mother and father for what they've done for us. We wouldn't have to say that to them and neither would they expect it, but it's just an understanding"

Mrs Dooley was delighted to see her five sons and four daughters take such and active part in sport. Apart altogether from Joe, Billy and Johnny, her other sons Seamus and Kieran also wore the county jersey; daughters Mary, Sandra, Patricia and Eilish played camogie for Offaly.

"I'm very proud of them all. They always seemed to be hurling. The first thing they did when they came home from school was to take out the hurleys. There's always great excitement around the place before a big match. It's a way of life here. We look forward to every game and talk about hurling day in and day out. I worry about them all and I'm always disappointed for them if things don't go well."

Most satisfying of all as far as Mrs Doley is concerned is the fact that success has never affected her sons. "I suppose you'd be worried in case it would go to their heads, but thankfully that has never happened. I'm glad about that."

Joe is married to Marie and they have three children, Shane, Aideen and Niamh. Johnny is married to Sinead since June this year. Billy is getting married to Fiona Maher from Kinnity in Offaly on the Saturday after the final. The wedding was originally planned for the second of September, but they decided to move it back one week, just in case. The Dooleys and all of Offaly are hoping for double celebrations.

Although there was always work to be done about the family farm, there was ample time, too, for young Joe to pursue his favourite past time. Life was different then and the whole world seemed young. Most evenings Joe would head off for a game; other times the local youngsters would converge on their own farm. Their sole aim was to play as much as possible before nightfall.

Offaly was not always in the front rank of Leinster hurling, and Joe Dooley's own childhood heroes were by no means confined to his own county: men like Eddie Keher, Pat Delaney and Tony Doran. The county won its first senior All-Ireland title in 1981. That was the catalyst. Incredibly, Offaly contested every single Leinster Final in the Eighties, winning 6 to Kilkenny's 4. The traditional counties found it hard to absorb the implications. Offaly, though, had arrived centre-stage and were in no hurry to move aside.

"In 1978, no one would have dreamed of Offaly winning even a Leinster title," Joe tells me. That's how quickly the whole thing happened. I can recall being outside Mass in Clareen one Sunday morning in 1980, and in jest somebody said 'maybe Offaly could win the Leinster this year' and everyone just laughed."

Joe Dooley's repertoire of skills soon came to the attention of those in charge of hurling in the county. He was corner forward on the Offaly team that won their second All-Ireland title in 1985 and, along with goalkeeper Jim Troy, was the only surviving member of that team that won in such dramatic fashion last year. By then, Billy and Johnny had joined their big brother in the forward line. With five minutes left to play, Limerick were leading by 5 points, and there appeared to be no chance whatsoever of an Offaly victory. Then came the most amazing turnaround in the annals of the final.

Johnny struck the ball to the net from a free. Limerick appeared to panic. Almost immediately, substitute Pat O'Connor scored another goal and Billy struck over some wonderful points. It is almost impossible to comprehend the drama unfolding before our eyes. Offaly scored 2-5 in the final five minutes and won in the end by six points.

It was a comeback of gigantic proportions. Captain Martin Hanamy once told me: "I remember asking Michael Duignan if what was happening was for real, or was I imagining it all."

Reflecting on that momentous day, Johnny Dooley recalls how he scored one of the most important goals ever in the history of the game. "It was a do or die situation and I took my chance. It sprung a great Offaly comeback and one which will never be forgotten.I was just delighted to be involved," he says modestly.

"Next Sunday's final couldn't possibly be as dramatic as that. From what I've seen of them, Clare have been very impressive on the way to the final. No one could fault their displays in any of the games. They're unbelievably fit and we'll have our hands full to try and curb their backline, especially. It's great for hurling to see a new team coming through."

Joe agrees with his young brother, emphasising that Clare will be extremely difficult to overcome. "Their backs, in particular, are very, very strong and their forwards are fit and forceful.The one thing about Clare is that they're finishing their games very strongly and no team, with the exception of Cork in the first round, has come close to beating them."

As soon as Billy and Johnny could walk they were out in the yard, hurling to their hearts content. Joe remembers his two younger brothers as exceptionally skilful. "They could make the ball talk from the time they were knee high". Damien White the local schoolmaster was a big influence, and so too was Mick Corrigan, who has since sadly died. Both graduated to the Community School in Birr. Billy won minor All-Ireland medals in 1986 and '87, and Johnny was on the team that won minor All-Ireland titles in 1987 and 1989.

Can this present Offaly team become the first from the county to win back-to-back All-Ireland senior hurling titles ? Joe Dooley is under no illusions and is only too well aware of the threat posed by the men of Clare.

"It's going to take a supreme effort to beat them. Normally, Offaly would have most of the neutral support, but on this occasion it looks like we're going to be on our own and that's going to make it harder. We'll be treating Clare with the utmost respect!"

COUNTY CLARE & DAVID FITZGERALD

Sixty-three years! And nothing to talk about only hard-luck stories. Words like heart-break were permanently linked with Clare hurling. Demoralising defeats by Cork, Tipperary, Limerick and Waterford for good measure in 1938, had taken their toll. It all amounted to a lifetime of misery for Clare hurlers around the fields of Munster.

And then it changed. Somewhere from deep within, the players in saffron and blue found the courage to win a first Munster title since 1932. The famine had ended and the Banner county went wild with excitement. Captain Anthony Daly held the Munster Cup in a vice-like grip. And then he spoke: "It's been sixty-three years of heartbreak and sixty-three years of the long road back from Thurles and Limerick, but this baby's coming home tonight!"

Manager Ger Loughnane's prophecy in the dressingroom in the aftermath of the League final loss to Kilkenny, that Clare would win the Munster title, had come true. His bold statement had a profound impact on goalkeeper David Fitzgerald.

"To say that, at the time, was unbelivable. The fact that he showed so much faith in us put the lads thinking. I remember talking with P.J. Delaney in the car park after the game and I said to him: 'Hopefully, we'll be seeing you in Croke Park in September'. He probably thought I was off my head. But Ger's words had already sunk in!"

The ultimate for Clare is to win the Liam McCarthy Cup and David is eagerly awaiting the challenge.

"We don't know what to expect because we've never experienced the atmosphere of All-Ireland final day. I suppose we have one thing to do and that is to concentrate on the game, but that is not going to be easy. We're not accustomed to the big build-up, so we're hoping it will work out for us. Offaly will start as hot favourites as defending champions".

Clare's first round win over Cork, when supersub Ollie Baker scored the winning goal, was one of the major highpoints of the championship for David from Sixmilebridge.

"That win was very special! My memory as a youngster is of Cork coming back in the last two or three minutes to pip Clare with a goal or a point And suddenly it happened that we turned the tables on them and pulled the game out of the fire. I thought when Kevin Murray got the goal for Cork that it was history for us. But Ollie saved the day with that winning goal, something he keeps reminding me of during training. He continually says to me: 'you wouldn't be here only for me.' It's all a bit of fun."

David admits that the tension of this year's Munster Final against Limerick was the worst he ever experienced. The players were only too fully aware of the consequences of a third successive defeat in the provincial decider.

"The pressure was phenomenal, much more than in the All-Ireland semi-final against Galway. There was no such thing as enjoying the game. We all knew that if we didn't do the business we'd be in trouble and it would take a long, long time to come back again. Thankfully, it all came right for us on the day."

The whole Clare squad trained exceptionally hard throughout the winter in difficult weather conditions. That tough regime under Mike McNamara had paid rich dividends in all of Clare's games on the way to the final. Clare have finished strongly all year and will be determined to do likewise on Sunday.

Winning the Munster title has meant that all the players have attained celebrity status throughout the county. That in itself brings its own problems. Everyone wants to shake their hands and of course the usual songs have been written about their deeds. But the players still have to play the most important game of their lives.

Hurling has always been a way of life in Clare, and David was imbued with the spirit of the game from a very early age. His father, Pat, is the Secretary of the Clare County Board and a widely respected figure in GAA circles.

"No matter how I play in a match my mother and father would never criticise me. They've always been one hundred per cent behind me and it's the same with my sister Helen. I would also like to pay tribute to John Lynch, Trixie Twomey and Gerry McInerney for all their help through the years."

David's uncle John Fitzgerald, a member of the famed O'Callaghan Mills club, had a huge influence on his career. He brought his nephew to all the games and spent many long hours teaching him the skills of the game. David won every under-age medal in the county with Sixmilebridge.He also won an All-Ireland Colleges medal in 1987 with St Flannan's in Ennis, the famous hurling nursery. He was on the losing side against St Kieran's Kilkenny, some two years later when none other than that master craftsman D.J Carey scored 3-3.

David Fitzgerald and his team-mates face the most daunting challenge of their career this Sunday. It promises to be a day of extreme emotion.But the Clare goalkeeper is ready for the challange.

"At the end of the day, we'll all be judged on how we perform in the final against Offaly. All the hype has to be cast aside. We've got to keep one thing in our heads and that is to concentrate on giving it everything for seventy minutes against Offaly"

For my report on the Final, see above page 119 to 124.

ANSWERS TO

BRIAN CARTHY'S CHAMPIONSHIP QUIZ

1 Pat O'Toole, Longford. 2 Paul Clarke. 3 Peter Canavan. 4 Nicky English. 5 Evan Kelly. 6 Peter Reilly. 7 Powerscreen International PLC. 8 John Meyler. 9 Derry in 1976. 10 Peter Canavan. 11 Terry Ferguson. 12 Pat Spillane. 13 Sandra Marsh. 14 County Donegal. 15 Limerick. 16 Padraig Horan. 17 Eamon Coleman. 18 Ogie Moran, Kerry. 19 Ollie Baker. 20 Paul Delaney and Michael Ryan. 21 Meath. 22 Joe Dollard. 23 David Kilcoyne. 24 Vinny Murphy. 25 He assisted his club, Oulart-the-Ballagh, against management instructions, in a mid-week club game. 26 Daithi Regan. 27 Liam Harvey Cup. 28 Dublin. 29 Antrim. 30 Tommy Doyle. 31 Noel Keith. 32 (A) Roscommon (B) Wicklow (C) Waterford. 33 1973. 34 Liam Currams. 35 Liam Griffin. 36 Seir Kieran. 37 1977 and 1978. 38 Wexford (Wexford scored 6-23 against Westmeath in the Leinster Hurling Championship). 39 Kerry (Kerry scored 7-12 against Tipperary in the Munster Football Championship). 40 Longford. 41 Limerick. 42 Waterford. 43 Right corner forward. 44 Four. 45 Donie O'Sullivan. 46 Former Taoiseach, Jack Lynch. 47 Jimmy Murray, Roscommon; Sean Flanagan, Mayo; Enda Colleran, Galway. 48 Peter Darby. 49 Pat Kenneally. 50 PJ Smith, Galway.

ACKNOWLEDGEMENTS
A special thanks to everyone who assisted with the publication.
The publishers would like to thank Fergus Cashman for all his assistance with typesetting.
The publisher would like to thank the following publications for their assistance: Donegal Democrat, Clare Champion, Kilkenny People, Roscommon Herald, Derry Journal, Dundalk Democrat, Northern Standard, Limerick Leader, Western People.
Colour Section Photographs: courtesy of Inpho. Black and White Photographs: courtesy of Inpho pages 6, 13, 14, 19, 36, 37, 40, 41, 44, 44, 45, 57, 61, 62, 63, 69, 74, 75, 84, 90, 93, 94, 96, 97, 102, 104, 106, 108, 112, 116, 121, 126, 128, 130, 131, 135, 148, 153, 156, 157, 159, 160, 180, 182, 183. courtesy of Sportsfile pages 16,17, 30, 31, 46, 51, 52, 64-67, 70, 72, 77, 78, 80, 82, 124, 126, 128, 143, 145, 146. Courtesy of John Quirke, photographer, pages 21, 23, 25, 26, 28, 32, 33, 35, 47, 169, 171, 175. courtesy of Paddy Cotter, photographer, pages 121, 149, 151, 154, 179. courtesy of Gerard O'Loughlin (Longford News), photographer, pages 23, 160. courtesy of Western People pages 85, 87. courtesy of Connacht Tribune page 89. courtesy of Limerick Leader pages 132-33. courtesy of Eamon Ward (Clare Champion) page 137. courtesy of Oliver McVeagh pages 48, 49, 54. courtesy of Down Recorder page 177.

Chasing Gold: Sportswomen of Ireland
Yvonne Judge

Irish sportswomen have taken enormous strides in the last seven decades.

This book follows the fortunes of Eleven of the Best:
Sonia O'Sullivan, Catherina McKiernan, Michelle Smith, Karen Nugent,
Angela Farrell, Rosemary Smith, Angela Downey, Caroline Barker,
Mary McKenna, Ann-Marie O'Brien, Sandra O'Gorman.

Many girls are devoting themselves to public sports which demand
violent exertion and a notable scantiness of clothing...
THE IRISH TIMES SUPPORTS POPE PIUS XI AS HE FEARS FOR THE CHRISTIAN MODESTY AND MORALITY
OF WOMEN IN SPORT, 4TH MAY 1928.

*Your magnificent achievement is a cause for pride and celebration throughout
Ireland and a great personal triumph.*
PRESIDENT MARY ROBINSON, 12TH AUGUST 1995 TO SONIA O'SULLIVAN, WORLD CHAMPION.

ISBN 0 86327 447 1

Hurling Giants
Brendan Fullam

Hurling Giants is a new classic from the author of the greatest hurling book
of all time. Packed with interviews, photographs, team choices, autographs,
statistics and text by the players themselves, this book captures and celebrates
views, memories and achievements from this game of speed and skill.

This completely new selection includes
— modern masters of the game
— the great camogie players
— giants of the former years
— and special profiles of the game's five 'Giants among Giants'.

ISBN 0 86327 444 7

Football Captains: The All-Ireland Winners
Brian Carthy

The greatest football book you'll ever buy. A unique portrait of fifty years of Gaelic football through the eyes of the players who captained the All-Ireland winning teams.

Each captain who held aloft the Sam Maguire Cup from 1940 to 1993 gives his thoughts on sport and the game, memories of the glory days, reminiscences on his greatest team-mates and opponents, with facts, photographs, achievements and more.

Fully illustrated in colour and black and white, a magnificent record of Irish football.

ISBN 0 86327 394 7

Giants of the Ash
Brendan Fullam

'A great hurling book, *Giants of the Ash* has the nation's history woven into it. Conversation courses through the pages as it flows through the living body of the game.' *Irish Times.*

Giants of the Ash by Brendan Fullam is the first in-depth study of the outstanding hurlers of the century.

Seventy-nine of the greatest players including Christy Ring, Peter Cregan, John and Michael Maher, the Rackards and the oldest among them, John T Power.

HB ISBN 0 86327 315 7
PB ISBN 0 86327 346 7

The Greatest Hurling Decade
Nicholas Furlong

The sensational years of Wexford's hurling glory - the 50s. It was a mould-breaking decade for modern hurling, an era of revolution and sensation for Wexford and the teams they met in this explosion of hurling talent.

The domination of Cork, Tipperary and Kilkenny was irrevocably challenged as Wexford, Clare, Limerick, Laois, Waterford, Galway, Dublin, Meath and Westmeath emerged into the mainstream. A riveting hurling memoir.

HB ISBN 0 86327 420 X
PB ISBN 0 86327 411 0

Ulster Football and Hurling
The Path of Champions
Jerome Quinn

The Sam Maguire Cup travelled to Down in 1991, to Donegal in 1992 for the first time ever, to Derry in 1993 and back to Down in 1994. Irish football has been taken by storm. *Ulster Football and Hurling* explores how the Ulstermen did it, the stories behind the scenes, the emotions experienced by these great players, managers and fans along the way both in hurling and football.
A beautifully produced book that explores, commemorates and celebrates the phenomenon that is Ulster GAA.

ISBN 0 86327 394 7

These books are available from all good bookshops or direct from
WOLFHOUND PRESS,
68 Mountjoy Square,
Dublin 1.
Tel: 8740354 Fax: 8720207.
Call or write for our full catalogue.